| DATE DUE | | | |
|---|---|---|---|
| | | | |
| | | | |
| | | | |
| | | | |
| | | | |
| | | | |
| | | | |
| | | | |
| | | | |
| | | | |
| | | | |
| | | | |

# Women
# Changing
# Work

**Recent Titles in**
**Contributions in Women's Studies**

# Women Changing Work

## PATRICIA W. LUNNEBORG

DISCARDED

Contributions in Women's Studies,
Number 112

GREENWOOD PRESS
New York • Westport, Connecticut • London

**Library of Congress Cataloging-in-Publication Data**

Lunneborg, Patricia W.
    Women changing work / Patricia W. Lunneborg.
        p.    cm.—(Contributions in women's studies, ISSN 0147-104X :
 no. 112)
   Includes bibliographical references.
   ISBN 0-313-26843-6 (lib. bdg. : alk. paper)
   1. Women—Employment.  2. Women—Psychology.  3. Sex role in the
 work environment.  I. Title.  II. Series.
 HD6053.L86   1990
 331.3'4—dc20      89-25673

British Library Cataloguing in Publication Data is available.

A paperback edition of *Women Changing Work* is available from Bergin & Garvey
Publishers (ISBN 0-89789-214-3)

Library of Congress Catalog Card Number: 89-25673
ISBN: 0-313-26843-6
ISSN: 0147-104X

First published in 1990

Greenwood Press, 88 Post Road West, Westport, CT 06881
An imprint of Greenwood Publishing Group, Inc.

Printed in the United States of America

The paper used in this book complies with the
Permanent Paper Standard issued by the National
Information Standards Organization (Z39.48-1984).

10 9 8 7 6 5 4 3 2

# CONTENTS

## IV. Skillful at Organizing

# PREFACE

This book starts from the premise that women do work differently than men, maybe not *very* differently but detectibly so. Going one step further, I reasoned that women in nontraditional, male-dominated jobs might not only do their jobs differently from male colleagues but that they might, over time, change the way that work gets done. Perhaps women's values and concerns, women's physical and social characteristics, would make a significant impression on the male-dominated workplace.

This is not a traditional research study. It is instead a feminist discourse in which the views of feminist writers are presented in prologues to each part, followed by chapters containing the evidence I sought out and found to corroborate those writers' ideas. This book documents, then, the unique ways that feminists have predicted and perceived that women would perform "men's jobs." It thus presents three viewpoints: first, those of the literature; then, the views of the women interviewed; and finally, my views based on twenty years of teaching and research in counseling psychology and women's studies.

*Women Changing Work* is biased and one-sided. I asked only five questions, and they are what the book is about. It isn't balanced in the sense of asking, as well, how nontraditional jobs change women or how male coworkers are not changing or how the women do their jobs just like the men. It's not about sexual harassment or discrimination. In fact, it slants away from the negative. This is a celebratory book about a be-coming-perceptible transformation, the reworking of male occupations based on women's unique life experiences.

The data come from interviews I and my research assistants did during a two-year period, 1985–1987. We had fun doing the interviews. It's okay to have fun when you do a feminist project. It's okay to tell an interviewee up front what your premises are, and it's also okay to change the interview if someone is giving you such dynamite material to one question that you don't care if you ever get to the next one.

So this book has several defining characteristics. It is positive because the positive is what I asked for; it is what I wanted to hear; it is what I want to pass on. The book focuses on an optimistic reality, not on equally true and real but depressing facts. Second, it's about data no one has gathered before. It thus represents an original, investigative look into women's behavior in the workplace. Next, I have tried to report in a straightforward, nonacademic style out of the belief that writing does not have to be pedantic to be taken seriously. Finally, it is written primarily for women but also for men. Without men's efforts, work cannot truly be transformed.

Some thanks are in order. Several wonderful women helped with the more than 200 interviews. I appreciate the contributions made by Karen Graber, who interviewed physicians; Anita Mann, who sought out veterinarians; Kris Morgan, who helped with the carpenters; Mary Mullen, who interviewed police officers; Debra Pierce, who talked to engineers; Pamela Thompson, who saw landscape architects; Lisa Watkins, who interviewed firefighters; and Debra Srebnik and Kristina Keilman-Vowell, who interviewed skilled craftswomen. The interviewer par excellence was Jennifer Brace, who interviewed all of the state legislators and most of the brokers.

In addition, as part of my Women and Work seminars at the University of Washington in 1986 and 1987, the following women conducted interviews: Jaclynn Beltz, Janet Blessing, Annette Diehl, Stacey Grigg, Linda Hartz, Lisa John, Kathy Kanner, Suanne Kinnamon, Mary Lou Laprade, Brenda Lar, Marla Levin, Angela Purcell, Mary Pedersen, Nancy Rehberg, Annette Sacksteder, Alayna Sheron, Karen Thompson, Becky Vit, Kathryn Walter, Shary Weber, and Lynne Wilson.

# INTRODUCTION

The idea for this book came from two sources. First, there were books such as *Women and the Power to Change* (1975), edited by Florence Howe. In it each contributor talks about how she believes women's values and sensibilities will make the male-dominated workplace more humane, less competitive, and less hierarchical. The university was the workplace these writers were concerned about, but I could see that any "man's job" should be open to the same reforming.

Second, once I had this idea in my head that the "ethos of caretaking" might replace the "ethos of making it," I read magazines and newspapers with a different set. I was looking for articles that might support the idea that women had the power to change work.

I started a file with case studies from the *Seattle Times*, articles about individual women who were the first to do this or that male job. Among my favorite clippings is one about Libby Riddles, professional sleddog breeder and racer, who was the first woman to win the Iditarod race across Alaska "with courage and with love," as the headline read. Another article describes the first female navy brig commander, who returned to jail in the evening to teach remedial English and mathematics. A third, from a British newspaper (Great Britain is where *Women Changing Work* was developed), talks about a woman British rail station manager who controls vandalism with flower beds, fresh paint, and neighborhood involvement.

When my clippings started spilling out of their folder, it became apparent that I could go beyond these individual stories and perhaps gather a collective portrait of the changes that were taking place in male jobs because of women. From the beginning the project has been called "Women Changing Work."

As I began this work I was well aware that there were writers who have concluded that women in male jobs become just like the men. A male writer who calls his book *The Feminization of the American Military*, for example, accuses women of assuming masculine attitudes toward everything by, for instance, driving fast cars, competing at sports, and devoting themselves totally to their careers (Becraft, 1989).

I became aware of the studies reporting that to "make it," women in men's jobs had to forego marriage and/or children. I've also read those books describing women who "have it all," reports that make me wonder how the average woman can possibly identify with women so overendowed with stamina, intelligence, and very often economic wherewithal. What do you and I have in common with Superwomen?

But the thing is, I said to myself, these disheartening reports cannot be the only reality. Suppose I go forth and say to nontraditional women that I am not interested in how you and the men are alike or how you've been changed by them. I'm not interested in learning more about women's lack of progress. I don't want to spend our time hearing about sex discrimination and sexual harassment, although I'm sure you've got your war stories.

Instead, I'm going to ask you some questions nobody has asked before. I'm after some very special knowledge. What I want to focus on is how you do your job differently than the men do theirs. How do your experiences as a woman, your values and perceptions, and your approach to life affect the way you go about your job? How might your behaviors and attitudes, and those of other women, be changing the men around you and the workplace itself?

## AMERICAN WOMEN IN MALE JOBS, CHANGING MALE JOBS

We definitely are making progress in getting more women into traditional men's work. Ironically, university faculties are one of the most resistant-to-change occupations. The professions of medicine, law, and engineering have made the most progress, the skilled crafts the least. Nevertheless, the increasing proportion of women during the past fifteen years in male-dominated jobs is a small bright spot on the American work scene.

Sometimes these opened doors seem like the only positive event for women in U.S. employment in the past two decades. Judging from Sylvia Hewlett's statistics in *A Lesser Life* (1986), our male–female wage gap hasn't narrowed in fifty years. Just as bad, the United States has made no progress in providing the family supports needed by working women—maternity and parental leaves and childcare. In contrast, other industrialized Western countries have both smaller pay gaps between women and men and expanding, government-paid-for family support systems that make it more realistic to have both career and family (Hewlett, 1986, pp. 14–15).

Hewlett accused American feminists of overemphasizing the Equal Rights Amendment (ERA) and abortion rights at the expense of obtaining family benefits (1986, pp. 142–143). But ERA and abortion rights have not been the only emphases of the American women's movement. I believe another important issue has been equality in employment. A very good reason for North American women pushing for equal pay and comparable worth and sex-discrimination legislation is that we live in a rampant capitalist society. We have not had in place, as have other Western democracies, a socialist government with a tradition of providing child benefits, public housing, free health care, and subsidized early education and childcare. We have no tradition of a welfare state to which people look for broad support. So American women have had no choice but to look to their jobs as a realistic way to take care of themselves and their families. Employment reforms have offered us the greatest promise of success in a conservative country now in the throes of ultra-conservative reactionism.

Affirmative action and equal employment opportunity have been successful in recruiting and training women for male-dominated jobs. Sex-discrimination and sexual-harassment legislation are responsible for retaining us in those jobs despite male resistance. As Hewlett (1986, p. 75) noted, between 1962 and 1982 the proportion of women engineers rose from 1 to 6 percent, of women physicians from 6 to 15 percent, and of women bus drivers from 12 to almost 50 percent.

Incredibly, then, we women owe our forward movement in employment to conservative capitalism. We also are in debt to the wider civil rights movement. Congress, in the 1960s, in facing up to the inequities for blacks in employment, took women along for the ride, literally as a joke. In writing Title VII of the 1964 Civil Rights Act, the "sex" category was added by opponents in the hope that it would defeat the bill. It didn't, and women, ironically, have benefited more than blacks from this civil rights legislation levied at discrimination on the basis of race, color, religion, national origin, and sex.

Other powerful forces that, paradoxically, aided American women in our search for job equality were an expanding economy fueled by the Vietnam War and growing consumerism. We could get jobs during the war without taking them away from men, and we wanted to work to be able to supply our families with unprecedented mounds of material goods.

In these ways U.S. women have entered male occupations. But what about my idea that we are changing those occupations? Why might we be feistier than women elsewhere, more pushy, independent, self-confident, more likely to change men?

Maybe our divorce rate has something to do with it. Sylvia Hewlett called it by far the highest in the world (1986, p. 67). We're on our way to two out of three marriages ending in divorce. Something like 4 percent of American families now conform to the ideal of yesteryear—employed father, at-home mother, and two children. Women on their own raising children is fast becoming the norm.

Maybe our higher level of education makes for greater feistiness. In the United States more than half of four-year college students are female, and half of all master's degrees and a quarter of all professional degrees go to women (Hewlett, 1986, p. 73). Is it education that gives us the self-confidence to challenge the status quo?

Is this combination of a government with no family supports, women entering the workplace in unprecedented numbers, women more often being single with dependents, and women with more education than their sisters around the globe what sets American women up with attitudes and behaviors destined to change the workplace?

## MY GOAL

This book is primarily for women. I'd like to see the interviews encourage more women to get into nontraditional work and to stay in it until, in time, there is no more nontraditional work, no overrepresentation or underrepresentation of either sex in any job. It can happen. In Sweden the government has special training programs to get men and women into nontraditional jobs. Technical ability is socialized; after all, why else did women in the 1960s, for example, represent only 1 percent of the U.S. engineers while they made up a third of the Russian engineers? Why were only 2 percent of our dentists women while more than 80 percent of the Russian dentists were women? Technical skills and technical interests are cultural, conditioned, and controllable.

I'd also like to see these findings help to transform male-dominated work. Wouldn't it be healthier, less frantic, if society valued women's ideas about power and money and success no less than it does men's ideas? Wouldn't it be more enjoyable to go to work where our ideas about egalitarianism and cooperation coexisted with hierarchy and competitiveness? Until we get men to lead balanced lives where they spend the same amount of time as we do rearing children and doing housework, women cannot lead truly balanced lives.

Although I was writing most of all for women, men were on my mind all of the time. How are we going to get them to lobby for more women in male jobs? To adopt our work styles and values? To support the structural changes we all need to make it possible to have a job and raise a family too? To that end the final chapter is about reforming men. It is a chapter to counter men's wish to preserve the dubious perks of patriarchy. It chronicles the gains men have already achieved due to the women's movement. It is further testimony, in addition to the evidence from the interviews, that men's work behavior is not static but evolving to be more nurturant and balanced.

## THE INTERVIEW

I asked the women five basic questions.

1. How do you approach your job differently than do the men in it, based on your upbringing and experiences as a woman?
2. What might be some small, subtle differences you've noticed in the way you do the job compared to the men?
3. How do differences in the values held by men and women in your occupation affect how they do their work?
4. What do you see as your strengths as a woman for your job?
5. How might increasing the numbers of women in your occupation change the job and the workplace?

Stop. Before you read any further turn to the back of the book where there are some blank pages and write your answers to the five questions. It won't take long, and it doesn't matter if you are in a female-dominated occupation. Even if you are a secretary, teacher, nurse, or administrative assistant, there have been some men in your job along the way—a male trainer or supervisor, maybe an intern. For question number 5, you can make it the changes that will occur with more women at the highest levels of your job.

It also doesn't matter if you're a middle manager who is trying to be as much like the men as possible or a banker totally cynical about a woman's point of view or even a woman who cannot bring herself to call herself a feminist. How do you answer the questions?

For myself, I was always very different from the men in my psychology department. I offered courses no one else would dream of teaching. I taught in a completely different style from the men. I did research that no one else was interested in. Most of the other women in this department were much more like the men, valuing grant getting and research over teaching, emulating the male style of all-knowing expert who imparts truth, and researching topics approved by establishment psychology. Still, as I think back on them, almost all of the women did their work differently. They only spoke up in faculty meeting if they had a point to make, while the men talked just to hear themselves. The women didn't disparage undergraduate teaching while the men avoided it like the plague. The women treated their graduate students more humanely and sympathetically, less exploitively and indifferently.

I hope you will think about and answer the questions not just once but many times. Doing so now, though, before finding out what I discovered, will give you insight into how each woman interviewed felt as she considered the premise of this book and thought about the questions, sometimes for the first time in her life—like my vet, Carrie Nemec, age 25, who was my first interviewee: "Okay, Carrie, tell me, do you think you do your job any differently than Dr. S or Dr. P or any differently from other men vets you have worked with?"

I remember how slowly and thoughtfully she responded to each question, each probe, slightly different from the last question. "Lots of cats and dogs like women more then men. It's because women are more often at home, I think, with their kids, so they do the feeding and walking, and animals are definitely submissive to size and feel less dominated by women. Also, I show my affection more toward animals. I try to put the animals at ease; I know how they feel. We [women] will baby talk them, get down on the floor with them, and I think we communicate with the owners better. I'm not afraid to express my emotions, to say that my pets are an extremely important part of my life too. I'll put my arms around owners if I think they need comforting."

## THE OCCUPATIONS

In selecting ten male-dominated occupations I wanted to cover the entire range of educational preparation required for jobs, from high school diploma to postbaccalaureate degree. I wanted results that would generalize across amounts of training and not just be limited, for example, to college graduates. The occupations are limited, however, to skilled jobs requiring either a formal training program or informal on-the-job training.

I also wanted to cover the entire range of occupational interests, and this worked fairly well with two exceptions. There is no arts and entertainment occupation represented such as jockey or symphony conductor. There is also no occupation that is essentially organizational. Women are making great inroads into middle management, and our style of managing is widely written about. So management, except at the highest levels, is no longer male dominated and is receiving lots of research attention as it is. For practical reasons the occupations also had to exist in the Puget Sound region and be of inherent interest to me or one of my volunteer research assistants, who had great leeway in choosing which occupations they would concentrate on.

The ten principal jobs we settled on were physician, lawyer, engineer, landscape architect, stockbroker, state legislator, firefighter, police officer, electrician, and carpenter. These were male-dominated occupations in that in 1980 fewer than 20.0 percent of those actively employed in each one were women. Using the 1980 Census of the Population data for nine of the occupations, the percentages that were women were: stockbrokers, 18.5 percent; attorneys, 13.5 percent; physicians, 11.7 percent; state legislators, 10.3 percent; architects, 8.2 percent; police and detectives, 5.8 percent; engineers, 4.6 percent; electricians, 2 percent; firefighters, 1.7 percent; and carpenters, 1.6 percent.

The 10.3 percent figure for legislators is for 1979 and comes from a little note in *State Legislatures* ("Number of women," 1987), which also tells us that women accounted for 4.0 percent of the state legislators in 1969 and 15.6 percent in 1987.

Why have these occupations been male dominated? What's masculine about them? As you might sense, lawyers, stockbrokers, and state legislators are in jobs where what is important is persuasive selling, aggressively talking people into buying something, either something tangible like stocks or something intangible like ideas and programs. Persuasive selling has long been associated with the masculine traits of dominance and aggression.

Science and technology represent two other areas of vocational interest that men have traditionally preserved for themselves. But physicians actually combine service interest with science, just as police officers and firefighters combine service interest with technical and outdoor interest.

Technical interest—this is the big stickler for women. Men characteristically have greater interest in things mechanical, and this is the factor that dozens of male-dominated jobs have in common.

Three occupations represent, more or less, "pure" technical interest: engineering, carpentry, and electrical work. That leaves the tenth occupation, landscape architecture, for which work is a combination of technical interest performed out of doors and artistic interest.

In addition to interviewing the 121 women in these ten principal occupations, I also interviewed 83 veterinarians, commercial airline pilots, pastors, owners of male-dominated small businesses, and women in a variety of skilled shipyard crafts.

I did not want to interview atypical representatives of the occupations and tried to find middle-of-the-road, mainstream attorneys, doctors, engineers, and so on, women working for very ordinary firms and businesses. I interviewed only one "cause" lawyer, for example, who represents students at the University of Washington, and only one engineer and one landscape architect employed by an agency of government.

The interviews always started with my stating my premise and beliefs. I would say something such as, "I'm doing a project called 'Women Changing Work.' It is my thesis that as women enter male-dominated fields such as yours, they change the way that work gets done. Now I have no idea what those changes might be, but you do. I also believe, in the day-to-day doing of work, that women and men may do the same job differently. Now I know you and the men in your field are very, very much alike, so what I am after here are differences, small perhaps but still significant differences. What I'd like you to do is think about..."

## THE WOMEN INTERVIEWED

The number of women who were approached and declined to be interviewed, by me or my assistants, can be counted on one hand. On the other hand can be counted the women who agreed but who then turned out to be somewhat antagonistic. I think we were successful because the women we contacted thought our thesis made sense and felt they had stories to contribute to a book about how women are changing work.

Some of the women were interviewed in their homes and our homes and in cafes, restaurants, and hotel lobbies. Some were interviewed in their place of business—emergency ward, law office, shop floor, or station house.

The environment for the interviews was informal, open, warm, and cooperative. There are no experimenters and subjects in feminist research, just participants working together. There is no deception or hidden agenda, no debriefing afterward to tell the victims what it was really all about.

All told, 204 women were interviewed, more than 10 in each of the principal ten occupations, except for 9 legislators. The youngest women were 2 eighteen year olds, one beginning police work and the other a shipyard apprenticeship. The oldest women were in their early sixties.

The average age of the 83 women in the miscellaneous group was 34. The average ages of the ten principal groups were: firefighters, 31; electricians, 34; engineers, 31; physicians, 36; police officers, 35; stockbrokers, 34; carpenters, 34; attorneys, 33; landscape architects, 38; and, in contrast, state legislators, 55.

Demographically, the women said they had entered these occupations at a later age than the men and believed they had a more varied education than the men and certainly more previous employment in a wider range of work. Whether or not these background differences will continue to characterize women entering male-dominated work, these women were convinced that they were different from the men to start with.

These are pioneering women. Pioneers are not devastated by being considered deviant, have a lot of self-confidence, and have good coping skills for dealing with rejection and hostility. They had survived a long process of screening and ordinary training and hazing plus extraordinary training to overcome socialized shortcomings, for example, weight training, assertiveness training, and remedial mechanical drawing. That we were able to locate them at all was possible because they had survived by doing a very good job. So their employers wanted to retain them, in spite of pressures to keep it a man's world.

Their greater maturity and at least passive identification with the women's movement means they understand the threat men feel working with them. Their sympathy for the men helps them survive. A police detective (age 30) said, "You have to give men time to grow and change and learn acceptance. You can't walk in and say, 'I've got the same qualifications as you, so go to hell.' If you come in with an attitude problem, you'll lose, because when things come up for the first time, the men make mistakes, because they haven't gone through it before."

This sense of history and politics also helps them survive when *they* are threatened by sex discrimination and sexual harassment. A carpenter, age thirty-four, active in her union, said, "The trades are hard. I really sympathize with these men. Most of them do not have a college education. It is the only thing they can do with their lives. They're taking physical risks every day. They ruin their bodies; they have bad backs, bad shoulders, and they're really stuck. The money is good, but they don't necessarily work year-round. I do have empathy for their situation, and I suppose that's helped."

## FOUR BASIC FINDINGS

To organize all of this material I first went through the interviews in each occupation and sorted quotes into however many themes emerged. As a result I had ten, sort of, "occupational chapters" consisting of themes found among the lawyers, the carpenters, the brokers, and so on.

"Our presence changes all kinds of things," said a 45-year-old broker. "It changes the language. It changes the way they conduct meetings, the way they address someone. The men just panicked. I mean, my God, what if I want to have a meeting with a woman broker in my office. Do I leave the door open? Will she know what to wear? My God, is she going to come on with the flowers and the roses? How do I act? What if she has a bad day? How do I criticize her? If I say, 'You shouldn't do that,' will she take it tearfully? Because the men were used to dealing with their wives and children, they weren't used to dealing with a female in a straight businesslike way. But now it is so much more relaxed. They're learning. We're learning."

Next, I asked, do any of the brokers' themes also appear in the other occupations. Are there some topics that appear across the board? My computer came in handy here. I pulled these common themes out, merging lawyer and carpenter quotes under headings such as "Listening over Talking," and "Cooperation rather than Competition."

Then I looked at the resulting headings and asked, do these headings have anything in common? Are there broad, global threads tying these topics together? Can I see underneath a deeply held value or a universal response to a particular situation or a basically female perception based on the same growing-up experiences?

The result was four major, dominant, higher order themes, and I organized the book around them. The major ways these nontraditional women did their work differently than the men did were through:

- A service orientation to clients
- A nurturant approach to coworkers
- An insistence upon a balanced life-style
- An attraction to managing others using power differently than men did

What underlies all four themes then became apparent, not that the themes had to have any ultimate, unifying source. But they do. It is women's lifelong socialization to be a mother and homemaker. All four findings are extensions of our cultural preparation to take care of other people, interwoven with taking care of a place called home.

I considered the irony of this finding. These women were outsiders, deviants, pioneers, gate crashers, women breaching the barriers. How could they possibly be altering the workplace through the socialized, maternal sex role?

Here were women who were like men in that they had to compete in school and training programs to get good grades and be certified. They were, by definition, competitive; were emotionally strong; and had the requisite masculine occupational interests. They were ambitious, hard-working, committed, pioneering women. What a paradox, then, to find that the major changes they were bringing to men's work were very sex-role stereotyped attitudes and actions, absolutely general and within the life experiences of all Western women. How deep-seated and complex our learning to be a homemaker must be.

The fourth theme, attraction to managing others using power differently than men do, was the biggest surprise to me. I had deliberately excluded organizational women, those employed specifically as managers. With very few exceptions, interviewees did not have job titles even hinting of administration. Why then should they be interested in managing the people around them and with a different idea of power?

For them, power was not control over others or the world. Power was seeing that resources got distributed fairly and helping people get control over their lives. A 49-year-old state representative said, "A lot of the men now accept women in their own jobs and in community roles, but they are very worried to see us move into a power mode. They are really worried because they are afraid something is going to happen to them. But they aren't going to be left out. We are just going to share some of that horrid responsibility. It is going to be a hard adjustment period for men, and it may take them a decade to get through it, to see it as being the helpmate, and being willing to take some of the terrible load off their shoulders."

## LOOKING AHEAD

Each of the four parts that follow is preceded by a prologue. The purpose of the prologues is to introduce readers to important feminist writings that bear on each of the major themes. My aim is to cite feminist theorists who thought about the question of women in male-dominated jobs and made predictions that these data bear out.

In the chapters themselves there is a blending of the women speaking for themselves with my thoughts and reactions as a feminist and a psychologist. Each of the four parts has three chapters containing minor themes found, in most cases, across all occupations. The blue-collar chapter is an exception, referring only to firefighters, police officers, carpenters, and electricians. Likewise, the chapter on leading, using our kind of power, refers primarily to the legislators and lawyers.

The twelve chapters making up the four parts are followed by a final chapter devoted to "Reforming Men." In it is more good news—evidence that men have changed and are liberating themselves from male sex-role socialization. This is where men tell other men how they benefit from becoming more service oriented, caring of coworkers, balanced in life-style, and egalitarian in managing the world of work.

# I

# Service to Clients

---

The four general themes in this book are rooted in our socialization for the roles of mother and homemaker. But this part and the next, "Caring about Coworkers," are the most obviously linked to the traditional role of a mother at home whose major task in life is to take care of her family. We learn it. Men can learn it, except, until now, most haven't wanted to.

Many people have written about the various feminine traits and behaviors that we learn as we grow up to be maternal and nurturant, among them Margaret Adams, Jessie Bernard, Betty Friedan, Carol Gilligan, Arlie Hochschild, Jean Miller, Adrienne Rich, Robyn Rowland, Dale Spender, and Joan Wheeler-Bennett.

I am, however, particularly interested in writers who talk about the possibility of conditioning men to be more like women, authors who not only believe such change is possible but who think that changing men to be more nurturant is a worthy feminist project.

Marilyn French is one of these writers. She is not the first feminist to make a plea for transforming society using feminine values, but her concentration on the value of nurturance and the pleasures of sharing and mutual compassion make her plea especially compelling. She emphasizes in *Beyond Power: On Women, Men, and Morals* (1985) how the male pursuit of power as control deprives most men of the core of life, which is sharing, community, trusting, and mutual affection (p. 297). Although French believes "there is no clear, right way to move," she might agree that male-dominated jobs are a good place to start (pp. 484–485).

Similarly, we must not be discouraged with men but continue the slow and difficult process of teaching them female values, said Lynne Segal in *Is the Future Female?* (1987, p.xv). Segal is dismayed that the new popular feminism seems to have given up on men just when men appear willing to embrace feminist ideas. Indeed, she says, feminist goals have become respectable and are genuinely supported by some men (pp. 38–40). Segal believes there are men who look to feminists as a source of change in society.

Segal warned against seeing two struggling camps—on the one side, virtuous women characterized by nurturance and cooperation and, on the other side, vicious men characterized by violence and competition—because, she said, our values are socially constructed and therefore can change. Neither women nor men are fixed and frozen (1987, p. ix). In particular, Segal believes that men should be as involved as women in the care of young children (p. 156).

The same optimism exists in Judith Bardwick's writing in *In Transition* (1979), where she suggested that we are moving toward a great humanizing revolution, moving beyond simply getting greater numbers of women into school, government, industry, and male-dominated occupations. This revolution is one of ethics and values.

Bardwick (1979, pp. 174–177) said we must question the work-driven style of the successful American male and traits such as competitiveness, independence, ambition, and assertiveness. Traits associated with maternal caring should be encouraged so that psychologically healthier humans result. Bardwick wants men as well as women to be emotionally vulnerable and dependent, men as well as women committed to relationships and community. Bardwick's revolution is about women's values, objectives, and styles becoming those of society and associated with people of both sexes.

In the United Kingdom Janet Richards, in *The Skeptical Feminist* (1980), called for women to take their caring activities outside the home for the good of everyone. If it is valuable to do social service activities for a few, why not for many? If it is a good thing to care about family meals, why not care about the running of the ministry of agriculture? If one's children's education is important, why not work within the whole school system to make it better? The most worthwhile work, she said, is "what does most good to most people," and that means outside the confines of the home (p. 169).

Richards' standard of what makes work worthwhile, "the most good to the most people," is shared both by women who do and women who don't join the women's movement, according to Robyn Rowland (1984). Women at opposite ends of the feminist continuum agree that society should cultivate women's caring values and eradicate male violence and aggression.

Not only can men learn to be nurturant, but Nancy Chodorow in *The*

*Reproduction of Mothering* (1978, pp. 218–219) told us that men must learn to share primary parenting with women. Equal parenting is, in Chodorow's mind, absolutely necessary if women are ever to achieve sexual equality. Our socialization for motherhood doesn't merely teach sex roles; it is the basis of male dominance and sexual inequality. Chodorow believes men can change and that there must be fundamental reorganization of parenting so that children are dependent on people of both sexes from birth on.

The three chapters in this part summarize what nontraditional women say about their greater service orientation to clientele—a generally more helpful attitude, certainly. But the features of service that are uniquely women's are willingness and ability to listen and respond to what others tell us they need and the ability to put ourselves in others' shoes, to identify with customers and clients to such an extent that their needs become our needs within the context of our jobs.

# 1

# THE HELPING ATTITUDE

My personality is 180 degrees different from the men. I have this technical background, how engineers think, plus a very feeling type personality. When I look at a project, I ask first, "who is this project going to help in the community?" Second, "how will the people working on it benefit?" Nurturing is a tremendous strength. If we ever see nurturance as weakness, we'll have lost a big part of ourselves. (Engineer, age 28)

Feminist thinkers and the man in the street alike know that, in general, women are more interested than men in caring for other people. Our traditional occupations are saturated with serving others: teacher, social worker, waitress, retail clerk, counselor, nurse, receptionist. When women in such female-dominated jobs take a vocational interest test, you see women's basic orientation immediately in their highest average score—social service.

But this interview project bears out another finding from the field of interest measurement: in male-dominated occupations women differ from men by having, in addition to the same great interest in technology, science, or persuasive selling, a higher level of service interest than men.

On the one hand, then, I was not surprised that these nontraditional women had such strong motives to be of service. But I *knew* these women. I knew how technically skilled, career-oriented, and persevering they were. So I had to ask, how could women with strong masculine work interests simultaneously have such a feminine orientation to work?

The most basic, core reason given by feminist theorists for this universal proclivity to care for others I'll call simply "The Motherhood Explanation." It is the Motherhood Explanation that sends women forth into the world, to engineering and police work, medicine and fire-fighting, caring very much about relationships, and taking care of people because of their early socialization for motherhood. How does it work?

According to the Motherhood Explanation, if mothers are to understand infants' wishes, they have to listen very closely to crying and wailing. What is being communicated—hunger, anger, thirst, discomfort, frustration, fear, wanting to be held close? Good mothering depends on listening patiently and picking up on unverbalized cues. Then the little girls who were attended to and gratified grow up modeling their behavior after their mothers, whom they see continually listening to what husbands and children ask for followed by seeing the pleasure of husbands and children at being given what they asked for.

This kind of listening isn't easy. Witness the difficulty described above trying to interpret an infant's cries. Some husbands' needs require even more careful attention. What is he trying to tell me about money? Oh, oh, silence. What's he worried about now? Oh, no, he's really angry. Wonder what it's about this time? Certainly, both boys and girls equally want to please their parents. But girls and boys are differentially rewarded by their parents for pleasing other people. Parents want their little girls to be sensitive to others' feelings, to be popular, to get along well with other children. All of this is necessary if girls are to attract suitable mates, about which parents worry far more with daughters than sons. Being good wife material means being good at taking care of other people's needs. So daughters observe and imitate their mothers' nurturance, and daughters have their aggressiveness ignored or punished.

A carpenter (age 30) talked about how she learned about mothering. "I had an ally relationship with my mother. She taught me to read when I was really little. We'd sit together in the same chair and read. She confided in me more when I was little than she probably should have. I was her confidante. I listened to what was going on in her life. It tuned me in a lot to relationships in the family. It really tuned me in to my mother and father's relationship. I sort of became the little peacemaker, the wrinkle smoother. If she couldn't run in when my father and brother got volatile, I would, and say, 'Stop this, stop this.' My relationship with Mom just tuned me in to be attentive to relationships. *My brother had to learn to be separate from Mom. But I didn't have to separate.*" (emphasis added).

This carpenter unknowingly put her finger on the greater importance to us of listening and of relationships. We learn that the most compelling relationship we will ever have is to an infant. We are taught from infancy to put infants' needs before our own. It goes along with learning to walk and talk and get a spoon to our mouths. It is girl children's first lesson, and it is taught by their first and most lasting model, from whom they do not have to separate, as boys do, to forge their sex-role identification.

Carol Tavris and Carole Wade (1984, pp. 69–70) in their summary of the sex-difference literature to date confirm that women's greater nurturance begins in childhood with greater affection and help for infants in little girls than in little boys. Helpfulness to small children is a task that most cultures assign to women, so little girls are simply picking up on society's expectations of them. Similarly, if little boys approach infants, usually to take something away from them, are they not also responding to society's expectations?

Tavris and Wade said that American boys typically are not taught to take care of or rewarded for taking care of children. Instead, they are taught to suppress their nurturant feelings toward infants in public. Men's socialization for parenting traditionally teaches them that women are the carers, and they are the protectors and providers. (But adult men can be resocialized at the birth of their babies and reinforced positively for expressing the nurturant feelings they've suppressed since childhood.)

A legislator (age 49) said that some men couldn't understand that she does her job to be of service, to serve her community. "They don't believe you, and they'll put you down for saying that; they'll scorn you with 'You are really in this for yourself.' Well, yes, it is a rewarding job and I enjoy it, but basically I wouldn't be there if I didn't want to do it for my community. This is a damn hard job with somebody always screaming at you, and it isn't exactly paying me a living wage, so why in the heck would I want to do it if it wasn't for some larger reason? I really believe my reason is that the community benefits. I bring *everything* to the job. I mean my husband will tell you that I haven't ironed a shirt in four years." That "larger reason" she spoke of, service, is very often primary for women.

What goes into this service orientation? There are seven aspects to it. First, the women said, our mindset is, "How can I help this person?" Second, they agreed that their approach to clients was more gentle, softer, and aided by voices that were softer to start with. Third, they said that clients came first, whereas male colleagues often placed company rules and pressures ahead of clients. Fourth, the women said they were very concerned about doing a quality job, and cutting corners for greater profit made them uncomfortable. After all, each job was for a real person who was counting on you. At the same time, they indicated, if someone wants to tap our expert know-how, we're more than willing to share it. Sixth, they gave me examples of how their expertise led them to simpler, less expensive solutions to clients' problems, a holdover from managing the household budget. Finally, the women claimed that they had more integrity than the men where clients were concerned. This popular stereotype, many said, was true.

## THE HELPING ATTITUDE

The police and fire services in most Western countries try to juggle the twin goals of control and service. Men traditionally have gone into both jobs motivated by the control side of the job. They have been attracted by the authority and the respect they expect to receive for their perceived role of risking physical danger to protect the public. Women, in contrast, are not motivated by the macho image. Rather, they are interested in the pay and benefits and in being of service to others.

Even in gun-toting America, the reality of these two jobs is far less control than service. Most police and fire work is hum-drum and routine, talking to citizens on the beat and inspecting homes and businesses. Very little time is spent in shootouts with criminals or putting out fires. But whereas men are bored with taking people's blood pressure at the station house, many women enjoy doing it and chatting with the public about health and safety.

The shift in emphasis from control to service is a continuing one. Women play a more visible role now in these jobs because physical strength is not as relevant to performance in 1990 as it was in 1900. Moreover, as public safety becomes even more accountable to the community, the service function will further eclipse the control function.

Women can thrive in these environments. Women have a more constructive attitude inspecting buildings and more sympathy when listening to crime victims. This greater helpfulness is the more evident because many women firefighters and police have left teaching, social work, and nursing for these higher paying blue-collar jobs.

A 28-year-old firefighter with five years' retail selling experience talked about this advantage: "I liked dealing with people, and I think most of the other women have had other jobs. So we have had experience in the business world and dealt with people before in a different capacity. One of the things I've noticed in dealing with the public on inspections is that some of these guys don't have any tact. They are real gruff and it's kind of like, 'Yeah, well, we're going to shut you down.' The thing is, *we're here to keep these people in business, to keep them firesafe. We're not here to bother the public or the businesses; we're just here to help them out.* I think the women have a little more finesse. If someone starts yelling and screaming at us, we're not as apt to yell and scream back. We'll listen to their side and try to accommodate them more" (emphasis added).

"Why can't I care about people and still be a cop?" a police officer (age 38) asked herself when she joined the service. "I decided I could be the kind of cop I wanted to be. So for the last ten years I have done a whole variety of things at the patrol level, jobs you can't do once you're promoted. For three years I did school liaison work. My goal was to make the kids aware that a police officer is a human being, not just an authority figure to be feared, and when I make arrests, I am not heavy-handed. For people with three or four arrests, you can communicate that when they're ready to pull their life out of the gutter, the cops are there for them."

In an entirely different arena, the lawyers and brokers told me a woman's first thought is, what can we do for this person? One of the lawyers reported she feels a deep responsibility toward anyone seeking her advice and hopes she will be able to get back to the client with, "Yeah, we can do it!" When she realizes she will not be able to handle someone's business, I was told, a women has a harder time telling the person. She agonizes over how to ease the rejection, whereas a male attorney can turn people down quickly with no regrets.

Because of the helping attitude, women brokers do not intimidate their male clients but encourage them to ask embarrassing questions, to say "I don't understand" or "I forgot what you told me yesterday." The conversation is more relaxed, informal, uncompetitive. Whether or not it is a stereotype, men believe a woman broker will keep *their* interests at heart rather than her own or those of the brokerage house. Women find they can be especially helpful to women clients because of shared life experiences that involve money, such as divorce, widowhood, and simply learning about money and finance later in life than men typically do.

A 40-year-old tax attorney described her work as very protective, shielding her clients from the "vagaries of strange laws and other people. I want them to be able to lead ordinary lives without being sued or having something totally unexpected happen to them. I just see perfectly innocent people all of a sudden in horrible tangles. Many of my clients are old; they just want nice, clean transactions, no excitement in their lives, no audits. Then these horrible things happen, laws being amended, updated, reformed. Men think it's a tremendous waste of time, but as a woman I care very much about my clients and their lives."

## A SOFTER APPROACH

Robert Fein (1974, pp. 55–56) said fifteen years ago that increasing numbers of men were spending more time in caring contact with their kids: first, because their wives were working and asked them to; second, because the women in their lives were asking them to examine the nature of masculinity and encouraging them to rediscover their caring selves through relationships with young children.

What have men gained from childcare? Fein mentioned honest, direct communication and an integration of one's childlike self with one's grown-up self (1974, pp. 60–61). He also said that caring contact with children counteracts loneliness, competition, ulcers, heart attacks, and premature dying (pp. 61–62). He mentioned work-related gains such as paternity leave, parttime jobs, and tax laws that now give corporations incentives to let employees meet family needs.

Encouragingly, the blue-collar women had observed what Fein observed. They said that because so many of their male colleagues' wives also have jobs, the men are developing latent nurturing skills that their fathers never had the chance to acquire. The men get the kids up and off to school, fix evening meals, and bathe children when their wives are at work. The lessons the men learn taking care of their own children have a noticeable softening effect on their interaction with others on the job, especially in interviews with children and women.

Women's lifelong socialization for motherhood, on the other hand, gives us an advantage in behaviors that show patience, gentleness, and kindness. Our elementary and secondary school socialization toward typical women's occupations reinforces other behaviors that express cheerfulness, politeness, uncomplainingness, and the desire to please other people. We are taught to be quiet, not loud; deferential, not demanding; well mannered, not rowdy like the boys; and soft, not hard. So a softer approach is what we take in relationships with others, whether at home or work, and we go on being softer even if we don't have children and even if we don't train to be secretaries or teachers.

A hospital maintenance electrician, age 50, said that she always thinks in terms of relationships between people and just naturally soothes customers. "My partner goes in to install outlets or lighting and won't even bother to offer an explanation. These people are our customers! So I say, 'Is this all right? Could you move to another area for a day? Would you mind taking a thirty-minute break? Why we're here is...' So people are glad to see me coming. I have a good reputation for getting the job done quickly and efficiently at the same time that I deal with people gently. So it's not because I can do the job any better; it is more in the manner in which I deal with people."

A carpenter (age 42) similarly deplored the work style of "blast through and get out." Women, she said, can't work that way because we are so aware of the effects of our presence on clients. "Everybody today is concerned about time lines. They want things done fast. I think it's better to do part of a big remodeling job, then let people live with it and see if they like it and want to go on. It's better to take time when thinking about changes. *Go slower, be gentler.* As much as we remodel homes, we spend time counseling clients to figure out what they want and to deal with the changes and stresses of having their home remodeled. The house is torn up, there's a lot of dust and clutter and noise, and it costs a lot of money. Sometimes I have a sense that we're as much therapists as remodelers."

A police detective (age 45) confessed that she has things worked out with her partner so that she deliberately plays the "nurturing and caring woman." "But it's also true. I do care about people even though they're breaking the law. So I play this role but it's true. Some are criminal criminals, and some are good people just trying to make it through the world. They're willing to say, 'I did this. Now how do I get through it?' They have no idea how to work within the system. You can reason with them and help them. I understand their problems and they relate to me as their mother, someone who sympathizes."

## PEOPLE ARE TOP PRIORITY

A woman legislator's priorities in making decisions are, first, her constituents and, second, her political caucus. Men's priorities are reversed— first, his caucus, meaning his buddies and peers, and, second, his constituents.

Similarly, men and women landscape architects have different design priorities. The women's are, first, is it environmentally sound? Second, does it meet the needs of all users—children, old people, the handicapped? Third, does it look good? Men's priorities are, first, does it look good? Does it make a statement? Second, is it environmentally sound? Third, does it meet the special needs of users?

"Our final product," said a 42-year-old landscape architect, "offers more amenities, more places to sit, more public conveniences. It is more of an effort to accommodate people than demonstrate our designing ability. We'd rather make other people comfortable and meet their basic needs than make a statement that might bring us fame."

For airline pilots of both sexes the top priority is safety. I talked to just a few pilots, not enough to learn what men's next priority was, but for the women, people came after safety. Their stories convince me that women fly planes differently than men do.

A 42-year-old pilot said she pays a lot of personal attention to passengers' and others' needs. "I remember we were to escort a body, and right before takeoff I discovered it wasn't on board but on the airplane next door. So I got the process started and the ground crew got the plane stopped and the casket put on ours. It all depends on how important you see another person's problem. I could picture that family waiting and mourning, and then we land and Grandpa's not aboard, Grandpa's missing. How could we do that to someone? They were already suffering enough."

For another pilot (age 30), passenger comfort clearly came before company policy. "It's part of being more concerned about the welfare of people. For example, on the way back from Hong Kong, a ten-hour flight, there was a woman whose seat wouldn't recline. This is a very uncomfortable position to sit in for so long, so I asked the captain if we could move her up to first class. He wouldn't do it. If I were captain, I would have done that. I don't care about what the first-class passengers might think. I'd have moved her up. Or take the matter of air-conditioning. The plan is to run with two systems on, the third off. If people complain about smoke or heat, I'll turn on the third, whereas lots of captains will say, 'Forget it.' "

Legislators use the same words feminist thinkers use in their writings, such as women having "a more compassionate attitude toward the struggles of human beings" or saying they are very concerned about people because "that is what state government is all about, helping people." Washington's legislators sponsor legislation on children's issues, schools, the juvenile court system, protecting minority rights, and all the people issues that have not been addressed legislatively by male colleagues. They say the only reason the men now vote for these issues is because women are there effectively advocating.

Most of the legislators interviewed say their constituents can call them any hour, any day of the week.

"If I weren't available, there wouldn't be anyone in this district to deal with the traumas in some people's lives. We are socialized to be caretakers in the first place. To me, my district is my extended family. They come to my door. I remember one woman who came with a huge book that she had compiled about a problem. She asked me would I just read part of it because she was so distressed. I started reading the darn thing, and my Lord, the first thing I knew I was half way through it, and the next thing I knew I am going to meetings the bureaucrats are holding to take away her childcare license. I got it stopped. I doubt very much that very many men would have helped her with that. But I dropped everything. I felt no woman is going to come to my door and expend that much effort unless it is pretty important" (State legislator, age fifty-eight).

## DOING A QUALITY JOB

One reason that nontraditional, pioneering women are spurred on to do a quality job is that if they don't, they'll be fired. But proving themselves isn't the only thing behind the women telling me how important doing a quality job is. It came up over and over again. What always underlies their high standard of performance is basic respect for people dependent on them: clients, customers, constituents, and community. For many women, these people feel like part of their families, and how do you treat your family? Your family deserves the very best, and you sacrifice to do the best you can for them.

This is why the matter of cutting corners to make greater profit makes women uncomfortable. Profit over people? This is also why the argument that "Everyone else is taking advantage of us, so why shouldn't we do the same?" is acceptable to so few of us. Because our work is done in a relationship context, even when the other party to the relationship is anonymous, that relationship precludes cheating the other party.

A cabinetmaker (age 30) shrugged and said that she can't afford the kind of furniture she makes. "But these doctors and lawyers are our lifeblood. If that's what he likes, then that's okay, and it's certainly okay if he wants to spend that kind of money. The guys have this predisposed attitude toward people we're doing the job for, before they've even met them, before they're even people, and it affects their attitude toward work. If they have the attitude 'he's a jerk and doesn't know anything,' the tendency is to let the quality of our work go down. It's their way to get back. 'It's good enough. He won't notice.' I won't settle for that. If it's not right, we have to get it right. So when they talk about 'this guy's a jerk,' I try to change the subject, turn it around to more positive things."

"As a journeyman, the quality of my work has to be the best I can do," related a 37-year-old electrician who had started another apprenticeship in a different area of electrical work. "But as an apprentice I always gear my quality of work towards whatever journeyman I'm working for. If he's sloppy, I put my pipe in sloppy. If he's neat, I do mine neat. He's my direct boss, and I'll do the covered stuff how he wants it done. Sloppy is faster. But if it's something that's going to show forever, I take my time. My panels and any work that is going to show are going to be much neater than that man will accept. I do that on my own standards."

## HELPING PEOPLE BECOME INDEPENDENT

Part of motherhood is teaching children to be capable, independent, confident persons who can get along without us. We are thus conditioned to teach clients and customers what we know and in the process to become more independent. Teaching is also a sign of respect for other people's intelligence and ability to learn. Women would rather spend time now with clients teaching than later treating unwanted pregnancies, scraping teenagers off the highway, or rescuing unattended children from fires.

The female firefighter's way of dealing with a business owner who is defensive and feels he's being harassed by an inspection is "to explain the codes and *benefits* to the owner of staying within the codes, such as insurance benefits. Using a *teaching approach*, instead of 'You have to do it. I have the authority to make you.' "

The female broker's way of dealing with people's money is truly to be a financial counselor or investment planner or whatever the fashionable term is today that implies caring and concern, whether it's there or not.

With women the concern is there. They believe that the clients' dollars are those people's dollars.

"It is not the brokerage houses' money; it is not Hutton's money or Merrill's money or Oppenheimer's money. Those people have a right to be given the best advice as to what to put their money in—period. I don't care who you are, the most important thing is to give that service. The other brokers around here say, 'I don't believe you tell your clients all that. Just tell them to buy it, it's good, trust me, and hang the phone up.' I really go through everything with them. After being with me six or seven years, they are really smart clients. So I don't have to do so many dance steps anymore. They understand my lingo because I have educated them over the years. I write pieces to them on what I am seeing. I always ask their opinion. It is important to give your client as much credit as you can" (Broker, age 33).

A young pastor proved that youth is no deterrent to teaching independence. It took about two years, but she finally got the women of her parish, most in their seventies, to challenge the church hierarchy. Several of these women had an angry confrontation with a bishop who had set a very inconvenient date and time for an important meeting. They demanded in the future that they be consulted in keeping with their important roles in the church. The young pastor felt this happened because she had used her power to empower these elderly women. Her mission was to free them to do things they never dreamed possible, to see where they were within the church and move beyond it.

Stunned by the lies she read about herself in the newspaper, a legislator (age 45) went to educate its editor. "I have often said that the best training I've had for this job was a year I taught in junior high. Anyway, after I got over my original outrage, I went to that editor and laid all this stuff out, just to make sure that he understood what was being said in the campaign by my opponent were intentional mistruths. He found it fascinating, my educating him to what was game playing and posturing! It made him look at my opponent in a more questioning light. He had been too accepting of some of the things he'd been told."

## GOOD SERVICE IS PRACTICAL

"Being practical" means different things to women and men. Our meaning comes from being practical in running a house and managing its budget. Our meaning also comes from seeing all problems as connected to people who need to be helped as quickly and inexpensively as possible.

The employees in one of my interview settings had complained to the maintenance people that every time the air-conditioners were turned off, the filters fell on their heads. The filters were simply applied on the outside of the machines and hung on by sheer suction, until the equipment was turned off, then plop. Our heroine, a 33-year-old electronics technician, got tired of waiting for the sheet-metal men to complete the design of expensive, custom-made, retrofit metal frames. One day she said "enough" and went to Woolworths and brought back some hookside velcro with a sticky back. She stuck strips of velcro all around the perimeter of the filter area on an air-conditioner and then stuck the filter material up against the strips. The filter gripped the hooks, acting like the loop side of velcro—an eighteen cent solution now rather than a thirty-five dollar solution sometime in the future. The entire plant adopted it overnight.

Our solutions do not have to be sophisticated. Homely will do as long as it does the job. We tend to grab materials close at hand, and we aren't concerned that we have found the "best" solution. Men put more emphasis on the process of finding an elegant technical solution; we are more concerned with simply finding something workable for the person who needs it.

On the other hand, we won't compromise the needs of a client to solve the problem quickly. We are willing to spend time working with a client on that cheap answer, probably because we enjoy the interaction and know that collaboration is likely to produce a more satisfactory solution.

An engineer (age 30) said that in her design work she was much more practical when it came to cost. "There are standard rules of thumb you can use, or you can use precise calculations. I am always wondering, what's the cheapest thing that is safe? So I'll take more time talking to the client. The men don't want to call and talk to someone, so to be on the safe side, they throw in stuff that is totally needless and much more expensive."

## A LITTLE HIGHER LEVEL OF INTEGRITY

A 45-year-old broker's daughter had followed in her mother's footsteps just two weeks before the mother's interview. "I told her there are two things I am going to tell you, and write them down, or blaze them in stone, or write them in lipstick on the top of your mirror, whatever you have to do. One is always be honest. Don't ever lie—ever. The other is when you make a mistake, own up to it right away. In this business you can't hide things. If you make a mistake, you have to immediately address it."

The brokers were unanimous that society believes that women brokers are more honest than men brokers, and they agree. The men's lack of integrity slops over into their personal lives or vice versa. "My office mate gave me a ride home," related a 33-year-old broker.

"There is this traffic divider where you're supposed to go right, get in the left-hand lane, and turn left to get back on Spring Street. Well, he looks at the divider and those poles and says 'Huh?' and just proceeds to drive right over the top of it. I screamed 'My, God!' and he said, 'Do you see a cop? Do you see a cop?' 'No.' 'See. Got away with that one!' What I am telling you is that he does that every day in some little way, some bigger than others. He'll do transactions when the paper work is not in. He'll do it anyway. We would say, 'Let's get the paper work in, and as soon as it is okay, as soon as all the signatures are in, and da-ta-da-ta-da, we'll do it.' That is why, so far, our integrity is pretty good."

"If we had more women managers in brokerage firms," she continued, "the priorities would change as to who gets rewarded, who gets the most money. We think our word is our honor and that it is the number one thing. That is really saying that I think women have more honor. Have you heard that Khadafi's private bodyguards are women because they can't be bought? Their sense of honor and loyalty are greater than men's. That's my credibility, Khadafi!"

The broker with the daughter, above, said her sales manager realizes that women are his secret weapon because there are no compliance problems with them. "We don't break the rules. We don't set out to break the rules. We just say, 'How do I do this?' 'Oh, okay.' Then we go out and do it and bring the money back. The men say, 'Ha, ha. You really did that?' I say, 'Yes, and it worked.' So we stay within the rules, while they tend to believe rules are made to be broken."

All the legislators, too, said the public perceived that women had more integrity and that they thought there was truth in that perception. They said our socialization teaches us to be more honest. So women are less likely to lie in campaigns, more likely to keep their word, and less likely to be on the take. Integrity also meant being prepared by doing research and not faking it and fighting for right even though you might lose personally.

"There was a truancy bill that I felt extremely strong about. There were no provisions for parental involvement—nothing. I felt so strongly that was wrong. One by one, the other side who were going to cosponsor my amendments fell by the wayside. The education chair said, 'Don't worry about it. That bill isn't going any place.' Well, I don't feel that any one person has that much power, so I ran my amendments, and I continued running them with a handful of people on the floor, and they voted for every one, if a vote was called for. But a good friend told me, 'You lost a lot of points today. That was as close to a filibuster as we've ever seen.' Well, if the others who said they would run the amendments had done it, it wouldn't have fallen to me. It had been a very bad bill, and when it came back from the Senate, they had incorporated my amendments; it was a much better bill. So if I lost points, I lost points. It mattered more to me that some kid who is being neglected by his or her parents already and is an outcast at school already not be sent to detention for skipping school and put in with kids who have committed all kinds of crime. I'll bet the chair of that education committee never forgets it as long as he lives" (State representative, age 58).

Part of integrity has to do with keeping confidences, and we are very good at it, the legislators said.

"There is a lot of counting that goes on behind the scenes. If you're not going to keep your word, they're not going to trust you again, the interest groups, your colleagues, the governor. It is absolutely a false impression the world has that women are gossips and rumor spreaders. It is absolutely the opposite. A Democratic woman and I ran the water quality bill two years ago, and we negotiated, whether they would vote for it, whether they would give us a vote if we needed one, the whole thing. To this day, nobody knows who those people were. I knew I had more votes if I needed them, and she knew she had more. But we never told anybody. We never let anything out of the bag. We didn't move until we were ready to move, and we were very successful. The only credit we got was in the local newspaper, which said, 'When the vote was over, these two women hugged on the floor of the House' " (State representative, age 49).

The lawyers are less sure about whether the integrity stereotype applies to them. They think the difference between the sexes is small, if it exists, but a 40-year-old attorney said, "Wait a minute," and went off to get the monthly bar newsletter. She held it out to me and said, "You know, *all* of the people who get reprimanded, disbarred, censured, and there are two to four of them a month, are males. It's amazing; it almost always has dealt with screwing around with clients' funds, using trust funds for personal reasons. It gets real easy to feel this money is your own. But I think women are more self-policing. We were always taught to be good little girls."

A good mother wouldn't steal from her children's trust funds. But we also have a different slant on morality than men have. Men are more concerned with abstract justice, women with what is right for the people involved. The right thing to do is a very weighty, complicated, caring decision because of people, because of relationships. Our different slant is what Carol Gilligan's *In a Different Voice* (1982) is all about.

One of the lawyers is a partner in her large, very conservative firm; yet she practices the morality of caring in relation to her clients, at great risk to herself within the organization.

"Women get all kinds of scrappy, little, complicated, incredibly weird business that the person can't pay for. Men won't take these cases. Instead, they'll give the person the card of the lawyer they hate most in the world. Often this business is with women who've signed something without getting legal advice, or it's some family affair for which they lack business acumen. I took one case where this woman was being shut out of the business she owned, so we did some self-help. We broke in and took all the files relevant to the case and loaded them into my car, and then we roared off, laughing in hysterics. It was totally irregular, right on the border of the criminal. But she was a very difficult client, and no one else in my firm would touch her" (Attorney, age 40).

## NURTURANCE IS NOT A WEAKNESS, UNLESS...

Nurturance is a good thing, but women are often manipulated to be nurturant when we should be assertive, independent, and selfish. We are so well socialized to be nurturant, and men are so well socialized to the fact that they don't have to be, that we sometimes fall into "the compassion trap." That is, we do all the service work for both sexes when we should, instead, insist that caring be divided equally and our other needs be met—needs such as achievement, recognition, and creativity.

To bring "the compassion trap" close to home, Margaret Adams in *Woman in Sexist Society* (1971, pp. 514–515) told a story on herself, how she, another woman, and a man had planned to spend a Saturday afternoon writing. They had turned down attractive invitations and were looking forward to a day of creativity and moving forward with their literary commitments. Instead, unexpected and uninvited guests arrived, and the two women entertained them. But the man didn't. He went right on with the original plan, remained cloistered in his study, had tea brought to him, and nobody thought anything of it. Margaret Adams said her tale has a moral, but she didn't spell it out.

Maybe the story has several morals. Maybe all three should have sent the interlopers packing. Maybe all three should have entertained. Maybe they should have told their guests what their plans were and spent an hour making tea and then splitting, back to their typewriters, leaving the guests and the rest of the household to entertain themselves. Maybe what Margaret Adams intended is that we all start saying we're fed up with nurturance being thought of as universally and exclusively female.

# 2

# CAREFUL LISTENING

You are selling your expertise of listening to someone else, of listening to their needs and what they are trying to do, and then matching that to what is out there in the market. If I have ten quality conversations a day, where you ask somebody what they want and you give feedback and give and take, well, you have so much business you don't know what to do with it. All it is, is listening. (Broker, age 45)

In their review of sex differences Carol Tavris and Carole Wade (1984, pp. 42–43) did not list listening ability, not as a physical difference, an ability difference, or a personality difference. Yet the women I interviewed told me, "Women are much better listeners. Everyone knows that."

From my experience in teaching, I know they are right. It always confounded me that in every class I ever taught, the men far outtalked the women. They could be very caring, social service-oriented, liberal men, but they dominated discussions. Unless we all worked very hard to overcome this phenomenon, three guys could clock more minutes than seventeen women in any seminar on anything.

Similar to behaviors that display integrity or show that people are top priority, listening is learned. We imitate our mothers' careful listening. We were and are rewarded for careful listening.

A 36-year-old police officer described how women of her generation simply modeled their listening behavior after their mothers. "We've had a fairly traditional upbringing with a mother who was at home, whose center was the home and family, and we model after that female. I think that our listening ability, the phraseology that stimulates conversation, the proper responses that encourage a child to unburden, those same responses work with the people, the clientele that you have to deal with. Especially when you're dealing with victims, the mothering experience has a positive effect on me as a police officer."

This lifetime of rewards for listening sometimes makes it a need that must be satisfied regularly. Some of us have to fulfill that need daily, even before clients knock on the door. A 33-year-old broker said, "I *have got to* go around in the morning and say hello to everybody, find out what they did the night before. I have to know who cut their hair. I have to be real social, have to say 'Hi' to everyone, and then I can sit down and work."

If we don't watch out, we can even get listening deprived. A shipfitter (age 37) was sent out of town with nineteen men to do a job that lasted six weeks. She didn't think it would be hard on her, but "after two weeks I was going to grocery stores just to stand in line to listen to other women. I was so desperate to chitchat. I can be one of the boys for eight hours a day, but you do have to have a little camaraderie with other women. I didn't think I'd miss it that bad."

But men also learn to be poor listeners. Why? What's behind it—the masculine ideal? This traditionally has meant dominating and controlling other people, succeeding at any cost, protecting your image, and striving to distance yourself from others. It, and this is very important, also means guarding against anything female or feminine in yourself.

Sensitive and sympathetic listening is not part of the old masculine ideal. Is passive, taking-in listening so identified with being a woman that men trying to live up to the ideal resist listening with their overriding talk? Are men poorer listeners because keeping their mouths shut and listening to others is unmanly?

This is the way men behave. Tavris and Wade (1984, pp. 235–236) referred to research studies that found (1) in male–female conversations, men do almost all of the interrupting; (2) men often squelch topics raised by women by minimally responding ("ummm"); (3) women gaze at and attend more to men while listening than men attend to women; (4) in male–female conversations, men speak for longer periods, whereas women smile more.

How much interrupting of women by men are we talking about? The figures are ninety-eight percent of the interrupting according to Susan Brownmiller's *Femininity* (1984, p. 121) or ninety-six percent as reported by Alfie Kohn in a February 1988 *Psychology Today* article called "Girl Talk, Guy Talk" (p. 66).

I think men's poorer listening ability is linked with one of the few conclusive sex differences researchers have found, aggressiveness. Men are more aggressive than women (Tavris & Wade, 1984, pp. 71–73). This sex difference appears as soon as children start to play with one another, at age two or three. Little boys from the start show more physical aggression, play aggression, fantasy aggression, and verbal aggression.

Is an interruption not part of using talk aggressively, as a battlefield, or using talk as another opportunity to challenge, argue, fight, and win? If you stand around listening, you're not chalking up points, carrying the day, having the last word, winning and succeeding. Men must learn that listening is weak, indecisive, inactive. After all, listening closes the distance between two people; it implies reflection and introspection. Listening means absorbing and considering and perhaps changing one's opinion. Listening must be very threatening to traditional masculine idealists, because if a man doesn't win, he has obviously failed.

Dale and Lynne Spender laughed throughout *Scribbling Sisters* (1986) over women's mythical talkativeness. Dale reported that in mixed sex conversations women talk only ten to twenty percent of the time, and when she measured column inches of newspaper reviews devoted to women's books versus men's books (as another indication of how ready men are to listen to what women have to say), women received less than six percent of the column inches (p. 32). Yet the editors were convinced that the space allocation was fair, and one editor even thought women's books dominated the reviews.

I don't think men realize how their socialization for verbal aggression gives them such a bad reputation in terms of being of service. High-pressured, pushy salespersons turn most women off, and I don't understand why other men reinforce it. In any case, one of the big, on-the-job differences revealed in the interviews is that women spend more time listening to clients. The women said more time was spent by women doctors with patients, women cops with robbers, women brokers with customers, and women legislators with constituents.

There were six ways in which the women told me they listened more carefully. First, they wanted to know as much about their clients as they could before deciding how best to help. Second, this was particularly true when dealing with women clients who had learned to give up trying to make their real concerns known to male experts and deferred to whatever men prescribed. Third, they said that because women are not used to being dominant it was easier to understand other people's points of view and they had discovered that client input produced better results. Fourth, the women police officers said that they saw the world differently than the men did and that the two perceptions together came closer to reality than the viewpoint of either sex alone. Fifth, the women did not think that showing compassion and sympathy was unprofessional, and they weren't about to lose their socialized sensitivity. Finally, they knew that just listening could be helpful and that sometimes nothing they said could be as beneficial as simply being a silent sounding board.

## TO LEARN EVERYTHING ABOUT CLIENTS

The women's attitude toward clients is, "If I don't really know you, how can I help you?" Men, on the other hand, tended to be eager to sell a preplanned package or one of their original ideas or their initial diagnosis. But this tendency made it more difficult to draw out information from clients or to accept what clients said nonjudgmentally.

In contrast, a women broker wants to know what your temperament is. She wants to know about your kids, your family, your goals. Before she is going to let you invest, she is going to do research tailored to your special needs. When this 33-year-old sends you her results,

"I expect you to read it. I think the thing that men and women differ on is the fact that I want to make sure if I get anyone into an investment that they understand it, and they have to give me a commitment, too, that they are going to learn right along with me. I don't want somebody to dump fifty thousand dollars into my lap and say, 'I don't know anything about it. You take it and invest it.' Uh-oh. I want you to be in control of your money, to make logical decisions. I am not going to ask you to read a lot of research reports, but if I do send something in the mail, when I call you about it, you at least should have an opinion on it. At least have some questions for me. I don't want to be in a position where I call you up and you say, 'Yeah, do whatever you want.' This is not the way I work."

Your family and financial problems are also important to a woman attorney. She expresses her emotions openly to make it all right for you to express your emotions. She wants to get at the emotional factors under the facts. She wants you to talk about how you're feeling, as well as what you're thinking. "I tend to be more interested in my clients, I care about them. I know that I get too emotionally involved with my clients, spend hours on the telephone listening to them, but these relationships are very important to me. I like working *really closely* with my clients. I like that. There are clients who want hardass nasty men, but I'm not that kind of lawyer" (Attorney, age 35).

An internist, age 47, said that patients perceive that women spend more time with them and are more thoughtful. "Patients have paid me that compliment. I spend an hour with each new patient and at least a half-hour in follow-ups. Some docs see one patient every fifteen minutes. So I spend more time listening, where I know some males who'll charge a sixty dollar fee to adjust medication. It goes back to the pressure men feel to be productive, to make big incomes for the high debt loads they have."

This perception of clients, that women will listen, can get to be a problem, but it's worth it. A 38-year-old general practitioner (GP) said, "All I can say is that I am more sensitive, I spend more time, I pick up on lots, and people really appreciate this. Sometimes people take advantage of me because I'm a woman. They think we'll listen to everything. So sometimes I feel very imposed upon, thinking 'If I were a man, you would never tell me this. Clearly, we have finished with your medical problem, the time has ended, and you are telling me this irrelevant story.' People feel comfortable because I am a woman, but it may also be part of sexism that people don't see our time as valuable."

One deputy sheriff (age 29) has such a reputation for listening that some people after dealing with her think, " 'This is my own personal deputy here. If I have a problem, I'll just call her!' I feel good that they call me and count on me to listen, but it can be a bother. I usually try to be real patient, maybe more so than the guys. I haven't got the heart to tell them I haven't got the time right now. So I end up listening to people a lot and sometimes that can be a problem."

A state representative (age 49) thinks our better listening starts very early but that raising children sharpens it.

"We listen to our children, adjudicate sibling issues and all of that. When you go to the legislature and have to listen to the issues, it is much better to be a generalist than a specialist. Most men are specialists. They have been an engineer or a lawyer. They haven't done a lot of volunteer work in the community. Women have had to be involved in a lot of different aspects of the community, whether schools or land use or children's issues. With that background it is a lot easier to get up speed on the issues than it is for the men, and it is a lot easier for us to go from one issue to another issue and not get too excited about, 'Well, that's not my field.' Then we solve problems by getting everyone involved in the solution. We come up with the right solution by listening to everyone's opinion and compromising. We bring listening skills to the situation, I wouldn't say 100 percent, but most women and very few men do."

## HEARING OTHER PEOPLE'S REAL CONCERNS

In theory, at least, as underrepresented groups are brought into white, male-dominated occupations, those groups get better service from those occupations, because, finally, there is somebody on the inside who speaks their language, who understands the nuances, who can read between the lines. The underserved should get better medicine, legal advice, representation in the state house, and service from city engineering departments.

Until there are more of the other minorities in white, male-dominated jobs, however, women will fill in through our knowledge of what it feels like to be in the minority. The lawyers told me they had more of a sense that the law should be fair. They thought that being female gave them a sense of identity with minorities, a sense that the law was not equal for everyone. Fairness was more important to women attorneys, they thought, than it was to male colleagues.

A 56-year-old state representative said that women are easier to talk to and less intimidating for all nonprofessional, nonskilled people who visit the legislature. "It's easier to come and talk to a woman than a man for those who are at all timid about the whole idea of talking to a legislator, which they shouldn't be, we are just one of them, but they are. We offer that kind of sensitivity and compassion that makes it easy for them to talk to us."

Hence a chief way that services improve in male-dominated occupations with more women is that we have greater sensitivity to other women's concerns. A broker (age 33) said it has to do with her ability to put herself in the other woman's position. "Years ago, we kept our money in the bank. Nobody taught us how to handle our money, not unless we were in a very unique situation with fathers or husbands or boyfriends. So I can really put myself in the position of knowing that I need to do something with my money besides keep it in the bank and not knowing exactly what to do. I ask questions that are going to create their whole life story, hardly without even asking for it. I throw the ball back in their court and make them feel comfortable enough to talk and talk and talk, hardly saying anything, and then at the end of the conversation I know everything about them. I know every amount of money they've got, and I did not take up very valuable time trying to tell them what they should invest in."

Women are sensitive about countering the deferrence and subordination of wives to their husbands in financial matters. The broker above continues: "Even though the male's always done the investing, it is important that I hear both sides. I always try to address the female, so she understands what is going on, and it is not in a patronizing way at all. I want her to know that it is okay to have her own opinion. I've inherited clients from brokers, and I'll call and I'll talk to Mrs. Smith, and she will say, 'You need to talk to my husband,' and I'll say, 'But it says here you have a joint account.' 'Well, he always does all that.' Then I say, 'But I'd like to talk to you.' I want to hear from the women in these kinds of accounts as much, if not more, than their husbands."

A woman physician more easily hears a woman describing pelvic pain, saying that her husband is clumsy at lovemaking. She more easily hears a woman describing the side effects of medication, saying the quality of her life is being ruined. She identifies readily with a woman having her face sewn up in the emergency room, and says, "Let me answer any questions you have about how you're going to look when this is all healed."

American women now prefer women to men obstetricians/gynecologists. Until recently, when there are finally enough women doctors to make comparisons, we never knew that women doctors listen more than men do. I guess U.K. and other European women have known this for a long time. But now American women are using our consumer's voice to demand the kind of care we want, and that means a relationship with the doctor who is going to oversee the birth of our babies. We want a human birth experience with someone who cares about us, so we are demanding women. The forecast is that male obstetricians/gynecologists will be a thing of the past in twenty-five years.

We also stand to gain a lot from the influx of women into the skilled blue-collar crafts. A 45-year-old carpenter talked about how different women in the trades are with women customers compared to the men. "Customers say they've had men carpenters tell them, 'Oh, no, you don't want it *that* way,' or 'No, it just can't be done.' Men want to do things that are familiar. Men don't realize how important some things can be to people. They're not willing to make things shorter for shorter people. They're not willing to take the time to think of alternatives. I think it's fun and a very important part of doing quality carpentry."

Another home remodeler (age 42) said the same thing, that clients are amazed that she pays attention to what they are asking for. "Last spring I was working with a woman who wanted her kitchen remodeled in a French country style. I didn't know what she meant, but I kept trying to figure it out. She said oak, so I kept thinking of washes we could use to make it more authentic, but I wasn't getting her meaning from her words. In the end she found a picture of the style she wanted, and we were able to work out an elegant kitchen she's really happy with. She told me she'd had men on other remodeling jobs, and they kept telling her she couldn't do things the way she wanted, but she thought they just weren't taking the time to understand."

## BENEFITING FROM OTHER POINTS OF VIEW

The legislators characterized themselves as public servants, there to listen to constituent needs. They said that a lot of legislation women were involved in had developed from a personal problem somebody had had. They said that now that the public knew they were there, the public came to them with their problems and also their ideas about what should be done about those problems.

A 55-year-old state representative had the following observations: "It is the thing we are taught from the time we are little, to listen and don't butt in. We tend to be more observant because of this. We find ways that we can participate, even if we are not initially invited to do so. The women who are like that are the very best legislators. They tend to make up their own minds, rather than to go along with the crowd. It is interesting that a woman's first priority in making decisions is going to be her constituents and secondly her peer group, her political caucus. I think that when it comes to the men, they are more likely to have their first priority the peer group and secondly the constituents."

It appears, then, that male legislators are less receptive to constituents' points of view, sometimes out of the belief that they know best. But in all ten of the occupations we studied, the men were resisting input from clients. In contrast, the women were using others' viewpoints to solve problems, and while they put themselves in another person's shoes, they nodded supportingly. They might reach out and touch that person. Because they were not used to being dominant, these women said it was easier for them to understand other perspectives and to see their potential values.

It also follows that women are not afraid to acknowledge that after trying to use client input for a better solution, it didn't work. We aren't afraid to say, "Well, I appreciate your side of things, but I'm going to proceed this other way and here's why." A 58-year-old legislator said that when people write to her, especially if they are angry over a vote, she always calls and explains, telling them she appreciates their input. "I only had one case in four years where they weren't absolutely gracious. Even though they didn't agree with me, they respected the fact that I had studied the issue and that there were variables they were not aware of. I do not compromise my principles. I am honest with them. I am not rude. I don't call up and say, 'Listen you SOB, I'm not voting that way.' Most politicians, if they get a hostile communication, don't even respond, or they send a form letter. I never do that."

A 30-year-old consulting engineer is very proud of her reputation as a troubleshooter because she gives and takes with the contractors more easily than the men. "I'm not afraid to ask them, the people we're consulting with, for solutions. I draw on all the relationships I learned as a girl child, for example, playing up to a fatherly older guy who might have the answer. I got called all the way to Alaska once when the guys said they didn't know how to solve a problem. I sensed that one of the contractors, a grizzled pre–World War II guy, *knew* how to solve our problems, so I had 'Dad' tell me. But the men were too proud to listen to what he had to say."

A broker, age 33, said many men brokers like to listen to their own voices but that women are really listening to what clients are saying and trying to understand: "What is going on with them? Why are they thinking that way? Why did they say no? Why aren't we going forward with the plan? What is the problem? Other brokers might say, 'This is the way it's going to be,' and come across real hard. I am more reflective on everything. I said this. He said that. What does this mean? Other brokers would be appalled that anyone would differ with them."

The greater willingness of the landscape architects to listen to clients produces better results. A 30-year-old said, "Our clients feel we are really listening to what they are saying. They feel that they are getting better service from a woman because of our ability to build rapport that is ongoing. We are more in tune with feelings. We were brought up to be that way. So we listen more to client needs. We also tend to do more research because we don't have all the 'right' connections that men automatically do, so we compensate. Having come from behind, we have to put more into it than the men."

Another 30-year-old landscape architect said, "I think that clients really understand the issues and have good input. I want to hear what they have to say, to hear what their needs are. Women have more respect for other people. Men want to meet the clients' needs, but they don't think the clients know what they want. Their ego gets in the way. Men feel they are *really good*. I get far less of the ego from women."

## A BETTER PICTURE OF REALITY

Particularly in detective work, having more women around encourages the attitude that there's more than one point of view that can be right. We are getting men to listen and consider others' opinions before making decisions. We model *not* being so definite that anything is *the* solution or the only solution or that my way is the only right way.

The women interviewed believe that men's seeming advantage—acting self-assured and confident and making quick, snap judgments—isn't an advantage. In spite of being absolutely sure that they are right, many times men aren't. So it's better to be willing to discuss various possibilities, in the first place, without trying to protect one's own point of view. In the second place, it's a strength rather than a weakness to be able to back down from one's position and agree with someone else's better plan of action.

A deputy sheriff (age 29) said that a lot of the guys have told her that "women officers handle stuff differently, that a woman's point of view is a lot different from a man's. Like I'll get a totally different impression of a situation than a male cop will. I'll see through someone's story one way, and a guy cop will see through it another way. I don't think the guys listen as *well* as I do, but that could go along with just the different ways we do the job."

"We can be tremendously more effective, more productive, more successful in investigations," said a 45-year-old undercover agent who thinks her job has great potential for women. "When I was younger, people assumed that my partner and I were living together, having an affair. This made people tell me all kinds of things. I could ask them personal questions, things about their background, more readily than he could. Now that I'm older and he is in his mid-twenties, I introduce my partner as my son and get them to think I'm trying to set him up in business. They are not suspicious of a mother, but a lot of it has to do with my ability to get them talking."

That male officers don't listen when they're interviewing is the biggest frustration of a 38-year-old investigator.

"Interviewing is a very important part of every investigation, and it really pays off in the long run to be able to listen to people and to hear what they're saying and to find ways to relate with them before we just start accusing them. If you can establish rapport with someone, you can get a lot more information from them. Most people like to talk about themselves, but the men are impatient; I don't know why that is. I actually interviewed a rape suspect for fifteen hours, not all at one time but at different times, and got to the point where I was holding his hand and praying with him and crying with him, and I think being able to be open with your own emotions makes it easier to relate on an emotional level with someone else and that really helps in interviewing."

A fledging 24-year-old attorney talked about her first deposition. She was one of four lawyers deposing an 80-year-old woman who was very confused and defensive. "They asked her lots and lots of questions. She kept denying everything, that she'd signed anything, saying dumb things like it wasn't her legal signature when everyone knew it was. Finally they left. I felt so sorry for her. I figured I'll just ask her again anyway and be more gentle. So I was gentle and, well, I can't raise my voice or talk harshly anyway; in time she trusted me and she told me the truth. She ended up admitting everything."

## LISTENING SHOWS COMPASSION

Sensitive listening is an important way we are changing the field of medicine. We go slowly and listen for emotional messages. The doctors say that if you do not deal with the emotional aspect, you miss an important part of every illness. Several quoted an adage about primary care being that branch of psychiatry where patients present physical complaints.

A dermatologist (age 39) had as one of her first patients a middle-aged man who had herpes on his penis. "He was completely destroyed by it. He thought his sex life was over, and I had to assure him that it wasn't. He said one time, 'You know, I feel you are just like my mother,' and I thought at the time, 'He could have said sister, friend, counselor, or that I was the most wonderful physician in the world.' It shocked me—'Mother!' But what was important was that I would listen to him in a neuter-gender way as mothers are supposed to."

Listening is also important for picking up on just what patients understand of what they've been told. Do they know how much medicine to take and when? Do they know what side effects to look out for? "I want my patients and their families to understand, and I'm willing to write things down, draw pictures, whatever it takes for them to get it. I will spend whatever time is needed to listen and then accomplish this. Especially men doctors from the old school don't listen as much—those great surgeons we met in school who had this idea they were God, the surgeon" (Geriatric physician, age 32).

Listening is changing the fire service as well. "Basically we deal with people. Before this, we women predominantly provided services as nurses, teachers, educators, all types of nurturing professions, and a lot of work we do is very caring, aid work, not necessarily fighting fires. Women bring a lot of caring to the profession. A woman five months pregnant says, 'I'm so glad another woman is here.' It's a relief, a comfort to have my presence there. Our aid runs are more like, 'How are you today?' and if the wife is crying, you go over to her. The men can learn to be more sensitive and not go about it with such a calloused approach" (Firefighter, age 33).

The women could not only easily take the point of view of victims but also that of criminals. A woman victim might ask, " 'How do you make your husband behave? Does your husband ever bug you? My husband drives me crazy. He won't pick up *anything!*' I can identify with that" (Police officer, age 29). Then another woman cop (also 29) turned around and empathized with a male criminal. "I've worked on so many burglaries, about 150, that I'm sick of them. But once you start listening to these guys, the more you want to work with them, the less you feel like sending them to prison. You'd like just to help them and make this the turning point in their life."

Body language is used a lot by physicians to show they are listening compassionately. They will put an arm around a terminally ill patient while he talks. They will hug a patient who says how much better she is feeling. They may cry as they listen to a patient sobbing. "I remember a friend working with a woman emergency room doctor. A woman came in aborting, and my friend told me of how the ER doctor cried with the patient who was telling her how much she'd wanted that baby. I was worried about crying with patients, but now I see it as a valid way of communicating with patients" (Family practitioner, age 29).

Women legislators, like the sheriff's deputy and GP quoted earlier, have to watch out that they are not too approachable. "People are more willing to share those very heart-rending stories with a woman. I know good and well that some women wouldn't tell men some of the stories they tell me. I hope that I never get to the point that these stories don't affect me. I hope that sensitivity is still always there" (State representative, age 55).

Another legislator (age 49) said:

"There are lots of people in this district who will call me and won't ever call the other two, because they don't feel so uncomfortable telling me, whether it is a mother image or sister image or whatever. Women won't feel there is something wrong with you if you have this problem or take a 'What's the matter with you?' position. There are literally hundreds of people who come to me with their problems who would never go to my colleagues. It doesn't mean the men couldn't have solved their problem. It just means they wouldn't have approached a man. They feel the men really won't listen with any sensitivity but that a woman will automatically have that sensitivity. You won't have to give her the whole nine yards. A lot of us have been there. We learn listening when we are a little tiny girl. We learn it because we just have to keep using it over and over again. It is part of being a woman."

The brokers talked about clients as people they have nice relationships with, rather than as business customers. These brokers maintain those nice relationships by sending friendly notes, visiting in the hospital, and keeping in close contact even when the market is down (which men tend not to do for fear they'll look bad). "You can get up in the morning, have a great sunrise, take a nice walk, and come in here and the market is down 100 points. So you babysit; that's all you can do. You spend a lot of time just holding hands, getting somebody out of a position they say they are too nervous about or getting somebody to just calm down and ride out the storm for better times ahead. Money is a very precious commodity to everybody, and it brushes off on you if you are the sort of person who really does care" (Broker, age 34).

## SOMETIMES LISTENING'S ALL YOU CAN DO

We are willing to listen, no matter how difficult it is, because we believe in the value of listening. We know people benefit from being listened to. Sometimes it's the only thing we can do for someone; sometimes it's the only thing someone else can do for us. Listening is a very important activity for women, one we bring to male-dominated work whether or not listening was part of the job before we came on the scene.

Crime victims find it easier to talk to women because the relationship feels less formal than with a man. The 18-year-old police scout found, to her surprise, that it isn't only children who prefer her but adults who have had crimes committed against them before. "Now that it has happened again, all they want is somebody to talk to, somebody who understands, who'll come across like they care."

There's another side to this. Several police and firefighters mentioned that the men sometimes get immobilized by anger when facing a horrible tragedy they can do little about. But we know we can always listen. "A man's anger sometimes gets in the way of his reasoning powers in child abuse or rape cases or in dealing with children. Again, the mother instinct in women helps. One time there was an accident where a man was killed who had left his three children at a campsite to come into town for something. A male officer was supposed to go up into the woods and get the kids, but instead, he asked me if I would go. Later, he came and apologized to me for not doing it. He said, 'How can you do that without crying?' I said I would cry later at home, but right then, those kids needed comforting and somebody to talk to" (Assistant police chief, age 55).

There are many situations in the fire service where listening's all you can do. A firefighter (age 28) talked about death and how she and the rest of her crew handle other people. "You kind of have to build up a hardness or coldness. There was a family and one of the members died for some reason and they were sitting around crying, and I just went up to this one lady and before I knew it I was putting my arm around her and just crying with her. The guys in my crew, they saw me do it and they didn't tease me about it. I was just listening to her, and she put her head on my shoulder and started crying, and it just got me going, and I was saying to myself, 'You can't be doing that.' Most of the men just turn around and leave the situation. It's easier that way. You listen to someone who is grieving, and it's hard; it's emotional. So they'll turn around and leave. But I'll be there if I feel they need somebody."

Another common situation is the call from a lonely old person who just wants someone to talk to. The firefighter above continues. "I'm not saying the women are more compassionate to these people, but I think we are. We have more patience with them. We deal a lot with children, and we can understand them a lot better. But it is hard on the aid car at four o'clock in the morning when you've been up all night and it's not an emergency run; it's a 'dud' call. Your bedside manner is poor, but I tend to listen to them a little more even if their problem is just loneliness."

## THE ARTICULATE WOMAN TALKER

In *Flying High*, a little how-to book about succeeding on our own terms, Liane Jones listed the characteristics of those high-flying women she interviewed who were the best talkers, the "inspired talkers" (1987, p. 39). Ask yourself, would men who are successful in their careers and also are considered articulate have any of these characteristics? Articulate women

Are good at giving and taking ideas

Are genuinely interested in what the other person has to say

Have voices that register emotion

Look directly at the other person

Show when they are impressed or amused

Are willing to learn new things

Pause to think and only interrupt to get something clear

Can you believe these are the marks of a good talker? You can if you are a woman, because an articulate woman talker is, basically, a good listener.

# 3

# NO US VERSUS THEM

---

When people get technical, it is because they want to hide behind the technical language rather than talk like, "What is your dream?" and "How are you going to get it? What do I have that can help you get your dream?" We don't feel as comfortable with the math and all that stuff, but it's very easy for us to say, "What do you want?" Men want to prove themselves by their knowledge. "Man, do I know this stock!" they say. "This stock has a P/E ratio of blah blah." Let me tell you, people don't care. (Broker, age 45)

Women at work are on one side of the fence, the fence separating the person who provides a service or product from the person being served. When we are not at work, we are on the other side of the fence. One moment we are the experts; the next moment we are women in need of expertise.

The way women tend to see it, everyone has some information or skill, so everyone sometimes gives and sometimes receives. But in the end, we're all equals. We see it that way; however, our male colleagues tend not to.

A 30-year-old engineer said the men encourage a mystique about their jobs that isn't deserved. Her attitude toward the profession is completely practical. "I have some information someone else doesn't have, but they have information I don't have. This attitude is very threatening to male engineers. They fear they will lose preferential treatment, automatic promotion to management, to being directors of corporate planning. So they don't want us women to blow this little myth they have that they're so special."

Before I consider why the women did not see a sharp line between the people inside and outside their careers, let's examine the reasons why there is a sharp line for men. Again, sex-role socialization provides an obvious and convenient explanation. Ruth Hartley, who is an expert on sex roles, has described vividly what happens to little boys as they get socialized to be masculine (1974, pp. 7–13). Sex-role pressures are put on them earlier than they are for girls, and the demands are more stringent. To be a male is to be manly, and manly means two things. It means being superior to women, and it means not being anything that women are. Thus the line between "us" and "them" would appear to be basic and integral to male sex-role socialization.

To be a man means being strong, bold, athletic, in charge, and able to take care of yourself. It means having more ability and better ideas than girls. To be a man means not being a sissy, weak, gentle, or afraid. It means not being feminine, female, or an inferior woman. Boys asked to write essays about waking up and discovering that they were girls used titles such as "The Disaster" and "Doomsday" and said things such as that everyone would then be better than they because boys were better than girls or that they would simply kill themselves (Tavris & Wade, 1984, p. 209).

When you add to all of this that boys seem to learn their sex-role identification by trying to figure out what "manly" is from mostly absent fathers and through punishment rather than praise, you really feel sorry for little boys. You can see why in later life it would be important for them to want to preserve the male sphere, the expert insider sphere, for themselves and cling to the notion of their superiority and the inferiority of those outside the sphere.

Now let's consider why the service orientation of women in male-dominated jobs is associated with a blurring of the distinction between professional and client. The answer again is sex-role socialization but at a level that transcends cultures.

Do women reject "we and they" and "foe and friend" because we have a lot more in common with one another, just being women, than men have in common just being men? By this I mean that I can look at newspaper photos and the television news and see women in police trousers, peasant shawls, Paris fashions, chadors, saris, army uniforms, and I know that we are all alike in one respect. Whatever our origins, whatever our attainments, we are alike in sharing a culture everywhere subordinate to men. We are alike in that boy babies are everywhere preferred to girl babies. Our subordination is a universal female commonality.

Universal male dominance, universal male preference—both are in the backgrounds of all women in addition to the fact that, in learning to care for a house and family, all societies try to teach us to put everyone else in that house ahead of ourselves. Our needs and wishes and priorities, in the crunch, we learn, come behind those of children and, many times, husbands, parents, and close relatives.

Women, therefore, are not only not socialized to draw the sharp distinction between themselves and men, as men are, but also go through the same equalizing, humbling, and unifying cultural experience of starting out, everywhere, as "small joys" compared to boy babies and of learning that others' needs are more important than our own. A raised feminist consciousness only intensifies identification with all women.

I need to say a word more about putting others' needs first. It was part of these women's service orientation, but it must not be seen as the sick, symbiotic, delusional trap that women's liberation seeks to free women from.

What I observed is that the women interviewed saw very clearly their needs, their families' needs, and their clients' needs. Clients' needs became their needs within the context of their jobs. There was absolutely nothing missing from their development as mature adults, nothing lacking in their own strong self-identification. Indeed, their careers are clear expressions of the fulfillment of their personal needs for creativity, achievement, independence, and recognition.

There were six impacts of their "no us versus them" attitude. First, they said women do a lot of educating and demystifying among friends and acquaintances, presenting facts, debunking fears, and dispensing with myths about how special they must be to have a nontraditional job. Second, they said they openly questioned why some jobs, including their own, are accorded such high status and so much better pay than other jobs. They reject the mystique and the idea that their jobs should earn more money than other jobs. Third, they questioned the clothes they were instructed to wear, "the uniform" of their occupation. Dressing more like clients helps blur the line between who's doing the job and whom it is being done for. Fourth, they preferred to talk plainly. They didn't like to use unnecessary professional jargon. They wanted to relate to clients in an informal, warm, inviting work environment. Fifth, this informality sometimes led to clients becoming friends, which was not something the women saw as wrong or to be avoided. Finally, their friendships with other women, typically, were for the sheer enjoyment of one another's company.

## DEMYSTIFYING OUR JOBS

Friends and relatives, not to speak of complete strangers, are very curious when they hear about nontraditional women's jobs. "How do you do it? How *can* you do it?" So the women tell them, matter of factly, that you go to school, put in so many hours, and build up skills and strengths. But the other women say, "No, I mean, how do you *do* it?" Then the nontraditional women say, "It's a job like any other job. There's nothing special about it. It's not that difficult, really. Any woman could do it if she works hard enough."

A Protestant pastor (age 38) remembered with laughter her daily noontime swim at the nearby YWCA. "After a couple of months, while we were showering, I struck up a conversation with another woman I'd seen there many times before—you know, basic information questions to find out a little about each other. When I told her I was a minister, she looked me up and down, in all my nudity, and said, 'Well, you certainly don't *look* like a minister! How do you do it?' So I told her."

These off-the-job conversations help to break down the barriers between us and them by countering myths about male work. This demystifying task is facilitated because these busy women have many outside interests and outside connections. The women said that they had a greater variety of school subjects behind them and broader employment experience than male colleagues. They read more widely and had a greater range of recreational activities from knitting to soccer. They had a wider range of friends to influence, clients who had become friends, clerks and secretaries with whom they went shopping and had lunch, and friends from school they kept in touch with.

Certainly, having babies and taking care of children are a big part of women's link with the broader world. Babies mean that many physicians in training also play the reverse role of patient. "Women start out in medicine with more independence because they don't fit in as men do. So they question the system and say, 'I'm going to take time out and have more leverage.' Men students are consumed by school, whereas women students stay interested in other things. Women have forced medical schools to let them take time out to have a kid. Women say, 'I'm going to do it now and you're going to have to live with it.' They really don't want to kick you out. The schools want you to stay and conform, but they will take your staying as a compromise" (Third-year medical student, age 23).

In some cases demystifying their jobs led the women to demystify the whole world of work and to expand their interests to other areas previously reserved just for men. A shipfitter (age 37) said that when her son graduated from high school she was going to make another change. "I've got the whole picture now. I enjoy the work; it makes me feel good, but I don't want to grow into a drone. So I'm thinking about another apprenticeship. I want to learn new things, do different things. Since I found out I can do this, I've figured out I can do anything. Once you figure that out, it's incredible how you feel about yourself. It's amazing.

I used to be the shyest little wallflower. I didn't use to look at people's faces when I spoke to them. So it has been a real transition for me, gaining this self-confidence."

When I talked to her two years later, the shipyard must have picked up on her need to grow and noticed the physical training she was going through to become an apprentice line person for City Light, because they had promoted her four times during that two-year period, and she was now a planner and had given up her intention to leave the shipyard.

## REJECTING MYSTIQUE AND MONEY

Another part of seeing no line between us and them is to question the special status attached to male-dominated work and why it is so disproportionately rewarded. Why do men's jobs command such high pay, women ask. Why do secretaries, sales assistants, and nurses earn so much less than engineers, brokers, and doctors? Aren't everyone's skills equally deserving?

At the same time that the women interviewed wanted to earn as much as male colleagues, they questioned the system that says, for example, a manager should get more money for administering work than the employees who do it.

An engineer (age 32) said that the most influential person with the public in her office was the receptionist. "And she is the lowest paid, and I think it's a crime! I don't think the men agree how important she is. But if you don't have a good person in that spot, the credibility of the entire department would go down instantly."

Conflict is inevitable for such women as they fight for better salaries for clerical employees and fight against men who want to hold on to status and mystique. The men are already afraid that if women are seen doing their jobs, they won't be highly valued and command the high pay they do: Here these uppity women are questioning why their jobs are so special and pushing for greater rewards for other women.

When one woman first came into the fire department, she was told that women's coming meant they'd never get any more pay raises. "This guy felt that before the job had mystique and people were willing to pay for it because of that. But if women can do the job, it's not as valuable. Now some of the men understand that, in a changing world, if you set yourselves apart in an elite group, instead of getting admiration, what you get is resentment and mistrust from the public. The diversification of the fire department makes it so the public views them as people like you and me but who take risks other people don't. The biggest change women are bringing is firefighters no longer being seen as some kind of super elite people" (Firefighter, age 32).

Readers might expect the medical profession to be a little more subtle, but when the monetary stakes are high, the argument gets absolutely vicious. A 1986 *Seattle Times* article by Richard Restak, M.D., said that because of the influx of women, in ten short years doctors will be just like nurses, "docile, compliant, and cheap." The best men, who would have become physicians, will become corporate directors instead, where they can be on the cutting edge of exciting ventures, feel important, and get wealthy.

Restak implied that good medicine is medicine that costs a lot. He insinuated that if you pay less, you must be getting inferior care. He said because women lack entrepreneurial spirit and will do medicine for less, doctors will no longer be able to get very rich. Then, because doctors can't get very rich, the best men will do something else with their lives.

Certainly, the physicians I interviewed were not using their special status to get rich. Many felt their families needed two incomes to get by. A 32-year-old physician said, "Women in my field, geriatrics, are not major breadwinners. This specialty does not make a lot of money. If you really take time with your patients, and you must when you are dealing with the elderly, you are not going to see as many patients per day as you would with the general population."

Women's deemphasis on monetary rewards fits in with our service orientation. It means that more clients can afford the services of doctors, lawyers, and veterinarians. It means that salaried firefighters, carpenters, and engineers are less likely to strike or otherwise disrupt service for purely monetary gain. Curiously, though, public service, male-dominated jobs probably will not cost any less as more women enter them, because we will demand other job benefits that may cost even more than take-home pay, such as day-care provision, parental leaves, and improved health and safety work conditions.

## QUESTIONING THE UNIFORM

A small difference between the United States and the United Kingdom is how seriously the two business communities take dressing for success. In America women typically wear an imitation male suit, that is, a conservative, navy or grey skirt and jacket, white blouse, and a tie of sorts. American businessmen have loosened up a bit and now wear pale blue shirts and even brown suits. But in Britain the men look pretty much as they did ten to twenty years ago, whereas U.K. businesswomen wear flowery dresses, unmatched skirts and jackets, different colored silky blouses, and don't try imitating men's ties.

In any case, to us onlookers of the business scene, the people in it seem to be wearing costumes they feel obligated to wear for the roles they play, and we tend to view such conformity more with amusement than admiration. I was, therefore, curious about the nontraditional

women. Would they conform or deviate in choice of clothes? The popular stereotype is that women are more clothes–conscious than men, but
on the other hand, these women were deviant to start with.

What I found was that how people felt about the "uniform" depended
on the job. In some jobs the men were far more concerned about proper
attire than the women. The men most concerned about what to wear
were the lawyers, next the brokers, and then the doctors and legislators.
Male engineers and architects were primarily concerned about clothes
if they had to go out of the office and consult with clients. Then, they
wanted to project the image of a conservative professional businessman.

Among carpenters and electricians of both sexes workclothes are jeans,
flannel shirt, sturdy boots, and hardhat, a uniform dictated by pure
practicality. But the women wore cleaner clothes than the men, and each
seemed to have added some feminine touch to the required costume.
Among the firefighters and police, the women were more concerned
about "proper" uniforms than the men, because unless a department
had researched uniforms appropriate for women's physiques, the
women were still shackled with shirts, trousers, and shoes designed for
men's bodies, things that did not fit properly or look as smart on women.

In the main, the women we talked to looked fairly conservative in
dress, conforming, but not rigidly, to the codes of their occupations. But
they had done a lot of thinking about the clothes issue, and they shared
their personal interpretations of the required uniform.

They proposed that the function of doctors' and vets' white coats was
something clinical and laboratory/scientific to hide behind and to put
distance between oneself and clients. They said the function of a dark,
three-piece, pinstripe suit was to state: "I am professional, responsible,
conservative—someone to whom you should pay a lot of money to represent your interests." The function of police and firefighter uniforms,
they said, was to communicate power and authority over the public. But
they felt that to the men, the uniform, whether three-piece suit or goggles
and hardhat, was to separate elite insiders from the uninitiated public.
Thus the distinction of us versus them was widened by what was worn
and bolstered the men's image as experts.

New women were counseled quickly by other women to conform to
dress standards or be ostracized by the men. Most, especially the younger
women, complied and thought they did get more "respect" from colleagues and clients alike when they imitated men's clothes. But as time
passed, and their self-confidence grew, many defied the code in small
ways and took real pleasure in doing it. A 45-year-old broker said the
women in her office prided themselves in not having the Wall Street
look. "They have been here long enough, they know who they are, they
don't need to be worried about their image. It is okay to let the feminine
side of us come out. But nothing is wild. We don't go way off the limb,

and nothing is red. Red is sex. That is the last thing you want when you are talking about money."

One physician (age 38) said she was unwilling when she started out to express her femininity because she didn't want to be looked at in any way except as a doctor. "Consequently, I had a great deal of trouble after delivery losing my postbirth weight. I stayed overweight and wore nondescript colors. But now I have gotten past that because I have proven myself and know that people take me seriously. So I've lost weight and wear pretty colors, and I no longer feel obliged to wear a white coat. I do wear a stethoscope, though, to show I don't work in the gift shop."

The broker above, age 45, who never wears red found her ideal in *Representative Magazine*. "It showed one of the most successful people in the business. She had gotten so successful that she could work out of her home. It had a picture of her sitting at home with the quote machine, antiques, her pink and blue flowered dress, sitting there with the phone and her little fuzzy poodle and her oriental rugs, and she is making a million dollars, and I went 'My god!' It just blew my mind. There was nothing wrong with this woman in her flowered dress; there was something wrong with me. I hadn't gotten the message yet, that you could be yourself."

Women police and firefighters are pressing for greater individuality in their uniforms, that is, clothes and shoes that fit well, that are comfortable and appropriate for the job, and that take personal circumstances into account, such as pregnancy. A police officer of seven years finally felt she had enough seniority to write a several-page letter to the director of public safety complaining about the women's uniforms and got a serious response. "Our uniforms were designed for men, and, well, these shirts and pants and belt really look stupid on women, and I've seen some other uniforms that look really great, so I've made my recommendations, and we need a special uniform for pregnant officers. They have said, 'No way, we're not buying special uniforms for pregnant officers,' so they put the women in dispatching (where the public won't see them), and they wear regular maternity clothes. This has got to change" (Police investigator, age 38).

I think the funniest story I was told concerning proper attire came from a 42-year-old landscape architect recalling her student days. "We had a group at the university that went crazy, the six women in my class. We had this visual analysis class, and our first presentation was on Halloween, so we said, 'Let's *be* our visual analysis.' We went dressed as the Farmland Environment, the Flood Plain, the Built-In Environment; somebody was the Bare Hillsides. We made up a song and dance and totally stunned the faculty with our costumes. They were so stodgy and boring. We were severely criticized by the two instructors as not being serious enough, so for the next presentation we went formal, white tie and tails, but they didn't get the joke."

## TALKING PLAINLY

The women interviewed for this book differed from male colleagues in that the women entered their occupations later. They were older when they started medical and law school, began in the legislature and brokerage houses, and joined the police and fire services. What they were doing while they were getting older was usually traditional women's work, teaching, social work, nursing, retail sales, and office work—and being mothers.

Thus the women came to male-dominated work with practice at teaching, informing, guiding, and explaining things in a language everyone can understand, and they wanted to continue explaining in a language everyone can understand. Physicians taught shy adolescents about sex and drugs as part of the annual physical examination. Police officers lectured in high schools about resisting peer pressure and held self-defense classes for other women. The brokers and legislators, most of all, talked about opening up their fields to laypersons by avoiding jargon and talking plainly.

Women brokers want clients to learn more about investments and to take greater responsibility for their own money. They like to sit prospective clients down and let them know that they will not do a "quick trade and out the door." Instead, they move quickly from talking about the market to talking about the client, where clients think they are headed. They reassure women, especially, that the field is not complicated. They do not try to wow people with how much they know or why the person ought to invest with them. They want people ultimately to turn money over to them because they are somebody who can be talked to and somebody who can teach others a little bit about the market without making it any more difficult than it is.

Here are two examples of women teaching male colleagues how to communicate at a people-to-people level and avoid technical gobbledygook:

"My senator asked me the other night how I thought his public forum went. I said, 'You've got to quit building the budget ten different ways. People just don't understand it. They understand *you* understand it and that's fine. But you have to put it on their level or you aren't communicating.' If there is one thing I get over and over again it is people coming up to me and saying, 'Gee, I can understand what you are talking about and how it is going to affect me,' and it is because I put it in their terms. I guess I am always out there teaching and listening. People in my district who have time to pay attention and read my brochures have a better idea about how government works and how we work for them and what can be done for them. The men in my district have done very little of that. They just don't approach it the same way I do" (State representative, age 49).

A broker, age 33, and two men had been commissioned by the New York office to give a seminar on mutual funds.

"We all thought, 'Boring!' But New York wanted to see if we could make it exciting enough to get some people in and do some business. So Bill gave this talk on the economy that was so far over my head; I mean no way! Then Bob came in with a talk about market timing that was very sophisticated. Then I got up and said I took a trip to the Orient last summer and that the Pacific Rim countries are a good place to be. My talk was completely elementary and very informal. I used examples of appropriate investment choices that really hit home with the local audience. It was embarrassing because after the talk people walked up to me and wanted my business card. The guys were visibly upset, and I told them, 'You're not approachable. People are too intimidated to walk up to you. You guys have to get down to earth, get around your egos. There is absolutely nothing magical or sophisticated about this business. Come to a level of understanding with prospective clients; explain things to people in a language they can understand.' "

## PREFERRING INFORMALITY

Women's preference for informality also blurs the line between professional and client. Male-controlled organizations disapprove of women's attempts to make the office homey and individualistic (plants, posters, photos, pictures). We are censured for adopting informal poses (heaven forbid, we should put our feet up on the desk) and casual attire (quick, take off your running shoes) and having unannounced visits from squealing infants or demonstrative friends.

Informality to women means having more fun at work, easygoing banter, a lighthearted attitude, warmth and color, a homelike atmosphere, and making friends with clients. Formality means restraint and strained conversations, protocol, a cool, intimidating atmosphere, and sticking strictly to professional relationships and prescribed roles.

A GP said that when she set up practice with a female partner and a male partner, the two women wanted to make it a homey environment so people would feel more comfortable. He thought the idea was crazy and unprofessional. What? An aquarium, toys, and a coffee pot in the waiting room? But they did it anyway, and it was a success.

One woman's law office had just been redecorated at great expense, and now she regretted that she had not been stronger about pressing for a homey atmosphere. "Now the offices are so off-putting and cold, clients are intimidated by them. Everything is grey and black and brown. The whole thing is really dark with a horrible white sculpture we paid a fortune for—very high tech, very expensive. Some people on the elevator asked me if Darth Vader lives here. I want an office that is warm and inviting with earth colors that psychologically people respond to. Why can't an attorney's office be like that?" (Attorney, age 40)

Another attorney, age 58, had been a judge for several years. She'd had an easygoing, relaxed courtroom demeanor. "Traditional courtroom etiquette is such that when the judge comes in, everyone stands. In fact, the bailiff says, 'All rise.' Sometimes people are stubborn, or they are mad, and they don't stand up. Well, I don't care. How seriously can you take something like that? But I know men who care a great deal. Matter of fact, I know a judge who put someone in jail for not standing up, for being contemptuous. You won't find that in women."

Next to a courtroom the most traditionally formal work setting is probably church. But even here, maybe particularly here, women are making it more informal. An article by Joan Scobey in *New Woman* magazine (1986) describes the highly informal rituals and prayers being invented by women clergy to celebrate children's first teeth or first steps. The women take their ministries, which involve song and dance, into homes, schools, community centers, and storefronts. They preach sermons that are personal and practical, and they run their churches by listening to all their parishioners and making decisions by consensus.

## THE THIN LINE BETWEEN CLIENTS AND FRIENDS

One of the consequences of women's greater informality is that they are more likely to develop friendships with clients. The women said they lived comfortably with this client–friend fluidity, even though some men pointed to it as another example of how women act unprofessionally and personalize the work situation.

Judith Bardwick's *In Transition* (1979, p. 49) asserts that to personalize relationships at work isn't necessarily bad. Certainly, if we are overly sensitive to whether we are liked or not, or take criticism of our opinions personally, then personalizing is negative. But if personalization is used to develop richer and more honest relationships, it is positive. Bardwick described how the president of a large corporation told her how much he was enjoying friendship with the women he was now hiring in contrast to the ritualized relationships he had with men.

Some women said they didn't have more friends among clients than the men in their office but that the quality of their friendships was different. The women were not motivated by what such friendships might do for business, whereas men were. The women seemed to make friends for the sheer enjoyment of it.

A very successful broker (age 29) said that she has a very close circle of clients. "Some are your clients first, but some cross over to being friends first. I know that some of the ties I have made will last beyond this job. I see this as a benefit. My clients become involved with me on many levels. It cements the relationship. They need to know that I am a human being, and one of the ways they learn is because I tell them things that happen in my life. A lot of times I relate it to what they have told me. I don't express my emotions or tell people those things because there's a business reason to do it but because I enjoy their company and I want to."

A remodeler (age 45) said she behaves in a customer's house as she does in a friend's house, so that the first thing that delights a customer is that she doesn't leave a mess, which clients have come to expect from men carpenters. "We spend a lot of time talking with our customers. They like having us there; they don't want us to leave. They keep finding new work for us so we'll stay longer. When we're working on stuff that doesn't take a lot of thought, like hanging sheetrock, we share a lot. We become an important part of our customers' lives, and we become friends and see them after the work's all done. Last Christmas we took baskets of goodies to our old customers who'd had big jobs done. It was neat to see them again."

## A LAST FEMALE COMMUNALITY

I started this chapter by talking about how women might feel more like one another all over the world because everywhere we are subordinate. Nowhere do girls grow up feeling as special as boys are made to feel. In every culture we are taught to put other people's needs before our own.

But there is something else women with jobs have in common. Roslyn S. Willett's chapter in *Woman in Sexist Society* (1971) observes that most working women perceive very clearly that their male bosses are not particularly bright. Working women gradually learn that they are at least as capable as the boss and better than he is in certain areas. Willett mentioned, as examples, women's greater responsiveness, insight, and ability to carry jobs through to completion (p. 514).

This truth about men is an important female commonality. Some men deserve the elevated status, pay, honors, prestige, and power that patriarchy has bestowed on them. But most of the men we come in contact with do not deserve them. They are not cleverer or more rational than we. They are not emotionally stronger or better at dealing with stress. They are not more effective or competent where we expected them to be, on the job.

Entering the work force in unprecedented numbers has given millions of women the opportunity to meet enough men to know that women are not inferior. The line between us and them is their line. But it's phony, and we all know it.

# II

# *Caring about Coworkers*

---

Who among feminist theorists predicted that the principal way women would alter male-dominated work was through our caring attitudes in the workplace itself? Who said that our major contribution to the humanization of work would be to make the milieu more collaborative, empathic, and egalitarian?

Myra Ferree's chapter in Beth Hess and Ferree's *Analyzing Gender* (1987, p. 336) points out that women's work culture, that is, the culture of female-dominated clerical and factory jobs, has always been distinctively personal and friendly. We celebrate births and engagements with our coworkers; we share stories and photographs of our families. We try to find things in common with other women despite racial, ethnic, and class differences.

So it is not surprising to find Ruth Halcomb looking at office life today and asking, in *Women Making It* (1979), "Are *we* responsible for these milieu changes?" (p. 152). Are *we* responsible for the greater emotional expressiveness, even occasional tears when the tension gets too high? Are *we* responsible for the at-home atmosphere, where desks are real tables, offices look like living rooms, and visitors are treated as if they were guests? Are *we* responsible for first names being used? For men dressing more casually? For an overall more friendly, informal atmosphere? Yes, Halcomb said that women's socialized sensitivity and empathy make us better lawyers, doctors, judges, and executives because we care more about our coworkers (p. 149).

Several feminists have addressed the impact of women specifically on male-dominated engineering, technical, and scientific settings. One is Rita Arditti whose chapter in Arditti, Pat Brennan, and Steve Cavrak's

*Science and Liberation* (1979) predicts that the scientific milieu will become more positive, nonelitist, and cooperative.

Another such writer is Elizabeth Janeway (1982) whose chapter "Women and Technology" (pp. 117–129) says that women entering technical occupations and the executive levels of industry bring the ability to relate nurturantly along with them. This is true not because women are better than men, or innately more loving than men, but simply because our society has asked men as they grow up to abandon these qualities and has required that women preserve them.

Nurturance, however, is a necessary human quality, and the workplace is a community like any other that has to provide emotional and aesthetic rewards in addition to material ones (Janeway, 1982, p. 122). Janeway noted that the feminine quality most valued in women students by a dean of engineering was women's working toward goals with coworkers using conversation, compromise, sharing, and emotional support (p. 123).

Natasha Josefowitz's chapter in Jan Zimmerman's *Technological Woman* (1983) calls on women in scientific organizations to celebrate their differences and to tell the organizations what they bring that is different, what was not there until women arrived. What might that be? They bring verbal and interpersonal skills, an ability to share data, communicate, and get people to talk about their findings and their feelings. Women, Josefowitz believes, can make an extraordinary contribution to the scientific community (p. 194). We do this by promoting cooperation among coworkers and being supportive of everyone in the group participating equally, rather than certain individuals dominating (p. 198).

Veronica Nieva and Barbara Gutek, in *Women and Work* (1981), pointed out that the modern work organization and society at large are drifting away from rugged individualism and the male norms of independence, aggressiveness, and dominance. Society is now headed toward valued female qualities and behaviors, and the female behaviors that are most compatible with the modern, interdependent work world are nurturance, cooperation, and supportiveness of the people around us (pp. 127–129).

In *Women's Reality* (1981, pp. 104–105) Anne Schaef said that women's reality is not the same reality as that of men and of the dominant white male system. In the white male system relationships are always one-up, one-down. Somebody has to be superior and somebody else has to be inferior.

In contrast, within the emerging female system, we women think of all adult relationships as potentially peer relationships, with everybody equal (unless and until men make it impossible).

Schaef's ideas about peer relationships are very important here because equal peer relationships with coworkers are what the women interviewed are striving for. Schaef characterized peer relationships like this. Peer relationships are not defined by sexuality; they are intimate and close but without physical sex (p. 115). Peer relationships are based in verbal intimacy and mutual, safe sharing, not on being superficial pals and buddies (p. 121). Power in peer relationships is not based on the scarcity model where there is only so much power available and the more one shares, the less one has. For peers, power is limitless; power actually increases when we give it away (p. 125). Communication between peers means honesty, not trying to stay one up. Negotiation means finding solutions good for everyone, not winning (pp. 134–135).

A woman's relationships *are* her identity according to Carol Gilligan's *In a Different Voice* (1982, p. 159). Gilligan said that our distinctive morality is based on fulfilling the responsibilities that go along with relationships. We judge ourselves on how well we take care of others and see that no one gets hurt.

My interpretation of Gilligan's work is that if we apply our "morality of responsibility" at work we will (1) put our responsibilities to people above what is officially "right," (2) use any power we have to be nurturant, (3) change rules to preserve relationships, (4) not let some people's successes mean other people's failures, and (5) be open and sensitive to everyone's point of view.

Elinor Lenz and Barbara Myerhoff devoted a whole chapter in *The Feminization of America* (1985, pp. 75–96) to "humanizing the workplace." They believe that attitudinal and environmental changes in relationships at work are two of the most tangible changes women have brought about. We are responsible for healthier, more homelike, and more individualized workplaces. We are responsible for men now having nonsexual friendships with women who have taught them to share their feelings and be comfortable and egalitarian with women. Both of these changes are attributed to the caring and comforting that are part of the feminine culture.

Part II takes us through a general outline of "the nurturant approach" and then focuses on women's respect for differences and diversity among coworkers. We then zero in on the ways that nurturant firefighters, police officers, carpenters, and electricians ameliorate the stresses of the blue-collar world.

# 4

# THE NURTURANT
# APPROACH

---

I think men on the job are really schooled not to honestly listen to
each other. I really don't think they hear each other. I think they
are afraid to hear each other, and I think that I listen to them, and
if I access the things that they tell me compared to what they tell
each other, they don't share *half* with each other what they share
with me—especially the way that they care about each other. I tell
them that I care about them; they're important to me, and they tell
me, but they don't tell each other. Their communication is inhibited
by their lack of willingness to honestly listen to each other. (Police
sergeant, age 36)

One of the landscape architects told me her profession was in a funny
stage right now, an intermediate step that the next generation of
women won't experience. This stage involves playing many roles. But
after hearing about the multiple roles that women in all of the other
nontraditional jobs are playing, I'm not so sure this is an intermediate
step. "Simultaneously," she said, "we're expected to perform traditional roles *and* to make inroads in the profession. So we have two sets
of mores which we can manipulate. I know when to be technical and
when to put my lipstick on. Whatever role it takes to get the job done,
I'll do. In the design profession you need a variety of roles to deal with
all the crazy situations involving government officials, contractors,
county executives. If playing up my feminine qualities and wearing a

hotshot dress will be more effective, well, I'm an expedient person!" (Landscape architect, age 39).

What are the many roles these nontraditional women had assumed? The interviews do not support the idea that the roles were primarily negative—the Bitch, Gossip, Flirt, Tramp, Groupie, or Fan that Glynis Breakwell described in *The Quiet Rebel* (1985, pp. 92–97), all of which are roles imposed from the outside. Nor were they equally unflattering roles of Iron Maiden, Pet, or Seductress revealed in Rosabeth Kanter's *Men and Women in the Corporation* (1977, pp. 234–236).

These nontraditional women weren't playing derogatory roles because they were resisting playing *token* roles. "A token role originates outside a woman and is maintained by the dominant male culture." The women may have been tokens, in terms of numbers, but most of the roles they played were positive. This is true because the women chose them. It was also the case because the men positively reinforced their role playing once they discovered it solved problems and helped get the work done.

The roles the women had taken on were often nurturant familial ones. They used these roles to channel a genuine, conscious concern about the welfare of the people they worked with. They familialized the workplace. They were replacing a rowdy fraternity with a relaxed, extended family.

Before the women arrived at the fire station, the men had enjoyed the regression of all-male camaraderie, acting like a gang of adolescents, uninhibitedly, without taking much responsibility for their social behavior. Even now, if there would be no alarm for a while, the men would get antsy and start harassing each other. "They become little boys, with all their practical jokes, and show their anger, like when someone invades their space."

The male firefighters had a much easier time accepting the women's nurturance of clients than of themselves. It was okay to express caring to the public, but it made them uncomfortable and confused when it was focused on them.

What roles were these women playing? "This place isn't like an office. You eat, you sleep, you play, you work very hard with these people. You live with them twenty-four hours so the men have to know, do they relate to you as a mother? Aunt? Girlfriend? Sister? They have to know which category to put you in. Bringing a lot of nurturing into the station really confuses them. They have a hard time trying to fit you into a category. We want them to see us as coworker/sisters because that's probably one of the most healthy relationships you can have in our job. That's the role we choose" (Firefighter, age 30).

The interviews gave me an image of the workplace as a stage with actresses and actors walking out of the wings, scripts in hand, each worker with the potential for playing many parts. Each can reenact old roles, learn new roles, assume several parts in the same play. This workplace drama can be participated in wittingly or unwittingly and enjoyably or not enjoyably.

But why would women display such incredible flexibility at role playing? Is it sex-role socialization again? Carol Tavris and Carole Wade (1984, pp. 222–223) said that the pressures on boys and girls to act in certain ways are uneven and unequal. More flexibility is granted girls, and adults punish boys who behave like girls more than they do girls who behave like boys. Until adolescence girls can act like tomboys if they want to, but boys can't act like sissies.

Do parents fear that if boys play female roles they will become homosexual? Or do they punish boys because they are acting out a lower status role? In any case, research shows that parents restrict preschool boys more than girls and set firmer rules for boys. It is no wonder that, later, women in nontraditional jobs are free to play so many roles and to recognize that, as in any family, there is the potential for close, intimate friendships with anybody in the group.

There were six aspects to the women's nurturant approach to coworkers. They created a homelike social and physical atmosphere because, they said, they had been taught to do this as part of their preparation for homemaking. Second, they liked to mix fun and work; that came from women's culture. Third, they did whatever they could to get people to express how they felt and to work out differences. They wanted an atmosphere that was easy and supportive. They thought that no matter how traumatic the events in their lives were, they must be talked about. Bottling up feelings of anger and frustration only injures one's health and that of everyone around.

There were two other aspects to their caring. One was teaching coworkers new skills and sharing their technical knowledge, much as they did with clients. The other aspect was teaching coworkers how to look after one another so that all the nurturing wasn't left to the women.

## THE SOCIAL AND PHYSICAL ATMOSPHERE OF HOME

There are two reasons that the women created a homelike social atmosphere at work. One is that women tend to feel responsible for good feelings among coworkers, much as we feel responsible at home for people getting along with one another. In our homes we don't want tension; we don't want people feuding or ignoring one another. So we get family members to talk about their problems, and we try to get people to compromise and accommodate so that no one feels like he or she has lost out. If there isn't a good social atmosphere at home, women tend to feel guilty about it, because we have been socialized to think this is our responsibility. The same applies at work.

The second reason is that just as women have been conditioned to "take care" of the emotional atmosphere of home, so men have been conditioned not to do this. The workplace can be a shambles, interpersonally and interactionally, and the men won't know anything about it.

Take the case of a landscape architect, age 40 (she occasionally gets called Mama, but that's all right), who said she is not only valued for her superb design work but because she keeps an eye on, and an ear open, to the nuances of people's feelings. "I read between the lines when people tell me things and smooth over conflicts between people in the office. One of the bosses was having emotional problems and taking it out on all the other employees. The other two bosses were totally unaware. I brought it to their attention and said, 'We've got to find some way to deal with this.' They do not listen; they do not pick up on cues. They were slightly aware of his problem but not aware of the total scope of the problem. A couple of people had left because of it, and the business was in a slump. Everyone knowing that this person was on the edge of a nervous breakdown helped, and the bosses are much more sensitive now."

Other women said they had the same sensitivity, a kind of intuiting about the people, particularly if things weren't going quite right. A 29-year-old engineer said, "So I'll go to the boss and say, 'I'm not trying to be a pessimist, but I *feel* this plan just isn't going to work.' The boss takes me along on important lunches to get good or bad feelings about the other people. For example, is someone we're interviewing going to get along with our people?"

An engineer (age 32) said she is more in tune, more perceptive. "Men are sort of in the ozone and don't know what's going on in day-to-day office life, the relationships that people have. On a project, I get a feeling, this is going to be great; everything is going to fall into place. Or I'll have mixed feelings which are hard for me to tell my boss, especially if the project is very visible and politically sensitive. But if people are not catching on or are unhappy or resentful, he's not handling them correctly, and he doesn't know it."

Another part of the social atmosphere of home is that home is where we can let off steam and unwind, get out our frustrations about work, and find sympathy. I was surprised to find that the women interviewed said they were more apt than male colleagues to release tension at work. This was not the same thing as men who get angry and blow up at work, pound the table, and swear at people around them. It was more like a 35-year-old maintenance carpenter who compared men who go around feeling uncomfortable because they won't communicate their feelings with how she behaved when she was a social worker.

"I worked in an office full of women, and I could go in and fall on the floor and say, 'Oh, I'm so depressed. I hate my job,' and everyone would talk to me."

A supervising engineer, age 32, said women engineers are more emotional at work, and she doesn't think there is anything wrong with it. "It can bring a lot of life to a dull office. We are more emotionally rowdy here and let off more steam than the men do. It can be good to let off steam and release the tension. The men walk around the office with clenched teeth and stressed and don't release their emotions. My boss is tense about a lot of things, and I don't think he blows up enough. He's my age and ready to have a heart attack because of his tension. I just had a performance appraisal, and my boss said I react negatively to new situations because it bothers him that I let off steam, but once it's over I can buckle down and get to work on the project."

As for the physical atmosphere of work, across the board the women said we are more aware of it. Women pay more attention to whether there are flowers and plants and whether they ever get watered. Women make sure people get birthday cards. We are more apt to put up pictures and posters, more apt to take action if walls and halls get grimy and the furniture gets to looking seedy. A physician said that the people she knows who have nice offices are women. "Men are oblivious to office stuff. Men do not know or care about what goes on with employees and physical surroundings."

A pleasant working environment was very important to the subjects in Rosemary Burr's *Female Tycoons* (1987, p. 104). A prime example is a woman who wanted people to come into her factories and say, "Isn't this a bright clean factory?" Her husband's attitude was, "This is just a factory and it doesn't matter." But her attitude was, "It's my factory and it reflects me." So she wanted pale grey tiles and shiny white floors that were cleaned every day. She wanted colors to be easy to live with, believing people who feel better work better. Her factory, like her house, reflected how good a home manager she was, a connection men do not make because they don't take care of their homes.

There is one work site, however, where the physical atmosphere presented the women with a special challenge, the fire station. The firefighters were in a quandary. The last thing they wanted was to get shackled with cooking and cleaning. They wondered how to stop the men from saddling them with the domestic side of the job. On the other hand, women are socialized to think that we are primarily responsible for keeping things clean at home, and now, "Here is this home away from home and it's a pigpen!"

The women were using positive reinforcement, late-in-life conditioning, resocialization, anything, to get the men to change. First the women did the dirty work and then they showed the men how nice things could be. Next they worked out the organizational details and made sure the work got distributed equally.

Stations that are more fit to live in are a major change the women have brought to the fire service. "I feel like I go in there and clean some things that haven't been cleaned in twenty years. If the men didn't have to clean the bathroom, they probably never would. After a while I would have to see it cleaned. I might not do it every day. I'm not a compulsively clean person. But I take more pride in how it looks than the men do. Sometimes I feel like I'm the only one to ever dust the place, and I don't do it very often. It's much more important to me to have it nicer, at least clean. The stations might be dungeons, but they can still be clean. The men don't care what the public thinks of the dungeon they're living in" (Firefighter, age 28).

A 30-year-old station captain agrees. "Some of the shifts we come to work after, it's like walking into a garbage dump. It drives me absolutely crazy; I can't stand it. I walked into a station the other day and opened up the refrigerator to put my lunch in, and I said, 'There had to be a woman who worked here yesterday that cleaned this fridge because I know none of you guys did,' and all of a sudden, here she comes, and yes, she had cleaned that refrigerator yesterday. But as captain I can make sure everybody gets to clean the fridge some time this year."

In the same way another woman introduced holiday dinners to the fire station, improving both the physical and social atmosphere. "We try to make the work place more pleasant. Christmas comes every year and nobody wants to get a Christmas tree, and I always want a tree, so I go get one. I don't think it's that the men don't want those things. I think it's just like cooking; once they experience it and see that it is fun and enjoyable, they eventually start taking the time. When we had our Thanksgiving dinner, I figured out who was going to cook what, and one of the guys went out and bought white tablecloths. That's unheard of. Another guy went out and bought sparkling cider, and they brought in buckets, filled up the buckets with ice, and they tried to make it more of a family atmosphere. It got the guys going, and now they take the initiative to do those things themselves" (Firefighter, age 35).

## MIXING FUN AND WORK

At the same time that the first women were admitted to West Point in 1976 the army and the academy were both reconsidering just how functional it was to degrade and punish people as part of training. So probably since that time the level of abuse of cadets is lower. Betty Friedan's *The Second Stage* (1981), however, makes clear that whatever the level of abuse was then, the women were more harassed than the men. She talks about their inner strength and the healthy mental attitude of the women survivors. They had stayed calm, serene, and good-natured and conveyed to their tormenters an attitude of "It's too bad you guys have a problem." The women wished the men could have the fun in their lives they were having (pp. 185–186).

Mixing work and fun is part of women's culture. We want to have a good time at work, and we want everybody else to have a good time. The work environments of the police, firefighters, carpenters, and electricians especially need cheering up, and many men are in the habit of being negative. Because of what the women have gone through to get these jobs, they have a much more positive attitude toward work. "It's not just a job. It's a job we really like and appreciate and like to do well."

Two stockbrokers commented on fun at work. A 23-year-old said: "I asked this other broker 'How's your new house?' and he loudly said, 'Don't change the subject. I have no time for that. I'm here to work and make money.' When I asked a guy in Los Angeles how the weather was, he said 'If I sat and looked out the window all day I wouldn't make any money!' Well, gee, can't you stop and smell the roses?" A 34-year-old said: "I just recently read a study in the *Registered Rep Magazine*. They did a study on brokers, female and male. They've always told us you've got to make a certain number of calls each day. But they found out that the number of phone calls had nothing to do with the amount of production created. In fact, the broker who spent more time on the phone with personal calls was the better broker. *The top brokers took more time for their personal lives!* Before last year I was work, work, work. Now I spend as much time playing as working." (emphasis added).

A firefighter (age 30) had been in charge of a team of three, a man and another woman. "We'd go out and drill and it was a lot of fun. We made it fun. We really enjoyed it. The guy, he ate it up. He thought he was in heaven. He was an older man and he was just in awe, and in addition to having someone to talk with, the concept of teamwork was *real*. Everything went real well on fires. Everything was real positive on aid runs because we saw things being done that we had always thought needed to be done. I love to have women work for me. I would love to work for a woman, having someone to talk to on a day-to-day basis."

Once, by chance, all three firefighters were women. "Right away, at 9:30 we went on an aid call, and the medic unit that got called suddenly realized that Engine 34 had only women that day. So all day long people just kept dropping in to visit, to deliver things! It was such a happy time. We sat around and shot the breeze about things we never can because men are there. We all had such a nice warm feeling and a freedom we'd never experienced before. The greatest thing was we got called to a fire in another part of town and we beat the other engine by coming in the alley, and we put out the fire, it was a garage fire, before they even got there!" (Firefighter, age 33)

## FREEDOM TO EXPRESS HOW YOU FEEL

The lack of emotional expressiveness associated with the male sex role usually features high up on male liberationists' lists of complaints. To illustrate, Janet Chafetz (1978) asked men students what the disadvantages of the male role were and the advantages of the female role. "Can't show emotions" was a big disadvantage to the men, while the freedom to express emotions was regarded as an important female right (p. 49). Most male disadvantages were things they had to do, like be the provider, succeed, get drafted, or fix things. But expressing emotions was the only thing men complained they could not do.

It was very important to the women interviewed that people got along and weren't hassling each other at work. So they let the men cry on their shoulders and tell them their problems, recognizing that the men didn't really expect difficulties to be solved but just wanted to let off steam. A few men's relationships with female coworkers had progressed to the point of trusting friendships, giving them an alternative to male–male friendships.

Often when the women first started their jobs, they were very guarded and reserved about expressing feelings. They were leery about being emotionally open, even to laughing too loudly at a television show; they conformed. The men never described their innermost feelings, so the women didn't either. They were cowed by talk behind the backs of nonconforming women who "wouldn't change one bit for the guys." The guys called such women nuts and crazy.

Gradually, however, one of the men, still tight-lipped in a group situation, would tell a woman his true emotions, one on one. For a woman who wanted to but was afraid to express herself, this was often the signal to start being herself, even in a group.

It always takes several weeks before a new group of men loosens up around a 26-year-old shipyard machinist, but then they take her under their wing. "When the threat disappears, it's almost like a family, you're in one big family. I've found that the guys can get a lot more personal with me than they do with the other guys. Men don't talk about their families to other men; they tell sex jokes. A lot of times they won't brag about their kids when you think that they would. Talking about family life is too sissified for another man. Yet, boy, they can't wait to tell me the cute little thing their kid did the other night. It draws me really close to them."

A 30-year-old consulting engineer said that the men she works with like the sensitivity and enthusiasm she brings with her.

"I love going out and working with architects and owners, making site visits, and they know it. So now it's okay for them, too, to like doing this. There's this certain behavior they're supposed to be, rigid, controlled, fit into this mold. The image is to be business-oriented, work-oriented, technology-oriented, but this is not what really happens; it's not reality. In practice, architects are difficult, and owners don't know what they want, and you have to talk to them, come to them. So I'm always saying something like, 'Guess what, guys, I get to go here. Guess what I got to work on. Boy, am I excited about this thing!' and when I get stuck, I'll say, 'Charlie, let me run this by you.' Guys don't do this; they stew all by themselves, wondering how to pull this whole thing together. To me it feels better to sit down and say I'm frustrated, get outside myself, ask someone else what he thinks. I think I have a tremendous amount of power in my office because I'm different, because I enjoy trips and projects and even talking to the boss. For example, when we're in a restaurant, I'm always the first to order, and if I see something I've never had before, I order it. Now they all try it too, they want to share . . . all this power I didn't even realize I had. I'm doing what I want to do, and now they're all able to enjoy hot cajun food."

That big sex difference, men's inability to communicate their feelings, really struck a maintenance carpenter (age 31). She was referring to the fact that women feel freer to talk about feelings to anyone, whereas men have been taught not to. "So it changes the workplace when the balance of women to men changes. Now there are four women and ten men in my shop. People say that with more women the atmosphere is lighter, more relaxed, more fun. Women make it feel more like home. It's just who we are. We're more comfortable with other people, and we like to have fun. That alone takes some of the men's uptightness away."

A 31-year-old flight engineer on DC-10s said the fact that women's ears are more sympathetic on average than men's changes cockpit talk. "Being a woman up there, guys will talk about something that's troubling them. Just being a woman I bring things down to a personal level in our conversation, and they talk in depth about children and the things that are worrying them. If there were three men up there, they would never open up like that. These guys don't have women friends, not even their wives. So they open up more when I'm there, even get tears in their eyes talking about their wives and daughters."

An electrician (age 32) thought that if you are going to help men feel free to talk about how they really feel, you have to give a little when it comes to sexist comments. "I like the guys to feel comfortable around me and that they can say whatever they want, within good taste. If they want to make a joke about something, that's fine. I've had them tell me I have a nice ass, and I don't get upset about it. It's okay. I feel like it's a compliment if they can be that comfortable with me and express what they think and not feel like they are harassing me or creating a threatening situation. I put up nice pictures in the shack, things like nature scenes, and on this last job I was on, I brought some lilacs in."

About anger, the women were not averse to expressing it or to others' expressing it. But the *way* that anger got expressed was crucial: We do not like the way men express anger, and we want them to change, they said.

The engineers preferred that the men would let off more steam rather than seethe quietly. The brokers wished the men would let off less steam because their style was to scream at the sales assistants. Anger is all right, the women said; it is just that men express it in such inappropriate ways.

"Appropriate" means a way that helps the angry person and does no one else any harm. It means releasing anger so that stress is reduced all round, rather than reduced for some people and created for others.

One carpenter, age 30, had a lot to say about anger. "Two guys here have really bad tempers, so bad that they occasionally throw things and cuss a blue streak. I said I don't like that angry energy that's coming out. I explained that it bothered everyone. They never knew their anger affected everyone else. They said, 'It's not directed at you,' and I said, 'It still affects me. I don't want to hear it.' So we have fewer temper tantrums. Part of it is changing because they're learning to help one another. We cooperate more and can avoid those situations where they get so frustrated they feel like throwing things."

She continued:

"I don't get angry about mistakes or doing wrong things. I was in charge of an installation, a really big project. We were installing a big display case for a jewelry store. The guy who put the slides inside the cabinets forgot to check. It took three to four hours, and it was all done wrong, and he just blew his top, started throwing things and cussing. He'd made a mistake, done the whole thing wrong. I said, 'I'm going to lunch. It's not the end of the world. We'll fix it.' I sort of take these things in stride. I know when to walk away from something. Know when to stop and get some distance before I go at it again. Other times I tease them out of their anger and frustration. I don't like to carry those things with me. [I] take a break until I can come back with better perspective. If I'm angry I talk myself out of it. It's not worth it to carry that around for a whole day."

She models a different way to handle anger, the way women are socialized to handle it. Men don't like us to be openly angry; anger in women is, historically, unattractive, nasty, and it means we are out of control. But if out-of-control anger isn't nice in us, how can it be nice in a man? The women's attitude is that most men can learn to inhibit temper tantrums and adopt more constructive and cathartic ways to be angry.

## WE SHOULD TALK ABOUT TRAUMA TOO

Society's two traditional objections to women in the fire and police services were that women were too weak, physically and emotionally. But women have proven these two stereotypes to be wrong.

On the physical score, women police officers and firefighters are not on average as strong as the men. But the women do the job just as well. So lesser strength and size are not valid objections.

On the emotional score, women police and firefighters have proven they are just as strong as men and that they have an extra strength to teach to the men, the strength to talk about feelings and problems—not just about good feelings but horrible, screaming, teeth-gnashing, and grievous feelings; not just about minor problems but divorce, drugs, alcohol, children, terrible pain and handicap, and death.

Men's unwillingness to talk about feelings has been a real problem in both these stressful jobs. The traditional stiff upper lip and work-it-out-alone mentality was completely counterproductive. In the traditional all-male group, with its hazing, horseplay, and obscene talk, if a man was going through a hard time, it was seen as a weakness. The other men backed off and excluded him, waiting for him to come through it. Then he could be part of the group again. The women contrasted this abandonment with our supportive way of relating to each other through good times and bad.

Turning one's back on coworkers' needs is counterproductive. It only makes more likely what men fear most will happen, that is, that they won't get the backup they need. But unspoken and unresolved problems hang over everyone's heads, waiting to affect job performance and threaten other people's lives.

A captain (age 30) talked about women's greater ability to communicate and to relieve the stress of death and sights normal people just don't see. "I think that's another area where women have really helped men. The fire service is now realizing that stress is an issue to be dealt with. I remember when I first came in, we would go to a fire and somebody would get burnt up, and the guys would come back and be real jittery. I'd want to talk about it and get it out in the open, but they would only want to kid about it, jokes about crispy critters, not being able to eat chicken for a while. But that is changing. Now the course of action is that we sit down and we say, 'Yes, that was a bad experience, but we did everything that we could do. But it still hurts, and we need to cry and say how it hurts.' "

Another firefighter, age 35, said the same thing.

"They used to teach you that you couldn't be emotional. If you came home from a fire where you saw something bad, nobody talked about it, and the divorce rate used to be really, really high. But the department has finally decided that people who see bad things can't just come back and not talk about it, and they have finally put together a program on dealing with stress. They've decided that if we're going to keep families together and we're going to keep firefighters happy at work, then we're going to have to talk and we're going to have to deal with it, and I think women, when they came in, wanted to talk about things and the guys didn't want to talk, and I think we're breaking this whole men and women thing down, and letting men be upset. It was so stupid. It was part of the reason everybody got so calloused."

"We've been doing a lot of work dealing with trauma situations on our police force," said a 36-year-old police sergeant. "We've started a support group for spouses and developed a spouses' night at our reserve academy, because the officers need to be encouraged to express emotions. It is essential to their health that they share with one another the feelings they are experiencing. I think my being on the force, my femaleness, so to speak, is part of what's made the difference here."

A 38-year-old officer described a colleague as the old-fashioned macho type. He was still hurting emotionally from having been shot years ago but wouldn't talk to anybody, his friends at the tavern or the police psychologist. "He's one of the straight and narrow, 'I don't want to talk about it' types. It's eating at him, taking a toll on his life. He's got ulcers. But it's so hard to draw his feelings out. I try telling him my tears dry, but his ulcers just get worse."

Jean B. Miller's *Toward a New Psychology of Women* (1976) takes several of our weaknesses, as judged by men, and points out how they are strengths. Being in touch with feelings of vulnerability and weakness and admitting them openly and consciously are, in her judgment, mentally healthy and positive (pp. 33–34). We are strong both for consciously tolerating feelings of weakness and because acknowledging these feelings is the only way to move away from them. The frankness and expressiveness of police and firefighting women support her view.

## DEVELOPING COWORKER SKILLS

Many women mentioned that, in contrast to the men, they more often taught others new skills, even when teaching was not part of their jobs. Instructing and guiding others, so traditional for women, was done gladly, enjoyably. Teaching didn't carry with it the conflicts associated with clerical and housekeeping tasks.

A 30-year-old litigator who does trial work for a large number of cases, all of which last a very long time, works with lots of other people, attorneys, paraprofessionals, staff, secretaries. "I believe in explaining, in keeping everyone informed so they can think for themselves. Explaining doesn't take that long, and if they understand what they're doing, they're more fulfilled. If you explain a little legal theory to a paralegal, rather than just have them find some document, they can find other things as well."

A young woman surplussed by a different department caught the eye of a Boeing electrical engineer (age 37). "They had her simply entering data into the computer. But she was so sharp, I talked to my boss and got approval to give her a raise to programmer. Then I taught her how to program. It was an advancement for her, and I got another good programmer. If more women were around, they would see that people aren't machines and treat them as people, and they'd get more work out of them and better quality too."

"A woman has to have an eye out for helping to promote a good image of women in the workplace, if I am going to help her," said a 31-year-old electrician (who got a telephone call while I was at her home offering her a community-college teaching job). "Our actions are very magnified; we're under such scrutiny that if you do things right, you promote a positive image of women. But if a woman is just here to get married or trashes other women, I try to talk to them about how we all have that responsibility to be serious, forthright professionals. It's a career, not fun and games. So I will only teach people who are not frivolous. But if she's serious, I'll do anything to help her."

Sometimes this teaching takes place in a team context. A deputy sheriff (age 29) said she loves to work as part of a team and likes suggesting things within a team. "I like everyone to feel like it is a team. If I'm sort of directing things, I'm recruiting ideas. I'd just as soon have them think the ideas were theirs. As far as being a true 'leader,' I don't stand out, and I'd just as soon have it that way. When I've had to train someone new, instead of 'Do it this way!' I leave it as, 'I do it this way.' So I'm real low-key about training. If I feel I need to correct someone, I kind of tease them, 'Why don't you try it this way, ha, ha?' in a real light manner."

Other behaviors that the women are teaching the men are to ask questions and listen to the answers. A blue-collar woman's way of compensating for lack of mechanical experience is to see the job as a continuing learning process. Even an experienced journeywoman won't bluff if she doesn't know how to do something. A 31-year-old electrician described how the men pretend they know how to do something when they don't, where "we always ask questions. We take pains to get information first. We use instructions as our first resort. Say, we're putting in something new. The women will take the instructions out of the box and sit down and read them, while the men go off and try to install the system. By the time we've figured it out and are ready to go to work, they're back, swearing and looking around for the instruction sheet, saying, 'Well, we've screwed up. Now let's read the directions.' "

Speaking of teaching men to ask questions and listen attentively, it is also important to teach them alternatives to the male style of speaking in order to argue and compete. Women's speech, in a group working together, tends to be collaborative and supportive. Women don't like any one person dominating a meeting. Women will take pains to see that everyone in a group says something. Women are polite about letting others finish what they are saying. Jessie Bernard (1981, pp. 382–383), in her discussion of women's skills at supportive speech, included an anecdote about a woman in a seminar who never did get to speak because she kept waiting to make sure the male students were finished talking. They never were.

## DEVELOPING COWORKER NURTURANCE

A carpenter in her midthirties is very accepting of the motherly role she plays. "If a woman is secure in herself and has a good environment on the job, she can be a mother to other workers. She knows when people are upset and can help the men understand fights with their wives. Women care for themselves and for others on the job, and they try to change policies to protect everybody. I feel more sympathetic and open to showing my feelings when someone does get hurt. While I'm busy showing concern for the individual, the men are trying to figure out exactly how the accident happened. Women supervisors are more understanding about sick kids and the other family crises everyone faces in life."

How can this carpenter transfer her caring to the men? This is what some feminist thinkers propose: that we teach men ego massage or "stroking," so that they can support us and other men. An electronics technician (age 33) has never resisted the in-house maternal activities expected of her. But she slowly has figured out ways to teach the men to do them. "When you first come in, they say, 'Gee, we need somebody to collect money to send out thank you cards, somebody to organize the Christmas dinner,' things that they view as a traditional women's role and they don't want to do. So I did these things, and now I have the guys trained to do them. The point is, I'm going to be here a long time, eight hours a day every day. So I'm going to make this a better place for me to be."

The women lawyers thought they were modeling more nurturant behaviors toward the staff for male lawyers. They said even the Queen Bees in the highest positions treated their support people differently than the men did, giving staff a sense of being colleagues and not ordering them around.

I was interviewing a 35-year-old attorney when she jumped up and excused herself in response to a slight knock on the door. She explained when she returned that today was her boss's secretary's birthday. She had reminded him of it yesterday and said she was going to take her to lunch. Would he like to join them? No, he didn't think it was necessary. But when he got home he told his wife about it and she had read him the riot act, so now he was knocking, one hour away from lunchtime, to say what a good idea it was, and yes, he'd like to come along.

This lawyer admitted how easy it was, when the pressure was on, not only to ignore caring gestures like remembering someone's birthday but to act disagreeably. "So I have told the support staff, if I start ordering you about and treating you inappropriately, tell me. Stop me. I'm very conscious that I want to treat people like human beings, not machines, but I can get so wound up in what I'm doing... That's what I said to my boss, 'I know how busy you can get, *but...*' "

We also pay more attention to how everyone around us feels and model for the men other ways of saying, "How are you feeling?" and "How are you doing?" "Once in a while I'll put my arm around one of them, or give him a pat on the back, if I know he's had a rough day," explained a carpenter, age 30. "In general, I show my concern by touching, reassuring, letting them know they're not all alone. I may have been standing across the room all day, but I've paid attention to how they *feel*. We've had a lot of tension lately because of a big changeover. We had a much larger work space before. We're scaling down. I think I've made us all more open about the changes and what we are concerned about."

A deputy sheriff (age 29) said she has made a detectable change in the way the men treat one another when they have an "owie" of one kind or another. They are more sympathetic and more willing not to tough it out when they are hurting.

"We had a new deputy, and we were all enroute to a burglary in progress and driving very fast and it was raining and nasty, and the new guy called over the radio, 'I've been in an accident' with a real shaky voice. I knew everybody else was in front of me, so I stopped by and made sure he wasn't hurt bad, because no sergeants had come by yet to check on him. So I patted him on the back and said, 'It's okay; the sergeant will be here in a minute. I just wanted to make sure you were okay before heading up to the scene.' You see, in the beginning, everybody was always trying to watch out for me, so I have wanted to make sure I did it for them as much as they did it for me. I like to let them know, I worry about you guys too. Now we have made checking on each other a standard procedure."

Similarly, the women engineers think they are teaching the men kinder ways of interacting. In one office, "if the principals want to announce something and don't want to tell people, the secretary is asked to relay messages! Part of the reason is, the principals are so poor in personal relations, they need women to help out. I'm the only woman high enough to override project directors' decisions, so I am very gentle in presenting my case when I have to override someone. I could care less about letting someone know they've made a mistake" (Engineer, age 34).

Sally Cline and Dale Spender's book *Reflecting Men* (1987) is all about how we as little girls learn to boost men's egos, to protect and flatter men's pride, and to placate and prop men up so that they suffer no loss of face, especially in public. They ask, why do we do so much to make men look good and feel good, especially when they don't reciprocate? "Reflecting," they noted, is something women do for men but men don't do for women (p. 186).

Now they could conclude that the solution is for us to stop reflecting—like the celebrated smile boycott of New York City receptionists in the 1970s. But reflecting behavior is good. It's congenial and productive. It achieves harmony. There should be more of it rather than less. So instead, Cline and Spender recommended that we teach men how to reflect us. I agree—at twice our natural size, especially when other people are around. Get men to help us feel and look important. Get them to come to our rescue verbally, through smiles and kind gestures as well, so that we never feel we have acted inappropriately.

## JUST LIKE BEING A SECRETARY?

I have in front of me a chapter called "Secretaries" in Rosabeth M. Kanter's *Men and Women of the Corporation* (1977, pp. 69–103). Here are a few things she said about secretaries in a big bureaucracy: Secretaries' desks show splashes of color and individual taste through posters and pasted up cartoons and newspaper articles. It is the secretaries who remember to celebrate birthdays. It is at their desks that people trade small compliments and where guests are made comfortable (p. 69). Secretaries do personal things for their bosses, " housework," such as sending Christmas cards, paying bills, and preparing refreshments. But perhaps their most important "office wife" duty is to be a good listener and interested in the world of their male bosses (pp. 89–90).

Can women simply not help it? Or do we truly enjoy it? Many secretaries believe their jobs are at stake if they don't play office wife. But these nontraditional women had little to fear. Many of them have secretaries of their own. But they still perform a round of caring and soothing activities, not as subordinates but as equals with male colleagues and as superordinates to support staff.

Should women resist this housework? Cline and Spender might suggest that first we try teaching our nurturant approach to men, especially when it comes to how to treat a secretary.

# 5

# RESPECT FOR
# DIFFERENCES

---

I was always an athlete, and I thought, Geez, I'll just show them that I can do it. Well, see, I'm still showing them. Strength comes into it as my inside strength. I have to make myself be the best I can be and draw on all my inner strength. A guy doesn't have to, because he has all the outside strength and so, in my head I have to know that I can do this job of firefighter as good as he can. I'm not as strong, but I have inside strength to know that I can do it. More women have that because we face and overcome more negative things that tell us we can't do this or that. (Firefighter, age 32)

Why might women have greater respect for differences than men? What early childhood experiences might lie behind it?

The socialization process we discussed in Chapter 3 is also relevant here. Ruth Hartley (1974, pp. 7–8) stressed that the demands on boys to be masculine are stronger and made earlier than the demands on girls to be feminine. Girls are said to "amble gradually" in the direction of feminine behaviors. Boys, on the other hand, are impressed early on with the dangers of deviating from the one right path. As a result, boys experience anxiety connected with the "right" sex-role behaviors that girls aren't troubled with. Hartley said that some boys experience virtual panic at being caught doing anything hinting of femininity. Furthermore, the picture boys have of how they must behave is, said Hartley, oversimplified and overemphasized. It is a black and white picture with little or no modulation (p. 9).

What better background can you think of for boys learning disrespect for people considerably different from them, people perhaps more different than women are? Or learning disrespect for the tiny differences boys notice among themselves, particularly features that affect physical strength and athletic skills—height, weight, and musculature?

Early sex-role conditioning obviously lays the groundwork for women's comparatively greater respect for differences. But two adult learning experiences also powerfully influenced these nontraditional women: the men's reaction to them from the time they embarked on their careers, in engineering classes, apprentice training, and the police academy, and the general tenets of the women's movement.

As for the men's reaction, when a person belongs to a minority group, especially if it's a very small minority, the person can't help feeling like an outsider. The majority makes you feel like an outsider, different from *them*. But you also notice differences, like the one in the quote above, not having outside strength but having inside strength. Women's learning to live with being an outsider is partly responsible for the greater respect for differences these nontraditional women held.

A police investigator described being an outsider as "sort of like a creature from outer space. I would really like to be able sometime to listen to all-male conversations, just to hear how they communicate with each other, because I know that the tone of the conversation changes when I join the group. I'm accepted on one level as an equal. But on another level, I'm not quite part of the team. I really try to work hard to build relationships with the guys and to keep those communication channels open. But I'm the one that has to keep making the effort. Unless I get up and walk across the room and make a point of joining in, it's just very rare for me to be included."

As for the second contemporary influence, the women's movement, this is a movement that wants to, and tries to, embrace all women's experiences and points of view. Feminists are not looking for an official feminist viewpoint. We do not believe there is only one explanation for women's subordination. We try to have respect for views different from our own.

True, we are sometimes uncomfortable with the many forms of feminism that exist and at odds with campaigns and causes that other feminists believe are so important. But we accept our differences. We reject conformity. We respect diversity. I've heard a gay woman tell a woman from an ethnic minority group that although it was true that she couldn't really know exactly what that other woman's feelings of being discriminated against were like, she had been discriminated against herself and thus had some idea of the other's pain and rage. What they had in common is that they were both outsiders. As a result, they were dedicated to respecting one another.

Thus in spite of the fact that tolerance and respect for diversity are difficult values to practice, feminists believe in them strongly. If we do not respect our differing views, how can we ask the dominant culture to respect our overall philosophy and to end the many forms of women's inequality?

Some of the women's movement cultural relativism had reached these nontraditional women. For one woman her beliefs in diversity and in being treated equally clashed. She was a 39-year-old state trooper who questioned women and minority-group troopers being given an unequal share of affirmative-action activities.

"Most of the minorities feel the same way the women do. We're both fighting the same battles. First, we want to earn what we get. Second, we don't want to be singled out in any way. This Black trooper and I were really irritated when we were told to come to the lieutenant's office, and they told us we had to go out and recruit people for the State Patrol. 'We want you to be *examples* of minorities in the protective class that can do the job and hold us up.' 'Well,' we said, 'you're singling us out.' You're saying, 'Oh, look at our, pat, pat, pat on the head, look at our nice little minority male and look at our nice little woman; see they can do it and wouldn't it be wonderful for you too?' Our contention was that even though we believed in it, we were not going to be singled out."

There were six sides to the women's comfort with diversity. It started with their insisting that everyone deserved to be treated courteously and politely. Second, they demystified their jobs by striving to bring more different people in, people who, like them, would succeed where it was not thought possible. Third, at the same time, they tried to get male colleagues to see the value of difference and of making changes in their own lives. Fourth, the women's advocacy for more pay for people in other occupations demonstrated their respect for and dependence upon them. Fifth, on the other hand, their advocacy of different ways to do the job definitely showed disrespect for the universal male standard. They did not believe there was one right way to do a job. Finally, they made strong friendships with women at work that ignored status and class differences and built on closeness and sharing and growing.

## BEING NICE TO EVERYONE

"I listen real well; most guys don't. I communicate different, which is sometimes a negative because I ask a lot of questions and they don't think I really mean it, like 'Will you do this?' instead of saying 'Do this!' That would be learning how to do it their way, and I won't do that. The guys are a little more open with me than they are to other guys. That's because supposedly we're more caring and we listen better" (Firefighter, age 32).

Women are nicer to other people because little girls are raised that way. Everybody deserves kindness and consideration, our mothers teach us, and the women said that just because they might have better jobs and higher pay was no grounds for them to be rude or indifferent to those less fortunate.

Blue-collar men have gotten used to being abused by employers. It's like unpleasantness is a job condition. Antagonism between management and blue-collar workers is so enshrined that the men automatically can shift their identification from oppressed to oppressor. The women said that when their male coworkers got promoted, their personalities changed radically. "They are no longer nice persons, almost as if they have been sent to some school that says, 'You will not be nice to anybody.' But I think that if you are kind and fair to your employees, you get equal treatment back from them. I always believe in please and thank you. I don't care who they are, the grungiest man out there deserves please and thank you. I've put in for foreman but I won't change" (Electrician, age 45).

Praise is another way women typically are nice to those around them. Even if the men did not reciprocate, the women remarked that they liked the men's work or they thought a man had come up with a great idea. A 34-year-old mechanic said, "In terms of making the world a better place, I think men and women both can use a little more encouragement, a stroke every now and then. You can work with a crew to come up with ways to make the work situation more pleasant. Every place I've worked is a little different when I leave from the way it was when I got there. I know that. I can see that. You go on a job and nobody says 'Please' or 'Thank you.' If I need help from somebody, I will ask them if they will please help me, and then I tell them thank you. The whole atmosphere changes. It's really noticeable, and I do that every place that I work. Whether it stays that way, or whether they go back to treating each other nasty, I don't know."

"Being nice to everyone" was especially important to the women when dealing with people lower down the company hierarchy. An engineer, age 34, said she is always sensitive to how the people she works with feel. "I help boost their image of themselves; I trust them and their working ability. I am more willing to listen to others' ideas and feelings, more willing to talk to people and care about what people have to say, what their needs are. I was the first woman engineer here, and I dealt with a lot of blatant and insidious sexism. I didn't have anyone to talk to, and I'd come home feeling terribly, like from a guy saying something like, 'Hey, that seminar was good and the speaker was even a woman!' Hard knocks have made me more sensitive to what I say, to people's feelings."

"We're more concerned about being nice, about treating people with respect," a 31-year-old lawyer told me. "I want people to like me, so I am chatty. In this office there are three secretaries, all older than me, one's sixty-six. These women were concerned about my age when the firm hired me, so I have made an effort to make them think they are doing me favors rather than expect things to be done for me. They use my first name, while all the men are Mr. So and So. I'm a fairly informal person, lighthearted. I hate to sound full of myself, but lots of people tell me that this place is not nearly as formal as it was."

I was impressed by the hosts of situations in which the women felt frustrated, rejected, lonely, and angry, but still tried to be nice. "Even now when I go into a new station I have to tell myself, 'Now, Beth, you are going to go in there and introduce yourself to every person before you sit down," sighed a 28-year-old firefighter, "because if you don't, they'll ignore you. If you just sit down and read the paper and drink your coffee, you'll go all day and nobody will talk to you. We aren't that way. With new people coming in, we show them the ropes and include them, whereas the men will let them sit in a corner for a year."

For readers skeptical of the survival value of being nice to everyone, Jane Silver's "Love Your Colleagues as Yourself?" (1989) is a review of a research project describing the ideal characteristics of the successful "Euro-Executive." This person must be cooperative with colleagues, have understanding toward different cultures, and be able to move easily between cultures. New-age executives and employees, said Silver, have also got to try consciously to like their colleagues. Ruthlessness, competitiveness, office paranoia, and the routine stab in the back must give way to sociability, warmth, and friendliness among colleagues.

## MORE DEMYSTIFICATION STRATEGIES

Some women in male-dominated jobs are "Queen Bees." Queen Bees enjoy being the token woman. They insist that other women be allowed in the group only if they endure an identical hard climb, undergo the same rough initiation, and accept the male mystique of the occupation. Queen Bees do little to promote greater numbers of women in their fields.

There were no Queen Bees in this bunch. Like the overwhelming majority of nontraditional women, the interviewees did what they could to bring other women in, such as a 56-year-old legislator who, when she had worked in city government, recruited women for commissions and committees as hard as she could. In the legislature now, she said, it is especially important to recruit women to run against incumbents in swing districts. "We've found that a good woman candidate has a far better chance of taking out such an incumbent, of either party, than a man does. Women vote for women in this situation. Women have an expectation that we (women) will be fair and not tied to some political regime that has existed forever. So this is the perfect opportunity for building the numbers of women in the legislature."

Women, as a group lacking in power, empathize with and support other groups who lack political and economic power—Blacks, Hispanics, the handicapped, the elderly. So in the same way that the women encouraged other women, they also brought in other kinds of underrepresented groups, such as the young, to their nontraditional jobs. Women officers acted as advisers for police scout and cadet programs, electricians staged trade fairs for high school students, and engineers talked to first-year college students.

The success of women, minorities, and the handicapped in a white male occupation helps to break down the mystique of that occupation. Such success suggests that anyone with training can do it.

The idea that a job can be done by different people began for a mechanic, now 31, on the farm where she was raised. "I've always tried to do a man's job. When I joined the army at 19 they tried to give me a cook job, but helicopter mechanic sounded better than cooking. My Dad was the one who was always out, being paid on a regular basis. So my Mom worked the farm, without which we couldn't survive on his paycheck anyway. That's where I got the idea that there's no difference between a woman's job and a man's job, because she was doing his job because he was doing something else she didn't have the skill for."

Medicine, too, should be open to anyone who completes the training for it. "Taking care of other people is no big deal. Who used to sit up with you when you were sick as a kid—your father? It's the most natural thing in the world for a woman to be a doctor. Once you have had the training, there is no reason why anyone couldn't do it. Just like the president of the Boeing Company. He has skills, and he does his job well, but it's not magic" (General practitioner, age 32).

What other demystification strategies were they using? Three young women who were just starting in the brokerage business were going about the job a whole new way; they were going to share their expertise and clients. Sharing clients and commissions, I was told, is unheard of among men. But these three did not want to pretend to be experts at all things. Instead, each had a specialty. One was cleverer at investment-planning ideas, one more knowledgeable about bonds, another more knowledgeable about stocks. They shared their clients. Each client's "risk parameters" and "investment destinations" were evaluated against their pooled investment knowledge and an overall best-tax-advantage program worked out. This cooperative, egalitarian style of serving customers contrasts sharply with how men compete with one another to hold on to their clients.

Another thing the women were doing was explaining to the men how connected they felt toward the public they served. They wanted the men to see the similarities between "us and them," rather than differences such as the guns they wore or the heavy hoses they shouldered.

An 18-year-old law enforcement scout thought our links to the outside were women's strength for police work. "Little kids aren't afraid of female cops. They'll come right up to us. Everybody knows female cops are more friendly and talkative. Just look at our body language. Men have their thumbs stuck in their pants (she demonstrates), where a woman lays her arm across her waist. Women *care* about people. Men will say they like people, but I never heard one say he cared. The old cops are kind of surrounded by a bubble, and the public's in a different bubble. Younger cops, though, want to be accepted by the public, you know, in the same bubble."

A firefighter (age 32) said that what she and the other women were fighting was the Jack Webb outlook. (The 1960s television character Jack Webb was a taciturn cop who spoke in a monotone and who only wanted "to hear the facts, Ma'am, just the facts.") "To these guys a public servant is a well-trained, educated, intelligent man working to keep the public safe, and the public is always getting in the way, being stupid and getting themselves in trouble. This mentality means you approach the public as an obstacle to get around. I see the public as one of us, and my job is to establish a partnership with them instead of trying to get around them."


## TEACHING MEN ABOUT CHANGE

"It will slowly change so that people are more comfortable with different combinations of people. They will start acquiring some of our good characteristics, such as communicating better with each other, working together not quite so much in competition against each other, more working as a team. I think just broadening their experience of working with other people will help them on aid runs, inspecting, dealing with people. I think they will learn by watching women work with the public" (Firefighter, age 32).

Women entering male jobs throws together the two groups that must be the most different in the world on the openness-to-change dimension: men and women. No, I don't mean that. I mean that we have a minority of women who, by definition, are extremely open to change and learning new things and a minority of men who are very conservative and dedicated to maintaining the status quo.

The women thought that men in very male jobs were particularly resistant to change. The men did not like new schemes for shifts and procedures. They resisted innovative ideas about pensions and leaves. They didn't even like new tools. They didn't like to see people questioning requirements and regulations, and they didn't like new people, especially if they were different from themselves.

It looks like resistance to change is related to how strong tradition is in a male group, be it an occupation or a whole country. Consider the following study: Yvette Walczak (1988) interviewed fifty-one men in the United Kingdom about their attitudes toward women and men. The men said it was easy for them to mouth egalitarianism but quite another thing to change their basic attitudes toward women. They said change was a slow process; they thought men needed extra help to change (p. 130). Although higher education, cohabitation, and working alongside women were responsible for changing some of the men, many said changes in their attitudes were women's responsibility (p. 133). The men thought that the women were rushing it, that women moved quicker than men. Thus men's objections were natural. Change takes decades, they said, and especially attitudes toward equality would take a very long time (pp. 135–136).

A 38-year-old police investigator shook her head. "I don't see very many men who are open to change. If you look at women's magazines, they're always dealing with self-improvement, with trying to understand yourself and trying to understand other people. If the men set self-improvement goals, it has to do with physical things or maybe education. But it doesn't have to do with personality or emotions. They could care less."

These women, in contrast, couldn't help but be open to change. In the skilled crafts, police and fire services, for example, women have had to figure out different ways to do the job that are not dependent on physical brawn. Because of that, such women are always trying to find other ways to do the job better.

Inevitably, the presence of women gradually opens men's minds.

"They're real into all the stereotyping stuff. Most of their wives don't work. The newer ones do, but the older ones, their wives didn't work and the firefighter worked two jobs. Their wives took care of the kids and all that. So to have us come on and do their job, it just didn't make sense to them. It does now because we've been on long enough. But it took a while. The station is where the issues come about and where you see most of the change. On the fireground, you usually never have any problems. You can't tell me there from anybody else. By how I do anything you can't tell, so there really isn't any difference out there. There are differences if they can tell who you are in how they treat you. A big difference is we have a better attitude. I always try to see the positive side of the job, and it seems like they always see the negative, and they're real structured in their thinking. Change is real hard. I think maybe women, well, we are a change; it seems that it's easier for us to accommodate that. They're so structured in their thinking. It's like: Blacks are over here and women are over here and religion is here. They're real into that and I don't think women are" (Firefighter, age 32).

A captain (age 30) thinks that when women get to the top, their public relations skills will make for big, positive changes in the fire department.

"If women were in positions of power, if they had influence on buying equipment and training materials, I think the department would be better trained, as far as up-to-date EMS (emergency medical service), first-aid techniques, firefighting techniques, and hazardous materials. I think there would be a lot more information going out to the companies to keep them well informed. There would be a greater push to buy new, quality, updated equipment. I know a lot of that has to do with the budget, but a lot of it also has to do with presenting it to the city council and fighting for it. Women would be willing to be much more progressive in trying to get state-of-the-art equipment. Our public relations would be a lot better. When you're talking to the business community, they don't like us. That has to do with enforcement of the firecodes, how they're enforced. It goes back to that officer who goes out to inspect that building and how he relates to that business person. Your PR would be better if there were more women in the position of going out and doing that."

One of my internist friends (she was 47 at the time), who is a very conservative and cautious doctor, contrasted how she spends her spare time with the men in her office. The men spend any time they take away from practicing medicine worrying about how their money can make more money. She, on the other hand, spends her time learning about herbs, homeopathy, and acupuncture. "Not that I want to practice these things, but I want to help people make wider choices. There are many other fields that have something to offer traditional medicine. Until recently, I clung to my role as physician and was stunned by how much others know and have to offer. I foresee a melding of naturopathic attitudes and the technology of allopathic medicine that would be a real contribution to American medicine, more amelioration, less harshness, and learning about these new possibilities is fun; it really is."

In woman–man relationships the cliche is that men want stability and women want growth. Men don't want to think about their feelings or "develop greater self-understanding." They like things the way they are, with women in a subordinate position at home and at work. The problem is that if women think there is a conflict between the sexes, there is a conflict—no matter how much men wish it wasn't there.

These nontraditional women fought men's attempts to subordinate them. The electricians asked, why should we do the paper work? The firefighters asked, why should we do the cooking? The brokers asked, why should we always be the ones to organize the annual picnic? They learned that the only way to get these housekeeping tasks delegated fairly was not to do them unless a clear plan for distributing them equally was negotiated, which meant the men had to change their ideas about who does office housework.

## WORKING FOR GREATER REWARDS FOR OTHERS

Women become fast friends with other women at work, regardless of levels and statuses. It's another side of the "no line between us and them" discussed in Chapter 3. Women are bound to identify with our friends' sex-discrimination problems, poor pay, poor advancement prospects, and burnout.

The low salaries of sales assistants was a real problem for the brokers who solved it by "taking care" of their own sales assistants. It is a system problem, however, since brokers don't have to give the assistants a cut of their earnings. One broker (age 33) said, "My assistant is a very dear friend of mine who I asked to work for me. Because if I'm going to work eight hours a day, I certainly want to work with a very dear friend whom I love, rather than some person that I am supposed to order about, and I also want her to participate in my wealth, so I give her part of my salary. But I'd like to have more power so I can help more friends down there, suffering in the trenches. When I make even more money, then I'll have two assistants, two great friends working with me."

A 45-year-old stockbroker had this fantasy: "One time I had the idea I would pass out flyers, anonymously, chicken that I am: 'SOS! Save Our SAs! Until [this firm] does something about it, it is *our* responsibility. SAs need cash compensation. Could you live on $15,000 a year?' I am aware of their grievances. They really get a raw deal. How inferior they are treated by the old timers! The most successful people making $400,000, $500,000, won't give their people $100 a month. They want to keep it all for themselves."

A physician the same age reminisced:

"I once challenged the convention that technicians are paid to do your work, and your involvement with them ends there. There was this tec who had been with my boss for a decade, taking care of all his work. I really enjoyed this woman. She was a very intelligent, competent person. She had helped me out a lot on a project, and I wanted her to be coauthor on a paper. It was such a little thing, but a nice thing. But he criticized me severely over it. I was very upset because here I was, doing what I thought was right, fighting for increased recognition of a coworker. But I've always been determined that the people who work for you should be acknowledged fairly. Eventually, he did learn and paid greater attention to rewarding tecs after that."

A 24-year-old attorney who had just joined her firm said, "I am more considerate of our staff than the men. I'll always ask, would you mind doing this? I sit in on salary negotiations because I want to focus on what a person needs, what's best for that person, not on what secretaries are being paid that year. When the firm was talking about the annual Christmas party and the men didn't think it was a good idea to invite the staff and their families, I was the only one to object. I got no support. But after the party the men said, never again without the staff."

## OPENING UP DIVERSE SPECIALIZATIONS AND STYLES

Many of the women's colleagues are very traditional, conforming men, following society's sex-role prescriptions down to the letter. It may take a long time before whole new careers enter their minds, but in the meantime, following the example of the women, these men can consider other specializations within their fields and alternative ways to perform their present jobs. The women might have been very conventional off the job in domestic arrangements, politics, and religion, but on the job they stood for individualism, nonconformity, breaking with the conditioning of teachers, guidance counselors, the nextdoor neighbors, and old friends.

"More women means more choices and options for everyone" was a delightful theme running through the interviews. One of the first things an electrician (age 31) told me was that having women on the job was good for the men; it helped them a lot; it gave them more choices, for example, not to swear and to be more human. "We don't put up a front with the men. It's like it's okay to be yourself with us; it's okay to tell me about your cooking recipes; you don't have to talk about hunting and guns. It gives them an opportunity to be a little bit more relaxed, and we're cleaning up the air for them when we hear profanity and say, 'I can't believe you just said that, you foul mouth.' There's lots of guys that don't like to hear that trash too. So with us they don't have to talk that locker room talk, and they don't have to put up with it either."

An academic physician in her midforties said,

"As we get more women in medicine, we all as individuals can find specialities that fit us. My girlfriend who is a surgeon is a real technical whiz, a very, very good technician. She's also a genuinely warm and caring person. Her patients love her so much. It's okay for her to be both, but traditionally, 'warm and caring' weren't okay for men. More women in medicine means increased tolerance for individuals. We'll reach new levels of comfort for different types of doctors, more accepting of people from different backgrounds. We need room for all types of doctors, like the older professors who didn't have the pleasure of raising their children. We need room for leaders, fanatics of both sexes who want to rise to the top and who need support systems. It needs to be okay for men to stay home and be househusbands."

A firefighter (age 32) wanted to see two "human values" reinforced more in the department, the value of everyone working together and the value of differences among workers, rather than that of "how well you fit into a narrow definition of how you're okay. I think women in the department will have that effect. It's sad when women adopt the old male values as a survival technique instead of humanizing the department. It's real important to never let them forget that, as much as I want to be accepted, I never want to be one of the boys. Someday people are going to value that people are different. Someday we'll see a respect for people's unique lives."

In regard to offering men a full range of work styles, a big contribution of women to the fire service has been an alternative style of fighting fires. In the place of aggression and raw brute strength, women use a host of different techniques that are logical and sensible. Men like to break down doors, they said; we would rather try the doorknob first or climb in an open window.

"Women are much more technicians. I can't go out and do something physically that some guy six foot two, two hundred pounds can do, without thinking about it. I can look at leverage points and use my skill and my head, whereas a guy has a tendency to use his brawn instead of his head. But that is changing, and the changes are a direct result of women coming onto the fire service. We're seeing less back disabilities as a result" (Firefighter, age 30).

The women were at first worried about what the men would think of their techniques, but when everyone saw that "thinking first" meant fewer injuries, the women went from defensiveness to pointing out the advantages of their different techniques. "Women don't typically have that 'kill-football' type mentality. I watch men just chomping to get in there, the old 'Put me in, coach, put me in.' By comparison, I was at first tentative, wanting direction, needing my male counterparts' approval. But I don't need that approval any longer. I do the job that needs doing, not caring what they think if I think about it a little longer" (Firefighter, age 35).

Another 32-year-old firefighter defended being passive and observant. "One example is on a search and rescue in a house. I went in with this guy, and he was just throwing everything around and just going nuts, and I was thinking, if there *is* anybody here, they're going to get killed, just buried in debris. We reason more before we do something and before we get hurt. Whether that's trying the doorknob before you bust in the door or squatting down to pick up a ladder rather than bending over with your legs straight. A direct result of having women come into the fire service is that safety and technique are now a major part of our annual evaluation."

Success in many law firms seems to come from holding certain common attitudes and values, but for appearance sake, some law firms have token staff members representing diversity. At the same time, the firms had no intention of using tokens' diverse skills and attitudes. "If women and Blacks have the same attitudes and values as the founders, then they're fine. To be a woman and Jewish is respected as long as it doesn't interfere with job performance in their terms. Unfortunately, the women currently at the top have changed to become just like the founding fathers. But when there is a critical number of women at the top, they will create a different climate. Real diversity will be valued instead of the appearance of diversity" (Attorney, age 29).

Another attorney who had just turned forty illustrated what all of the women expressed. She goes way beyond tolerant. She enjoys differences among people, appreciates differences, sees differences as strengths. She related: "Another partner and I were discussing a possible lateral hire. He said, 'You know, *he*'s not one of us.' 'Why?' I asked, 'My feeling is he's a good guy.' 'Well,' he said, 'he *bikes* to work; he may even be left of center.' This guy is my best friend and he makes these incredible value judgments. The longer I am in that firm, the more different I get from them. I'm trying not to hide how different I am. I can't be a total fake about these things. But there's a thin line between being honest and being one of them, which is very important."

Several of the electricians think the workplace atmosphere, because of women, has become noticeably more natural and realistic.

"Things have already tipped. More women on the job is now more acceptable to the men, and it's much more comfortable and easy going. I feel a lot less uptight, and they do too. They don't feel they have to take care of us or worship us. Having women on the job is much more sensible. I've finally proven myself, and now the guys phone me to do extra jobs, and that's where I really make my living. That's real respect, and those things didn't happen ten years ago. Our major strength comes from how well we've progressed as a group, how fast we're progressing, and it's getting faster and faster. Men now accept that women want to do this. Men accept the fact that that's okay, and they're getting more and more input from women about how to do the job whether they want it or not" (Construction electrician, age 30).

## SHOWING THE STRENGTHS OF WOMEN'S FRIENDSHIPS

It has become something of a contest lately, writing about the differences between men's and women's friendships. Whose is deeper, closer? Which is better—male bonding or female bonding? Neither type of friendship has to be superior, but it's worth looking at the differences, because looking expands the choices we all have.

If men did adopt women's friendship style, the workplace would be very different. Women's friendships have the special qualities of a direct sharing of feelings, a need for closeness, an identification with what the other woman is experiencing. The flip side of this intimacy can be keen disappointment when our friends and we don't grow at the same rate, intellectually or emotionally. But the cosiness and love women give one another is viewed with wonder by some men. (I recommend Susie Orbach and Luise Eichenbaum's 1987 book, *Bittersweet*.)

We like to share and trust, reveal ourselves, and not worry about being ridiculed or betrayed. Many physicians said they were more emotionally expressive with their friends at work than the men. "I am very emotionally expressive at work. I like hugs. Most guys can't handle a hug and never hug nurses or each other. Also, I won't go along with the pecking order. I don't adhere to it, and I call everybody by their first names, which really bugs the men" (Physician, age 32).

A police investigator (age 38) described building this kind of friendship with a man. "I have one investigator that I'm good friends with, good friends with his wife too. We two just do things together. We worked several cases together, and after that we go to lunch together, go work out at the gym, things like that. If I'm going to have friends who are police officers, for a while anyway, they're going to have to be male." Similarly, a 39-year-old state trooper marveled at the changes in her conversations with men as they become friends. "We sit around now, and one of the guys will be talking about recipes and cooking, and it amazes me that they will listen to what I have to say, that they'll listen to me tell a story, that I can share things now."

Another example of women's friendship at work involved the creation of a formal organization for women to provide friendship and personal support, and also to work for reforms to benefit both sexes, as well as to recruit more women. The organization is the Association of Female Fire Fighters (AFFF) in Seattle. Elsewhere in this book the firefighters talk about how they take women's issues and make them "people issues" to negotiate with management. But I mention the AFFF here because it got its start in female bonding. It started from seeing other women die and facing one's own mortality. "First I went through the whole macho thing that I can't cry, and I don't need to go to anyone for help. But then I decided I would talk about it, and it was amazing how much better I felt after I talked to my family and friends. That really marked the beginning of our organization. I wanted to bring all the women together because here were women firefighters dying, and we hadn't even got to know each other. A lot of us decided we needed each other to talk to; we had to trust each other and not be like the guys who can't let others see their Achilles heels" (Firefighter, age 33).

But perhaps the most important aspect to women's friendships that changes the workplace is that women make friends with other women regardless of the jobs they hold. Women feel free to bond with all other women at work.

Physicians, surrounded as they are with ninety-nine percent women support staff, are in a particularly good position to bond with other women. A GP, age thirty-eight, said, "I share everything with my staff and ask their opinion on nonmedical things. Part of it is women's insecurities about making decisions. In the past my indecisiveness has driven my staff crazy, because people tend to think of you as less a boss if you ask their opinion and more as a friend, just because you are a woman. They feel like they can get away with doing what they please, instead of what you ask them. So you have to work that out. My staff now is great; they respect me, think I'm a great doctor, and like me as a person."

"I have had positive feedback being a woman doctor," said a former nurse. "I haven't experienced resentment from nurses, even the ones I used to work with as a nurse. But it's hard for me to ask people to do things. This on the one hand is good; why should I ask a nurse to get something? Why can't I get it myself? So I am uncomfortable delegating and less clear about authority. We see ourselves more as coworkers; for example, I eat with the employees who are all women. Male doctors aren't comfortable doing that" (Physician, age 36).

Another medical doctor, age 32, insisted on giving interviews to a very large number of people for the position of her office assistant. The important requirement seemed to be a kind of bonding factor. "Although they all had good qualifications, I relied on my intuition to choose who I felt was right for me. She is not only great, but we have become personal friends as well. We definitely have a team approach, and she shares in decision making when appropriate. She calls me by my first name, which is rarely done between doctors and their assistants."

The women supported other women in their professional growth by giving ambitious staff more responsibility and encouraging them to get more education. "I have a special bond and support of my mostly female staff. We have things in common; we're mothers; they can relate to my problems and I to theirs, the joys and sorrows. We all work on things together, lots of team work. I am better than the men at respecting the abilities of these other people, realizing their capabilities. There is a female tec here who I know could be a doctor; she is that sharp. I see this in her, where men might not see the qualities as well. I know that if certain things hadn't gone the way they did, if I hadn't made certain choices, I might be a tec rather than a doc. So I want her to grow and expand" (Physician, age 43).

## IF YOU RESPECT DIFFERENCES, YOU CAN BE DIFFERENT YOURSELF

Consider this story of close mindedness told by a 31-year-old firefighter. "The guys are real quick to judge others. They'll say just what they think, while women, if they can't say something nice, don't say anything at all. One guy at the station had his girlfriend lighten his hair. The guys really spoke out and gave him a bad time, while we didn't say anything, even though we may not have liked it. But the men are more opinionated. They have tunnel vision and can only look at things one way. If someone does something differently, they can't deal with it. But being a woman in a man's job, you have to be open to new things."

Given these men's early sex-role socialization, we can understand why they were so negative about a little hair lightening. But how can we get them to imagine the freedom to each of them as individuals if they could overcome that rigid socialization? How can we get them to see that if all men respected differences, they would all be free to be different themselves, no longer slaves to attitudes and habits laid down before the age of six?

Women need men's open mindedness to forge new forms of working. We need male champions of our causes, men who won't mind being thought deviant, different, and a traitor to their sex if they support day care at the work site, parental leaves at birth and to attend to sick children, flex time, job sharing, or institutionalized parttime employment with prorated benefits— all of those radical, new, deviant ideas that many men are intolerant of because they believe they are not part of being manly.

# 6

# BRIGHTENING THE
# BLUE-COLLAR WORLD

Years ago I worked for a construction company that pitted people against each other, and the fear of losing jobs caused a lot of competitiveness. If something went wrong a lot of shifting of blame went on, and there was not a lot of information sharing. I was one of two women hired because the company thought that the customers, the husbands, would rather have women working in their homes with their wives. The two of us fought the company about the competitiveness. They found us very difficult, always pushing and questioning. The men just accepted that that's how it was; either put up with it or don't work. Women don't think they have to work all the time, and we're willing to risk our jobs to try to make changes. I couldn't believe how accepting the men were. I kept asking, "Why don't people talk about how awful this is?" (Carpenter, age 45)

This quote raises the question of why men accept the stress of company-imposed competition among workmates? Why don't men object? Is it because they are afraid of losing their jobs? Or is it a matter of learned sex roles again?

Phillip Hodson (1984, pp. 94–96), a British marriage counselor, noted that among male traditionalists, blue-collar men have the worst situation because they are taught early to put up with gross unpleasantness for the prize of machismo. They are taught that heavy manual work makes them real men, whereas white-collar men are effeminate, doing women's work. Hodson said that both parents are responsible for teaching little boys that men must amount to something in the world, that men must have influence over some portion of the world at large, some external achievement. Both mom and dad present life as a competitive contest with the little boy set against everybody else. He is told that his emotions are unimportant in this contest and that only the world outside matters. He is taught to keep his emotions to himself, since one of the rules of the adult game of work is not to let anybody get a hold over you.

Hodson called this childhood socialization process the "self-selected slavery" of working-class men, because if parents didn't teach little boys that they had to be "muscly drudges" to be real men, it would be much harder for employers to get them to do that drudge work. The boys would consider other jobs appropriate for themselves rather than only those that improved technology destroys daily by the thousands.

There's also an adult socialization process that keeps men mired in miserable situations. This process affects men of all classes. It's the idea that real men do not ask for help. Helen Franks' book, *Goodbye Tarzan* (1984), is about the many different times men don't ask for help when they need it, such as when they are going through divorce, death of a spouse, job loss, or middle-age transitions. She has a whole chapter devoted to men's belief that going to the doctor's is a sign of dependency. Franks said that male doctors, who have the same sex-role socialization as male patients, prefer to explain everything in physical terms and don't want to see men as having emotional problems. Male doctors expect men to cope as a real man should by being cool, tough, and rational, and thus their male patients' anxieties and depressions go undiagnosed and untreated (pp. 145–147).

The quote at the beginning of this chapter brings up the question of how many women it takes to bring about change in a male-dominated employment situation. Judith Bardwick in *In Transition* (1979, p. 58) said that it takes "quantum numbers," that is, enough for normalcy. She said that only then can women think innovatively and use their different priorities, perceptions, values, and coping styles to create change. She believes our presence must be normalized before we can press our out-sider solutions. In any case, two women carpenters weren't enough for real change.

Many women still lack the self-confidence required to survive in the change-resistant trades. For many of us, still on our way toward becoming self-affirming and self-worth judging, having other women around is necessary to endure the situation as it stands, let alone change it.

On the other hand, the skilled craftswomen we talked to certainly did not have quantum numbers around them. Furthermore, many were hired as tokens because of affirmative-action pressure. Working isolated from one another and looked upon disdainfully by the men, inside themselves they were nonetheless strong. They did not behave as tokens.

Most of the women had been in other areas of the work force when they decided to change direction toward the trades. This decision gave them a sense of conscious control over their lives. "Men get into carpentry because their dads did it or because 'anybody can frame a house.' A lot of men feel real stuck. I've had several men say, 'Why are you doing this? If I could do anything else, had any other skill, I wouldn't be here.' We have more determination and commitment because we made a conscious choice. Our hardships make us look at that decision and affirm the choice. Women don't survive very long if they only want the money, while the men feel trapped because they need the money" (Carpenter, age 34).

The women's hardships gave them special sympathy with the men's hardships. They understood completely that job insecurity was the major reason that the men were so threatened by the women's presence and why men tried so hard to keep up the macho image.

"They have to keep up the illusion that there are only a few women who can do the job. They say to each of us, 'You're the exception.' Because there's not a whole lot of status or job security there, there are no rewards for good work. All they know is, 'I have to be the strongest and biggest SOB this company's got. I'll climb up there; I'm willing to go to any length to keep this job,' and the company's attitude is, 'You guys are a dime a dozen. Hump it; work harder.' So they're all threatened by unemployment, and management uses tactics like this one. They had me and my partner build a section of wall. We had one week. Then they had another pair do another section. Whoever did it slower 'goes down the road.' The way you get 'in' with the company is stay late and don't complain, do what you're told, and don't make waves for the employer. If you stay late and ask to be compensated, they say, 'You're lucky you have a job with us' " (Carpenter, age 30).

This excruciating, demoralizing situation is why the women were understanding when the men lashed out with some form of sexual harassment. But some said, "All that's changed in the last fifteen years. Their attitudes toward us have changed. I used to walk on the scene, and they'd drop their tools and stare and point. Now their conversation isn't as loose; they're not talking about who they slept with and making lewd comments about people walking on the sidewalk. They're less raucous, more toned down; no more naked women in the job shacks or *Playboy* magazines where we're supposed to be eating lunch. Some men never did appreciate any of that, and now they have a good excuse to cut the other men off, so I don't get labeled as a complainer because I don't like it" (Shipyard electrician, age 34).

The women talked about seven major ways their behaviors were changing blue-collar work. First, they said, we're not embarrassed to ask for help. It just doesn't make sense to us to hurt ourselves. This makes it more acceptable for men to ask for help. Second, it's more acceptable for men to mess up. Third, we must find ways to make up for our relative lack of physical strength. Our adaptations are always more sensible for the body, any body, including male bodies. Gradually, smart organizations, such as the fire service, adopt them for all employees. Fourth, they said women bring a calming influence to bear just by being there. Fifth, they enjoyed the process of the crafts more than the men, at least more than the men would admit to. The crafts stayed novel for the women; there was always something more to be learned. But then, daily job satisfaction is as important to women as good pay. Sixth, many of the trades are tied to life at home—plumbing, carpentry, electrical work, home construction, and home roofing—and the home has traditionally been women's sphere. Finally, as the quote that starts the chapter illustrates, they said they were willing to fight for right. They said they were feisty to begin with or they wouldn't have survived.

## IT'S OKAY TO ASK FOR HELP

It's not okay for men to ask for help. Asking for help is something women do. Men must avoid acting in any way like a woman, even if acting like a woman makes sense.

The origin of our asking, and they're not asking, for help is another instance of very early socialization by both women and men, mothers and fathers. But I think that once we're adults, it is men who do more of the conditioning. It is men who abuse other men for acting like girls and men who leap to do physical and mechanical things for women as courtesies.

I also don't think women's asking for help with mechanical tasks is based so much on the experience of trying and failing in girlhood as it is based on our not being allowed to try in the first place. As adults, we certainly get rewarded by men for letting them help us. It obviously pleases them.

About our not being allowed to try in the first place, one of blue-collar women's biggest problems is a man's conditioned courteous response. New male acquaintances reach automatically to take a woman's toolbox away so that they can carry it for her. If they see a woman having trouble turning a wrench, men are more likely to take the wrench away rather than give her information on how to turn it more easily. A woman has to be very careful when she asks for help so that she is told how to fix a machine and that the helper stands aside and lets her do it.

Women apprentices sometimes get inferior training because instructors and foremen shunt them away from tasks they fear the women do not have the strength for. Women journeymen sometimes get channeled into the lighter, less physically demanding jobs out of this same misplaced protectiveness.

Some women perceive this protectiveness as an advantage and just let it go. They rationalize that they do other things for their male helpers to compensate. But if a woman ever hopes to get promoted, she has to do everything connected with a job, including the heavy tasks and the shift work. In fact, most foremen do not knock off points in performance evaluations if a woman asks for help doing a heavy task. Getting assistance makes more sense to them than someone who tries to muscle it alone and gets hurt.

Even a small carpentry shop has heavy physical tasks. One five-foot, 30-year-old woodworker told me: "I'm a small person, and a lot of things I can't do by myself. I've convinced at least one guy in my shop that if I can't, he can't. The threat of injury is too great. I hurt my back once, and I don't want to do it again. So I ask for help when I need it. The guys nine times out of ten won't ask for help. But that's changing with the people I work with. They feel more now that if I can't do something, they shouldn't be trying to do it alone."

Especially on big construction jobs every carpenter needs the help of others. "After a while I realized I could do things the smart way—using tools and equipment or getting help, rather than muscling everything—building something in place rather than pushing it around after it's built or pouring concrete in place instead of dragging it over later. Many men have 'carpenters elbow' from jerking things around. We have seen how a man's strength eventually works against him because he pushed too hard, so we use our heads, like rolling a piece of plywood across the floor on its edges, end over end, instead of carrying it" (Carpenter, age 30).

Another woman is now in a position to change things for others:

"I'm moderately strong but not as strong as the men. I ask for help or find a machine to help me, or I'll refuse to do something if it's too hard. Lots of the men go to chiropractors after work. In the beginning I decided I wouldn't ever see a chiropractor for a work-related problem. I'd rather get laid off than hurt. You've got to say no if you begin to hurt. Now I oversee others, and I yell at them if someone picks up something too big. I'll say, 'Go and get some help!' It shocks people when I say no. They say, 'You won't do it?' and I say, 'That's right. I won't do it without help.' It's worked well for me, and now I'm starting to see some men say no. Today a truck came in to be unloaded, and we just looked at each other, rolled our eyes, and called for a forklift" (Carpenter, age 36).

## IT'S NO BIG DEAL TO MESS UP

A 39-year-old crane operator, who has had lots of harassment in her time, described the qualitative difference in the way the men harassed her versus men crane operators. "I can do something wrong and they'll say, 'Oh, well,' but if a man does the same thing, it is really bad, and the guys say, 'That's not fair,' because they get harassed more about their skills. If a man does something wrong, they'll yell, 'Hey, why can't you do nothin right?' They know they can't talk to a woman like they can to a man cause we'll get upset; they know we'll cry, so the shops treat us better. It's a terrible way to treat people, to make them feel crummy by saying, 'Can't you do nothing right?' "

Taking the sting out of messing up is the second way the women said they are brightening the blue-collar world. But it's also an attitude we are bringing to the white-collar world. It is the opposite of male egotism that says, "I'm terrific at everything I do and never make mistakes." It is probably also related to women's lesser self-confidence, which means that even legislators and brokers sometimes have to push themselves out the front door despite the fact that they know they have the ability.

About women's relative lack of self-confidence, I've done research with women and men whereby I asked them to estimate how many different abilities and skills they had compared to people of their own sex. It taught me that women underrate their abilities, even at simple skills such as addition and subtraction. Men, on the other hand, demonstrate an amazing amount of ego. They say they can do everything very well and that they possess a high degree of all skills, even skills traditionally associated with women's activities such as drawing or doing fine detail work. I concluded that this sex difference does not stem so much from a deficit on women's part as it does from men's totally unrealistic, out-of-proportion, so-sure confidence.

What I never before appreciated, however, until I did the background reading for this book is that this male ego, this exaggerated male self-confidence, is accompanied by a horrible fear of failure. Women don't want to fail, but men *really* don't want to fail.

Women have learned to live with society's expectations of the weaker sex, that we are not as good as men at some things and more likely to fail. But we also learn it's not the end of the world if we fail. Thus we live less uncomfortably with failure when it happens.

The women interviewed were surprised and dismayed at the fear the men had of making mistakes, particularly in front of clients. Male brokers wouldn't answer the telephone when their advice hadn't panned out. Male lawyers were totally undone by losing in court. Male legislators liked to have all their votes counted ahead of time to make sure they were going to win. The women felt there was no need constantly to be on guard about failing and that when it happened, it wasn't a catastrophe. But for the men it was life or death to lose.

"If problems arise in trading, following through all the way, my girlfriend will laugh," said a 27-year-old broker. "Men will fume, explode, swear, and really throw a fit. Whereas this gal will sit back and laugh and say, 'Okay, I'll let the client know. We'll work on it from there.' She doesn't connect problems in the office with her own ego. She has the ability to stay separate from the problems and not put her ego on the line. She follows through on her work with clients, admits when she's done something wrong, and doesn't blame it on others."

The brokers thought they could admit being a lot less the expert. One 32-year-old woman said, "I can be a lot less the expert. I ask clients questions and get their input. I can let my hair down a little bit. That is how we are unique. We can kind of come down off our pedestal of being the almighty financial wizard and let clients know that we have made mistakes, too, in our own investments, so not everything we are going to do is going to come off."

A GP, age 36, laughed at the way "acting as if you know what you're doing, even if you don't, is valued in medicine; I mean in front of patients. You get positive feedback during training for sounding confident. I act the other way. Say knee pain—I don't know anything about it, but you're not supposed to tell a patient when you don't know. I like to retain the honesty of what I know and don't know, without putting myself down."

"The entire purpose of my job is to make decisions. All the designers' work feeds back to me. So I make lots of wrong decisions. I make mistakes on a daily basis," recounted a 39-year-old landscape architect who works for the county. "I accept that, and I'm able to say I was wrong, but the men don't often say, 'I was wrong.' I'm also more open to trying something different, doing the end run, punting, because again, if I'm not always successful, I'm not as upset as a man would be."

In the blue-collar world the men "say stupid things like 'I never make mistakes. I've never been laid off.' Women don't do that. Men have woven a fabric of being Superman; each is stronger and more macho than the others. They'd never admit they lost a form and all the concrete poured out. We admit our mistakes. A woman I work with now came in recently and just said, 'Yeah, and I dropped the chainsaw in the water,' and we all laughed. People get laid off all the time, so it can be important to the men not to admit mistakes. But women are proud to be carpenters. We've fought a tough battle and made it. The men don't want to admit they're carpenters because it's like a fallen trade" (Carpenter, age 34).

Worse than that, a metals inspector, age 25, told me she was baffled that intelligent, knowledgeable male welders and shipfitters were content to stay in their trades forever. She speculated that "maybe they don't want the disappointment of failing if they try it. Maybe once a man gets shot down, it's too hard. I know it's tough for the men to make a mistake.

It's embarrassing, especially if they've been around for a long time. Probably a lot of men would like to get out, but they don't want to take the risk to go any farther."

## PHYSICAL FITNESS IMPROVEMENTS

The third way women have influenced blue-collar work has to do with a big sex difference between women and men, upper body strength. But what sometimes seems an advantage to men can work against them.

One of the reasons women are less aggressive, body chemistry aside, is that because of our lesser physical strength, we learn early there are other ways to compete than through brute force. As little girls we take stock of our physical limitations, the real ones and the supposed-to-be ones, and of our socialized intellectual advantages. Then we refuse to compete if the fight is unfair and we are bound to lose. Thus we avoid wrestling matches and enter spelling contests with gusto.

Women have to accept their physical limits earlier in life than men do. In contrast, many men hope in vain, way into their twenties, that they will get taller or heavier or hairier chested or more muscular. But we faced up to the fact that we were the weaker sex about the age of three. From then on we have grown used to the idea of physical weakness as something that applies to everyone; it is something relative, shifting, not terrible, and compensable.

Each woman had found different ways of coping with physical limitations. "Women are *not* taught that we should be able to do *everything* and that we are wimps if we can't. I learned as a little girl strategies for dealing with my lack of strength, and as a carpenter that just continues, like using leverage and tools and vehicles to help me" (Carpenter, age 31).

"I see height and strength as one of the reasons I have to do things differently," said a 37-year-old electrician. "I have to carry things differently than men. They lift a rack of pipes and put them on their shoulders and carry them a distance. I put the pipes on my hips, like I would carry a child. Most men only wear one tool pouch, but I wear two tool pouches, one on each hip to balance the weight I carry. It's easier on my back, and it's very comfortable for me. I can carry a lot of weight on my hips."

The women will not muscle things in if there is a better way. "The invention of the forklift equalized men and women at work. Women find the easiest, simplest, most time-saving, body-saving way to do something. Now and then I'll say, why don't we do it this or that way, and sometimes they take my advice. Other times they just muscle it. Women on the job, though, is good for their backs" (Electrician, age 31).

One interviewee talked about setting a nice pace for others. "I'm not going to run up and down the ladder and run to get material. A lot of that type of thinking is pressure people put on themselves. I've not had anybody who expected me to work like that, and if they did, I wouldn't work for them. We all have our own pace that we're comfortable working at. It's not worth it trying to push yourself beyond your own capacity" (Electrician, age 32).

She continued that she no longer tries to prove herself as she did as an apprentice. "Well, I'm really pretty lazy. I always look for the easiest way to do things. It's funny, they will try and muscle something into shape and I'll just look it over and say, 'I gotta do it this way.' I stand there and analyze something longer than they do. When I was going through the apprenticeship, I overdid a lot, and then slowly I got away from that mentality. This older fellow, probably in the trade for forty years, saw me trying to lift seventy pounds by myself and said if you want any kind of longevity in this trade, get help. There is no reason for you or anybody else to lift that. That night I had tense, tight muscles in my back and right then said, 'From now on I ask for help. I'm not going to ruin myself.' "

One of the first things most women police officers learn is their physical limitations because of smaller size and lesser strength. "Each person draws the line differently, but if you're big and strong, you're more likely to stop listening and to say sooner, 'Now we're done talking and we're going to do it my way.' My strength is my ability to talk people into things, to defuse angry situations. I take that extra time and use my wily womanly ways to get what I want. I'll put my arm around a big tough biker, and say, 'Come on now, sweetheart, we're going to get in the back of my prowlcar.' It's a sexual thing, but it works better than pounding the pudding out of him" (Police officer, age 38).

When a firm is owned and run by women, physical and mental fitness can be a top priority from the beginning. "One of my partners at the beginning was upset and frustrated a lot, and I spent a lot of time listening and talking. With all the women I've worked with, there's been a real awareness of emotional and health issues. We also work very hard to take time for ourselves. A few months ago we decided that each of us would get a massage every month as a business expense. We all have outside interests, and there's acceptance for saying, 'I'm not going to work next week. I'm going skiing.' I'm aware that we need to do more playing together. Business has been so busy lately that we haven't spent as much time having fun together as we should" (Carpenter, age 42).

We are definitely having an impact on male-dominated jobs in the area of physical fitness. Both police and firefighters mused that when the women's movement pressed for admitting women to these services, strength requirements gained in importance, as a way to keep women out. "But when they got to looking at everyone, they found some very strong women, *and* some men who weren't so fit, whose aerobic and cardiac fitness weren't what they should be. The scientific evidence was that the more physically fit firefighters were, the longer they could keep them working with less disabilities to backs, knees, cancer, heart attacks. Now we have a physical fitness program—see, a negative requirement that got turned around to positive, and another positive is that the environment has changed; none of that harsh game playing which is so detrimental. The older men say, 'Gee, it's nice not to have that stuff around anymore' " (Firefighter, age 33).

## THE CALMING INFLUENCE

Why should the mere presence of women calm things down in the workplace? The women said it does. Male firefighters play fewer mean tricks on one another, carpenters and electricians cut down on the obscene language, brokers don't shout as much, and legislators have fewer tantrums on the floor.

Is it because when men are being naughty and feel that they are being naughty, an authoritative woman walking into the room brings out an unconscious response as if Mom has walked into the room, Mom the peacekeeper? Mom who will be unhappy and disappointed if you keep on behaving badly? Mom who frowns on fighting, who listens to both sides, and who tries to resolve things fairly and peacefully? Mom who soothes and rewards if you are a good boy?

"This one guy acted like a mean son of a bitch; he yelled at everybody. He couldn't ever see that he frightened everyone. I know he's a marshmellow deep down, so I say things like, 'You're beautiful when you're mad,' and he laughs and is more reasonable. The work environment is much better now. He jokes and isn't such a hard ass" (Engineer, age 31).

There is one particular job where women's calming influence has also been noticed with clients, the job of police officer. The combination of our Mother image and the admonition that "it's wrong to hit a lady" means that women police officers often have a pacifying effect on men suspects. A rural cop said that "the guys have told me that even drunk people—you know drunk people don't know who they're scrapping with—don't seem as eager to take me on as they do the guys. As a rule I don't have to fight near as much. My sergeant has written in my evaluation, 'She seems to calm things down just being there.' The public just doesn't feel threatened by me" (Deputy sheriff, age 29).

But in terms of changing the way work gets done, the main beneficiary of women's calm is male coworkers, because women model how calm works better than confrontation. "I was dispatched to a party with about seven male officers, and one of our partygoers was very uptight. Lucky me, I got to deal with him. He was very drunk. As he was ventilating, getting his anger out, I was very patient, and he was yelling and screaming, and I could see one of my fellow officers in the corner of my eye putting his fist to the palm of his hand, just ready to pop him, telling me (by this sign) not to put up with that garbage. But it was all right. I handled it. I'm not a fighter, but when I have to, I do. This was not one of those times" (Police officer, age 28).

She and the other women officers know that they may lack the physical strength that their "customers" have and from the beginning of an encounter attempt to use talk instead of brute force. Talk *does* work and is now recognized as women's "nonconfrontational style" to the extent that women are influencing men officers to be less aggressive, to call for backup more, and to use talk rather than toughness.

Then there are those skills brought from the women's previous work lives that prove directly transferable to police work. Here is one from teaching.

"I'll get to an accident scene, and everybody will be angry, and I think, 'I've seen this before.' I can come in and I can say, 'All right, you be quiet and you be quiet and we're not going to argue about this. There will be no argument. We'll be sensible adults and we're going to talk about it. If you're going to argue, you can go stand in the corner,' and I've said that to people, and they look at me like, 'Oh, okay,' and if they turn around and start in again, I just say, 'Quiet! I don't want to hear it. We're not going to argue about it. We'll discuss it, but we won't argue about it.' The younger guys coming out have more liberalized views of women, and they figure if I can do it this way, fine, let me. The next step is to get them to try it" (State trooper, age 39).

## ENJOYING THE PROCESS OF A CRAFT

Too many blue-collar men just accept that "a man's gotta do what a man's gotta do," including putting up with poor working conditions. Too many men accept the employer's view that employees' labor is a commodity like any other for which employees try to get as much money as they can, while the employer tries to pay as little as he can.

They, the men on both sides of this adversarial equation, forget so easily that work can and should be done for more than money. Women seem never to get men's equation quite right in their heads. We women tend to think that work should be satisfying. At the very least it should give us good people to socialize with if the work itself is hum-drum.

But men seem to feel it is futile to insist on personal fulfillment and minor daily pleasures at work. Is it linked to the obligations surrounding the sole breadwinner role? Is it because work has become so much a privilege that men don't think they have any rights any more? Can't blue-collar men put aside those early lessons that work has got to be hard? That there has to be a basic opposition between employer and employee? That it is next to impossible to get even little things changed to make life more bearable?

Women don't have this early socialization for the sole breadwinner role. Nor do women think that work has to be taxing and wearing. After all, women know from the control they have over house and children that they can go about their work in many different ways, some more fun than others. What's wrong with trying to make it as easy as possible?

For many blue-collar men, it's impossible that work could be self-fulfilling; for the blue-collar women, it's impossible that it should not be self-fulfilling. So off to work go tradeswomen brought up with the idea that work can be satisfying and that if it isn't, they can find little ways to change it so it will be.

One woman who sold her restaurant to enter the trades said that she enjoys her work more than anyone she knows and that is one of the big differences between her and the men. "To me, going to work is when I'm the child; I get to go play. When I'm home, I'm in charge; I have to make this house work; the responsibility is mine. Whatever decisions have to be made, whenever things go wrong, it's totally on me. But at work, I'm the kid. I get to say, 'This is what I want,' and the employer can say, 'No, it's too expensive,' or 'Yes, you can have it because it's a good idea,' and I get paid for it too. I get to go play and have fun and meet people and build and create things. It's just a great time" (Electrician, age 37).

Many skilled craft jobs have the built-in satisfaction of doing the whole job from beginning to end. This is a very satisfying, creative, in-control, tangible-end-product kind of work. A 40-year-old fabric mechanic at a shipyard explained why she loved her job. "I get to go out and design what's needed, make a drawing, not a perfect scale drawing, but I can give it to someone else and they can make it, or I make it myself. Then they want it installed and I go install it. You get to do all the phases of a job, not like an office job where you get one little piece of paper 6,000 times a day. I feel a sense of accomplishment a lot of times, but I also think, I can do it better the next time. I don't know what else I'd want to do. Growing up I wanted to be a nurse. Well, I make a lot more money than a nurse, and I don't have near the day-to-day problems they do."

Once on the job, women enjoying their work makes the workplace an easier place to be. "I try to be very light and in a good mood, and I enjoy my job tremendously. It's a wonderful job, and people enjoy that. I look forward to more women carpenters for the camaraderie. Very quickly I've become friends with the women in a nearby paint shop just because we are women and we can go to lunch and talk about the same things" (Carpenter, age 35).

The women said that they will truly love going to work on the day when half of skilled craftworkers are women. "I could get support for who I really am, not just as another worker. There would be much more flexibility for mothers and more job sharing. Carpenters would be healthier people who enjoyed their work. Quality would go up. There'd be a sense of, 'If it's worth doing, it's worth doing well,' in contrast to all the 'Oh, that's good enough' I hear now" (Carpenter, age 34).

The women struggle to understand when the men complain that they don't like working. "I stayed home a month not long ago, and I stayed home seven months a couple of years ago, and it was real good for me because it let me see how much you don't get done at home, and it let me deal with the frustrations of not having any money and day in and day out not accomplishing anything. So I recognized better that the job gives me a sense of accomplishment that I can't get at home. Like lifting pipe—I've packed eighty pounds of pipe, and it's fun when you're feeling up to it, and if you have a crummy day, you can at least say I worked today, and you always make the same money" (Electrician, age 34).

Another woman tries to teach each male partner how she feels. "I ask, 'Where will the job take us today? How difficult do you think it will be? Who do you think will cross our path today?' I enjoy working with another electrician and I try to get him to enjoy my company and to see that two heads are better than one. I grew up to be a helper, and I like the feeling of helping, so I'm good at organizing materials for jobs, and I let the guy more be in charge. I and another journeyman can get three times as much work done and be glad we were assigned together" (Electrician, age 50).

## THE HOMEMAKING ORIENTATION

Pauline Hunt's chapter in Janet Siltanen and Michelle Stanworth's *Women and the Public Sphere* (1984) notes how quickly self-doubting, docile, former housewives get radicalized when they return to blue-collar work. Such women will support a closed shop if the women they are joining have worked for years to get one. They will walk off the job if working conditions get too bad. They will even take time off if their dog's having pups is more important. The women bring with them the spontaneity and assertiveness women feel when they work in their own homes. Hunt described how two women bookshop employees carried on as if they were still at home, doing the ordinary tasks in an easygoing way and, in between, totally reorganizing the shop without anyone asking them to do so. Their homemaking orientation brought them the self-satisfaction men complain is lacking in work (pp. 47–53).

For other women the homemaking orientation means paying attention to detail and being meticulous. One of these perfectionistic tradeswomen said, "I'm more meticulous than the men. When I was training, they said all the time, 'We're not expecting a visit from the president, you know.' But in the long run it saves you, trying to be perfect. I like things to look good because *it's my name on it*. I have to make sure my work is above par" (Electrician, age 31).

Women aren't rough and unthinking working in their own kitchens. So, said a 31-year-old carpenter, "we wouldn't go wild with a crowbar or sledgehammer if we were tearing something out. We're more likely to pay attention to whether or not there are people around. Women spend more time thinking things out ahead of time, like, if I'm putting in a cabinet that's going to be close to something else, I am more likely to check that the door won't hit something else. People always say to me, 'I like working with you because you think things out.' "

The women interviewed enjoyed their nontraditional jobs because of a sense of conscious choice. Men are drawn into carpentry, they said, because of their physical size and strength or because their dads did it. But most of the women had been to college or tried other jobs before deciding on carpentry. This raised the quality of their work. Then, just as in maintaining a home, they wanted to enjoy themselves as much as they could, and that means taking time, and sometimes less money, to do a quality job and enjoy yourself in the process.

The women regarded the homemaking orientation as a great advantage. "One way I'm different from the men is that I always put the tools back in the shop, so I just know where things are. Like at home, I know where my kid's tennis shoes are because he'll be needing them, and in the back of my mind I know where the wrecking bar is, even if it's in a pile of junk in the corner. The men are always asking me where stuff is" (Carpenter, age 34).

Another advantage stemming from every woman's job as a domestic is a questioning of rules that say this dish must be fixed this way, and clothes must be washed this way, and there is a "correct" way to clean house. Similarly, what if you don't have the requisite ingredients or the right tools? "There are lots of rules in this trade. 'You must do it this way.' 'It's always been done this way.' Lots of times the old ways don't work very well, and you have to wonder how the rules got made. We are much more likely to ask, 'Why do we have to do it this way?' and make up a way that works better. I think I approach carpentry in a softer way. Emotionally, when I come onto a project, I treat it differently. I don't elbow my way in, I treat the wood differently, more softly, creatively. Men are less likely to let their creativity show than women are. But being around women softens them up on this. It seems that they appreciate our creativity and its results, and it makes them think about creativity" (Carpenter, age 45).

Women builders think of variations and improvements customers have given up asking men carpenters to do. "In this culture we all live in houses, most of them built by men. Any woman who's attentive to her surroundings has noticed things about her house that don't meet her needs. As a female person I bring knowledge of what works for me that men might not know about, for example, heights of counters. In the business there are standard heights which are often too high for women. Or storage spaces—unless you're an active user of rooms, you don't know what's needed, like easy access to utensils in the kitchen, especially large storage containers and baking sheets, and lots of storage with easy access in bathrooms. A woman will think of all these things" (Carpenter, age 42).

## WILLINGNESS TO FIGHT FOR RIGHT

Most of the blue-collar women in this project were strong union supporters. The women I talked to at a big shipyard were all either active in the equal-employment-opportunity (EEO) and affirmative-action programs, or they belonged to formal women's networks in the yard or informal support groups outside the yard.

A 36-year-old shipyard electrician described her shop EEO committee as concerned about equal rights for everybody.

"Doesn't matter if it's a guy or a gal, 25 or 50 years old, black, pink, yellow, or green, we all have our rights. If somebody's harassing somebody, physically or mentally, or making gestures, we try to bring it to the attention of management and try to get it straightened out before it becomes a formal complaint. There are twelve of us on our shop committee, including three women, a couple Blacks, and one Mexican. I've been the chair for three months. At the meetings there isn't any chair unless we get off the subject too far. I told them that at the meetings we're all equal. We should be a committee. I don't think the chair should run the meetings and make all the contacts because once they're gone, nobody else knows anything. I'd like us all to be in the public view so everybody out there knows who we are, where we're at, and how to get ahold of us."

Because they frequently had a college background and previous, different work experience, the skilled craftswomen were more and more being asked by their shops to represent them in safety and health battles with management. "I was recently elected safety representative of my shop. In any kind of bureaucracy there are wonderful ideas, but the problem is implementing them, because you're fighting red tape. Today we had a chemical hazard meeting, and there were two women and fifty guys, and these guys are really concerned about chemicals, plumbers taking out drains with mercury and acids burning them. When there are infractions, there's lack of communication, and paperwork gets lost. Safety is not easily implemented. As a female in a leadership role I try to be serious, have all the facts, *not* be soft-spoken, and be *very* flexible" (Carpenter, age 35).

A minority group electrician, 31 years old, said she is a very strategic fighter. "You have to pick and choose your wars. When I do, it's for a good cause. I won't take up something at the drop of a hat: I'm no troublemaker. I'm very congenial and easygoing and don't get excited, so when I speak up on an issue, it has an effect. Like this one time, everybody was there, including the general foreman, and we were getting our orders, and somebody said something racist. So I said, loud, so everyone could hear me, 'We're not going to have any of that racism on this job. I don't need to hear anything racist. This first time's on me; the second time's on you.' There was this big quiet. Later he apologized."

Some of the women's willingness to fight for right comes from both their and Blacks' having to prove themselves over and over in the trades. "The Black men I've worked with have gone through the same things I have. In some ways we feel a comradeship. On one job I was on there was a Black man who was the shop steward, which was a real break-through for him, on a large job with all white except for him. I have to admit I did some coaching of the rep to get him that position. But he was qualified, and I was real pleased with that. He had helped me before when I had been sexually harassed. He could understand where no white man I ever talked to could understand" (Electrician, age 37).

A caucasian electrician, age 30, said: "This guy I was working with at a fish hatchery job said how glad he was he got me, instead of some nigger apprentice. So I said, if you'd got a Black, would you have said how glad you were you'd got him instead of a girl? We were going to have to be together for seven days so I told him to stuff it; I did not want to hear racist stuff or sexist talk. You don't have to ignore these guys, even if they're your heroes. If you don't like it, you let them know. But I got fired; the apprenticeship board didn't like it, my being rude and disrespectful to my foreman."

A major way the women fight sexism is by rejecting sexually explicit language, pictures, and behavior. A 50-year-old maintenance electrician objects strenuously if her partner ogles women going up and down the hall. "This constant interest in the other sex is amazing to me. I told them it embarrasses me the way you ogle women. 'I don't look and leer at men. I hate the way you visually undress women walking down the hall.' They like to tell me it's a natural, healthy interest!" The minority electrician quoted earlier pointed out that women give nonswearing men more choices. "Lots of guys don't like to hear that gutter talk, pornography, sexually explicit stuff. We're cleaning up the air for them, too, so they're not subjected to listening to that trash. Most people function better in coed situations, and women are starting to get a history. Some of us have been doing this for ten years already."

Health and safety were other big areas where the women were fighting for better conditions, and this will be taken up in the next section in the chapter dealing with stress. Here I only want to remind us of the sacrifice women make when they stand up for worker rights. "You're not supposed to squawk about health and safety. You squawk about health and safety, and you're down the road. It goes beyond just not making waves for your employer. You can't make waves for your coworkers. So they get to have such insensitivity to one another. They all have this 'Everyone wants something from them' mentality. 'Everybody's taking something from them.' I finally got tired of *not* making waves. I couldn't take it anymore, and I started making waves. But the minute I opened my mouth, I knew I was going to be branded as a harpy and a whiner and a women's libber for the rest of my career with that company" (Carpenter, age 30).

It seemed to me as though some of these women would end up in union leadership positions. They were that strong. A 26-year-old welding inspector was also a shop steward because

"I know what I'm doing, I'm confident, and when the heat is on, I can handle it. Unless you know what your rights are and the tricks to keep management off your back, you get to the point where you can't handle the pressure any more. I was dealing with this case, a woman they were trying to fire, and one day they accused her of being drunk, but she hadn't been drinking. That was the final straw. After a weekend of crying, and her husband couldn't handle her deep depression anymore, on the spur of the moment she handed in her resignation. It was somebody I was personally dealing with. I know I could have saved her job. I had so many precedent-setting cases, she had nothing to worry about. I really felt bad about it. I don't want management to see me as a threat. I want them to see me as helping them to get on the trail again, moving again, making things better here for the workers *and* for management."

One woman said that she hopes in ten years to have established her credibility with the union so that she can do labor-related work for the electrical worker's union or for the Washington State Labor Council.

"The people who produce and really work hard in this country have been traditionally downtrodden and looked upon as lower class citizens when they're not. I had an interesting thought last winter working on a bridge on the freeway. Here I am standing on this bridge freezing, so cold in that penetrating wind, and I see all these nice people in their nice cars driving into the city from their nice warm homes on this nice smooth highway to those nice office buildings on the skyline where they'll ride up elevators to sit at their nice desks, and they think that all this has just been bestowed upon them, and they have no idea of what somebody went through just so they could get into that nice car and work in that nice building. People take so much for granted, and they think nothing of the people who put it there for them. That's been the struggle of labor, to gain that recognition we deserve, because *we* built the city. The lawyers and doctors that get those great wages, where would they be without that efficient, clean, fancy operating room or those plush fancy offices lawyers work out of?" (Electrician, age 32)

## WE BELIEVE IN ORGANIZING

Joyce Gelb (1989) said that women are now 30 percent of the unionized workforce and that the percentage of women currently unionizing is greater than that of men. Women are also increasing their participation in union leadership. In 1982 33 percent of the locals' presidents were women and 45 percent of the local union offices were held by women (pp. 77–78). The future of organized labor in the United States depends on its ability to organize more women, especially women white-collar workers and women in the rapidly growing service and retail–wholesale trades.

Just getting more women into unions helps close the wage gap, and pay equity is a top priority of women unionists. Getting more women into steward and officer positions means that childcare and flex time will become a part of contract negotiations. But why else should men's unions bring in more women? Unions, in fact, actually win more representational elections when they stress "women's issues" (Gelb, 1989, p. 80).

The blue-collar women we came to know want to work in their unions. They see nothing monolithic or impervious to change about either unions or the companies they work for. They are ready for all kinds of structural alterations to improve work life for both sexes.

If they could just get the men out of their masochistic stupor! But in the meantime, until they can get men to the union hall, they are making things better in small ways—with Halloween candy, Christmas trees, Thanksgiving dinners, and slumber parties.

"I remember one time there were four women firefighters working together at the same time, and we all said, 'Oh, we've *got* to go upstairs and have a slumber party.' Well, the four of us went to bed before anybody else, and we were laying up there laughing and talking, and pretty soon we had them all up there laughing and talking and having pillow fights. That doesn't happen very often. It's just that men, they bring a certain perspective, and women bring another perspective, and that's why I think it's nice that we work together" (Firefighter, age 35).

# III

# *Valuing Balance*

---

Many feminists who have written about living a balanced life have been particularly interested in women managers, starting with Margaret Hennig and Anne Jardim in their 1977 classic, *The Managerial Woman*. After giving all kinds of advice about how to succeed in a male-dominated organizational culture, Hennig and Jardim concluded their book with a wonderful outburst about what American corporations will gain from accepting more women managers.

Everyone will be healthier and happier from balance. Balance means paternity leave and no penalty for refusing to be transferred or relocated. Balance means success through horizontal as well as vertical career paths, a better quality of life at work, and the freedom to express feelings as well as ideas (Hennig & Jardim, 1977, p. 232). Ultimately, balance means a four-day work week, followed by a three-day work week, so that we will have everyone working for a shorter duration and earning less money (p. 238). Therein, they argue, lies the survival of individuals, families, and corporations.

Judi Marshall's *Women Managers* (1984) brings to mind Hennig and Jardim's marvelous analogy for prospective women managers: Traveling in the male world is like going to a foreign country. Women have to learn the language, study maps and read guidebooks, and figure out the best way to get from place to place. We aren't surprised that we often feel frustrated, frightened, and lonely. We know we women come from one tradition and that these people come from another. We may continue to think our culture is better than theirs but also that if we keep hanging in there, some day we may enjoy this foreign culture (Hennig & Jardim, pp. 214–216).

Judi Marshall's women were enjoying the male world by treating work as only one of life's important areas. From women's culture they had brought the value of leading a life "dominated by wholeness." Their personal, honest, authentic style of managing demonstrated that the personal was political. They preferred cooperation over competition, valued relationships and connectedness to others, and tried to keep balance in their lives (1984, p. 196).

Virginia Novarra in *Women's Work, Men's Work* (1980, pp. 46–47) did a lot of thinking about our distinctive contributions to men's work. I especially like the way she took attitudes and behaviors men label negatively and showed how they are positive and beneficial to society. Absenteeism, for example, demonstrates how responsible women are, since women's absence is most often caused by attending to sick children and domestic crises. Similarly, "lack of ambition," she said, is really balanced living and "lack of loyalty" a sense of proportion. Indeed, women's sense of proportion about work, home, and community gives us a full life to fall back on when we are unemployed or made redundant. In contrast, men are extremely vulnerable to unemployment because they have so few interests other than work.

Perhaps because women are making steady inroads into middle management, there are more and more books comparable to *Women Like Us* (1985) by Liz Gallese. She discovered, six years later, that fully two-fifths of the women from the class of 1975 of Harvard Business School were ambivalent about their careers and not very ambitious (p. 249). She found it shocking that this many women had "done the unthinkable." They had either cut back their responsibilities or left work entirely (p. 26). Gallese called the women's attempt to live balanced lives and not forfeit everything to career a "thoughtful and intelligent attitude" (p. 251). In contrast, she described the hundreds of male chief executive officers (CEOs) she knew as one-dimensional, colorless, very boring people with no interests beyond the narrow sphere of their businesses (pp. 84–85).

Jane Adams (1979, pp. 202–206) studied sixty "women on top," many of them company and organizational administrators. She asked, "Do you see yourself as capable of becoming CEO?" and "Do you want to be CEO?" Only 50 percent responded yes to both questions. Why? Because CEOs don't live balanced lives. Half of these very successful women had backed away from male success. They wanted to be in control of their lives, not imprisoned in a job around the clock. They wanted to have a *life*.

Five writers who focused on the workplace as the arena in which to achieve balance are Elinor Lenz and Barbara Myerhoff, Janet Giele, Roslyn Willett, and Jean Lipman-Blumen. Lenz and Myerhoff (1985, p. 82) see our home and work lives being brought into balance through fluid, flexible time arrangements including parttime, flex time, and job sharing. They predicted that the time clock will end up on the "ash heap of industry," as a variety of work schedules are adopted to meet individual needs.

Giele (1978, pp. 111–112) likewise sees balance coming about from structural workplace alterations involving time changes and social benefit changes. It is in women's interest to work for both—for job sharing, flexible hours, parttime work, and shorter job tenure, as well as for the social benefits of maternity leaves and day-care centers that allow women to approximate men's traditional time patterns.

Willett (1971, p. 531) said that women understand very well what many businesses do not understand, that attentiveness to human working rhythms is more productive. She believes that a rational work world has people working on schedules they choose, with employers paying for the fraction of the usual eight-hour day worked. Freedom and flexibility mean increased productivity in addition to balance.

Finally, Lipman-Blumen (1983, pp. 83–84) advocated in-house training programs for men and women leaders to teach women how to use competition and power and to teach men how to develop relational skills. She did not urge women to become pseudomen and men pseudowomen. She said that both sexes need greater balance and freedom in their styles of achieving. In particular, men must feel free to be noncompetitive and supportive.

Lipman-Blumen also said that men should have the options of less rigid career paths, freedom to enter and leave the labor force at different career points, and nontraditional work. If men are to achieve balance, they need these opportunities to the same extent that women have them.

Among the writers who have focused on the home as the arena in which to achieve balance, Willett (1971, p. 530) said that home maintenance activities must be equally shared by partners and children. It isn't balance for married women working full time to carry the greater burden of the routine chores of a household.

Carolyn Heilbrun's *Reinventing Womanhood* (1979) literally insists that the only way to accomplish balance is if childcare is shared equally between women and men. We can change the sex-role conditioning of today only by men making the same practical commitment to nurture children that women make. Like Nancy Chodorow (1978), Heilbrun sees the origin of male dominance and female subordination in the practice of fathers not sharing the raising of children, equally, on a day-to-day basis with mothers (pp. 193–196).

Susie Orbach and Luise Eichenbaum (1987, p. 173) called for men to discover balance and connectedness by developing their potential in the domestic sphere. By spending more time at home men can undo their alienation from their children and partners and counteract the stress, competitiveness, and emotional constraint of their jobs that too often lead to illness and death at an early age.

Part III starts with "The Balancing Act." The main objections to balance, from the male point of view, are that men would make less money and have to do housework. Next is a chapter on the women's ideas about the structural changes we need and figuring out some way to get men to participate in them equally—the flex time, parttime work, job sharing, and parental leaves that feminist theorists call for. Part III ends with a chapter on one benefit of balance, "Not Living with Stress."

# 7

# THE BALANCING ACT

---

To me this job is the best thing that ever happened to me. I've been a divorced, single parent for eight years now. I've had to be the nurturer and the breadwinner, and it's made me strong. I had no lifelong aspiration to be a firefighter. I needed employment and this came along. Yet, it's funny; I don't give a rip about the money. I just love going to work, sometimes to the detriment of my family. But that's my decision, and I live with it. (Firefighter, age 35)

I am going to begin this chapter with two aspects to the balanced life women try to live and would like men to share in. The first is male sex-role socialization, which predisposes men to place career first and family second. The second aspect to balance is the great distance between balance as women's ideal and as a reality in women's lives.

Who teaches little boys *not* to balance? Their dads do. Men learn to put career first, making a balanced life out of the question, from their largely absent fathers. Phillip Hodson (1984, pp. 121–134), in the chapter "Families Need Fathers," described the sadness and regret of middle-aged men who finally realize how much time they devoted to their jobs and how little time was spent with their children. Hodson quoted U.S. research to the effect that the typical father spends twelve minutes a day interacting with his offspring (p. 128). As a result of this physical absence, fathers are seen as role models who have left behind instructions for their sons to "obey your father" and "make your own decisions." Well, normal boys make the decision to get out of the house and stay out of the house trying to be a success like Dad. Furthermore, they can't use their mother as a role model for balance because that would be too feminine. Until fathers spend more time with their families, boys have no choice but to put career first.

As to the second aspect of the balancing act, the gap between balance as a prized value and a practical reality in women's life-styles, I remember a cartoon of a rich, middle-aged couple sitting across their big dining room table, and he is saying to her that he completed a $300,000 business deal that day, and she had got the cleaning lady to polish all the silver, and that meant they each had a productive day in their separate spheres. This is a portrait of imbalance, of the separate spheres some women and men still live in.

Most women today, however, do not concentrate their labors and love in the home. Instead, they divide their energies among home, work, recreation, self-development, and relationships. Many women today wish men wouldn't put so much energy into being the bigger breadwinner and would see that there is more to life than getting ahead.

The reality, however, is that the balanced life women try to live is a sham. It's a sham because we women spend too much time doing housework, too much in the sense that men do not share it equally. It's not balanced to do two full-time jobs, the paid one and the unpaid one, but that's what too many of us accept. Why is this? Some writers believe that we don't want to let men share housework and childcare, that these are the things we are good at, that this is where we have control and power, and we don't want to give them up.

The more important reason for this imbalance is men's monumental resistance to doing domestic chores. They like being taken care of. They like not having to clean toilets, scrub floors, scour pans, dust, vacuum, wash, wipe, polish, and wax. It is so nice having all these things that Mom did for them being done by some other woman. Besides, he makes the most money. *His* job outside is more important for the family and more demanding. So when he's home, he's naturally tired and deserves to rest.

Have you ever thought about the possibility that men drag their feet about pay equity because if women made as much money, men would have to do more housework? They'd have to, because pay inequity is their favorite rationalization for not doing housework. The logic is, making more money means having more power. More power means not having to do the same amount of dirty work around the house.

It's fashionable now for men to recite the negative connotations of being work centered. It's smart to poke fun at the hard-driving businessman who devotes himself totally to his job, neglects his wife and children, and has no life apart from his work. But if balance is such a healthy, progressive, human potentiating idea, why are women the only ones trying to practice it?

We women are going to have true balance only when men share housework absolutely equally. Unless a balancing woman lives with a balancing man, spending exactly the same number of minutes on housework and childcare, she is living only the illusion of a balanced life. In the name of balance, we plug away at our employers for innovative arrangements—flex time, parental leave, flexible vacations, job sharing, parttime work—arrangements that men will continue to ignore until we collectively insist that they use them to the same extent that we do and not just for the delights of childcare but for the drudgery of housework as well.

Curiously, the women interviewed for this book seldom mentioned doing domestic chores. Their relationships with, and responsibilities toward, their children (taking them to school, the doctor, scouts, or sports) were what they talked about. In retrospect, I don't know why we talked so little about shopping, cleaning, cooking, and laundering, which take so much of women's time.

What balance turned out to be for these nontraditional women was a time–money tradeoff. They went to great pains to explain to me that there is this big sex difference that relates to balance—money versus time—and they would rather make less money and have more time. But this is not the position men take.

## THE DIFFERENTIAL IMPORTANCE OF MONEY TO WOMEN AND MEN

One of the biggest sex differences in values, according to the women interviewed, has to do with money. Men place far greater value on money than women do.

A 25-year-old veterinarian told me that for women vets, enjoying their work is more important than making lots of money. "I'll probably not go for the big fancy practice. I'll always give up money to enjoy every day. Happiness is more important. I don't feel the pressure to make money that men have ingrained in them. They feel so responsible. Society certainly doesn't allow money not to be an issue for us women, but I don't think we will go for it to the same extent. We have so few years on this earth; it's more important to me to see the world, meet people. I fight settling in, living the ordinary American dream. I want to experience all there is to life, not make a lot of money. I resent living and striving to get money that circumvents really living life."

She continued: "I have to be *me*. I won't put up with a job I don't like for the money. I have less restraints. Because I'm an outsider, I don't have to conform to their ideas of what success is. I won't compromise myself. I can get what I want, and it's too important that I like what I do. I have more freedom to be really me. I work for sense of accomplishment. Work is three-quarters of my life, a big, big part of my life, real integral."

Here is my summary of what these nontraditional women said are the attitudes of the sexes toward money.

1. *How much money.* Women want enough money to live comfortably now and in old age. Men want to make a lot of money.

2. *The inequities in money.* Women are more practical and philosophical about who gets more money and who gets less in America today. Men take making less money much more personally.

3. *The meaning of money.* Women's self-worth at work is tied up with doing quality work and having caring relationships. Men's self-worth is tied up with how much money they make and how much they spend.

4. *Work goals and money.* Women set work goals in relation to other life goals, independent of employers' desires. Men's drive for money makes them vulnerable to employer manipulation of work goals.

5. *Ethical behavior and money.* Women care more about quality work and service to clients and would rather make less money than be unethical. Some men are driven into unethical work behavior to make lots of money.

After two o'clock when the stock market had closed in Seattle, a 45-year-old broker kicked off her shoes and shook her head when I asked about money. "A lot of the really big producers from a dollars and cents point of view have practices I consider unethical. To be successful, that is, one of the top 5 percent, means you're unethical. My friend asked her sales manager, 'Is it possible to be successful and honest?' and he said, 'Why, yes, so-and-so is and so-and-so and so-and-so'—eighty brokers in this office, and he could only come up with four. I'm proud that I was one of the four names he mentioned, and I'll never be in the top 5 percent because my ethics hold me back, and it's amazing what we *don't* give to charity, the United Way campaign. I've seen the figures. It makes me shake my head." When she asked her sales manager how the firm could afford the lawsuits brought against the top producers, he said it cost far less to defend them than they were worth.

Just because men are salaried does not mean they escape the male value that success is how big your paycheck is. A federal police officer (age 45) told me that money is not paramount to her colleagues because they could all go elsewhere and make much more. "But for whatever reason, the men feel they should automatically get more money and more respect than I feel I should. They expect they should be paid at a given level because they believe they are innately worth a certain amount. They have no doubt. Women don't have to compete in the money arena to be worth something. *But men are worth what they make.*

They assume that because they've put so many years into the job, that equals their capability and they should be paid accordingly."

Women firefighters said that they are more organized with their money, save more, and think more about investments that will give them security in their old age. In contrast, the men talk a lot about money and are very competitive about spending it. A 28-year-old observed, "For example, last night the Seahawks were on, and this guy goes, 'I'll bet you my billfold for your billfold,' and one guy had a hundred dollar bill and the other had three fifties. It's their idea of I'm better than you because I've got more money than you." The women joked that when they first wheeled into the fire station parking lot, they thought they'd have to buy pickup trucks to fit in. "The men have a lot of adult toys, skimobiles, motorcycles, fishing equipment, trucks. They want bigger and better things right now, new motorcycle, new fourwheel drive, new pickup. Money is real important to them, and they spend it as fast as they can" (Firefighter, age 35).

A carpenter (age 30) reflected on the different meanings the money her parents earned had to the children, which meanings got handed down along gender lines. Her brothers learned her father's meaning, she her mother's meaning. "My father was a workaholic, always making money. He'd tell my brothers, 'You don't want to be a teacher; you'll never make any money.' He was always hoarding his money and buying things for himself. His money was his money. But my Mom's money was *our* money—for new shoes or the movies or taking us out for hamburgers. Our college money was from her, and I'm that way with my pay. My pleasure comes from spreading it around."

The landscape architects described the irony of men who can see clearly how their wives are exploited by other men, yet won't change the same behavior in themselves. "No one goes into this profession thinking they are going to make big bucks, but the men voice a concern about needing money more. They say its unfair that their wives tend to be in lower paying clerical kinds of jobs; yet they don't see anything wrong with the clerical women in this office being paid so little" (Landscape architect, age 40).

The veterinarians think the difference in attitude toward money is due to the way we are brought up, that is, that men want lots of money and we want just enough to pay the bills and save for the future. A woman in partnership with two other vets said: "For me, comfortable is okay. I don't need to get rich. Men do seem to value profit more than women, the older vets especially. Profit and expansion vary with the individual, but I think women do not want the practice to govern their lives as much" (Veterinarian, age 30).

When a woman insists on earning money at her own rate and in her own style, the result is sometimes a kind of uneasy truce between her and the men in power. A 29-year-old lawyer talked affectionately about her previous mentor in a high-powered New York law firm. "She divorced herself from the run for partnership. She will never be promoted, and she gets no strokes from the hierarchy. They leave her alone; she leaves them alone. Now all they care about are her billable hours. She opted for autonomy. She deals with very high-powered clients, and fairness and concern for everybody's point of view guide her work. She takes the time to teach the people around her. What she gets out of it is enormous personal gratification and a good living, a comfortable lifestyle. Over money she opted for a personally satisfying balance—time for money."

The women said nothing about money and male sexuality. So did they miss the most important aspect to men's preoccupation with money? According to Robert Gould, psychiatrist, in "Measuring Masculinity by the Size of a Paycheck" (1974, pp. 96–100), for men, money is sex, their sex. Money is virility. Moneymaking power is sexual power. He said that's why men kill themselves when they lose big on the stockmarket. When they lose their masculine image, life is no longer worth living. That's also why, when women make *real money*, men say we are castrating! It's a threat to masculine identity. I don't know. But it surely makes having just one measure of success (especially when it so externally controlled and ephemeral) a tenuous way to judge oneself.

## TIME FOR FAMILY RELATIONSHIPS

What did the women want more time for? The time would be used mostly for family relationships.

A broker, age 39, noticed that her female colleagues spent more time on the telephone talking to their spouses and children. The men were more likely to shove their families aside until the market closed. "If my husband calls me, I am very reluctant to say, 'Hang on a minute.' I am more likely to hang the phone up on a client, only because I am always thinking about him: what is wrong; does he need me? He would say, 'Excuse me, but I am busy right now. I'll call you back in a few hours,' and that's what male brokers do too."

It was typical of these nontraditional women to work long hours when starting their careers. But they didn't think of themselves as workaholics for doing this. It was just the right thing to do at that moment in their lives. Later, when they were established, balance surfaced. They could now afford to see work as just one of three or four important things in life, instead of *the* thing. The women then started to care less about men's ideas of success and to give more time to family, community, and their own hobbies. They also saw no contradiction in saying, at this later stage, that their families came first (when push comes to shove) and, simultaneously, that they were trying to keep equal their families' needs with their own needs (for career, personal growth, recreation). Somehow they were trying to balance two opposing values or ideologies, one "family," one "individualistic."

When women join the police and fire services, they typically put the rest of their life on hold. They put off balancing until they've proven themselves. It is interesting that their temporary work centeredness was much more wearing on other adults than on their children. Some relationships didn't make it. "I was really bad when I first started. I was married, and I put work right up there at the top. I'm a new deputy, and everyone's waiting to see how I'm going to do. Total strangers would say, 'I hear you're the new female deputy, I really want you to do well,' and I'm really trying to, breaking my neck really trying to. My husband felt like my work was more important than he was, and I couldn't argue with him. 'Right now it is.' He wanted to make such an issue of it, I said, 'Fine. I don't really want to be married.' Now I'm seeing someone who works in the same business, and we have more in common, and when I have to work late, he doesn't say, 'You chose work over me!' " (Police officer, age 29)

At other times the right thing to do is to spend more hours at home, for example, when children are little. Even when childcare can be arranged, women often pass up promotion to work parttime. How much is this because society reinforces the idea that kids need us more when they are small? How many polls have I read, taken at any time during the past fifty years, in which men and women, young and old, think that a mother's place is with her children when they are young? So women try to arrange it, even when they don't really believe their children will suffer without so much of Mom.

Women get good at having a "long-term point of view," a belief that everything will even out in the end. Some women balance on a kind of year-to-year basis. "If I don't achieve my career goals this year, next year I will." But the guilt associated with not doing as much at work is not nearly as great as the guilt associated with not being there for your children, particularly if they are going through some crisis.

An engineer (age 34) talked about the conflict no woman with children can escape, wanting to be two places at once. "I like being an engineer. I enjoy my job, having control over what I do, making important decisions, having more power than women at the tail end of the organization with more pressure, lower pay, and very little appreciation. My only dissatisfaction is that I would like to spend more time with my daughter. My friend is upset because she was passed up for promotion, but she only works parttime because she has a new baby. We want both, so we have hard decisions to make."

A 36-year-old police sergeant goes back and forth, sometimes compromising her job when her family needs her and at other times compromising her family for her job. "If you try to constantly have perfect balance, you'll go nuts. You hope that your boss understands when your family comes first and hope that your family understands when your work comes first. So I let my family know what's going on when I am called out. It might seem funny to some people that a six-year-old living out in the country would understand rape. But I felt it was important to explain it to my kids so they knew I wasn't leaving them for petty things. When I left in the middle of the night, it was for really serious, important things."

A flight engineer (age 30) on a Boeing 727 said she could be making more money as a copilot flying out of Chicago, but she stays in Seattle as a flight engineer "because I'm not in a rush to go anywhere. I'd be gone a whole lot more, and at the moment the kids are little and we're building a house, and I want to be able to pick and choose when I fly. This way I have a better quality of life. Success is being the best that I can as a pilot and to have a good marriage and raise healthy, happy, emotionally stable children. That's it. I really enjoy my job unless it starts infringing on my time off. My responsibilities as a mother definitely affect my outlook on the job."

## TIME FOR DOMESTIC RESPONSIBILITIES

The women also said they needed more time to take care of their homes. I disagree. Women don't really need more *time* for housekeeping. We need more *help*. We need the others we live with to do their fair share. We need domestic equality as much as employment equality.

So why don't we ask for what we really need, more help? Why do we sabotage the solution by taking an unequal share of the responsibility? Is it *our* sex-role socialization this time? Or is it the adult rewards of feeling indispensable and uniquely knowledgeable? Or our adult punishments of guilt and feeling neglectful? For how many women is sharing really threatening?

I read the letters to the editor of a magazine that had run an article about how husbands still don't do housework. Men had written in to say they did do their fair share but that their wives weren't satisfied with their ideas of clean. Rather than nag them, they said, their wives simply took on an unfair share. But, hey, it wasn't the men's fault.

Not one woman talked about a husband who is really, genuinely trying to do his fair share. Instead, these women had fairly old-fashioned expectations of how much housework women and men should do. They seemed resigned to doing more, which is such a traditional attitude, when their jobs are so nontraditional and unconventional.

An attorney (age 34) thinks that the average woman lawyer lowers her ambitions because it is the only way she can do the full-time job at home. "As time goes by, time gets more important to women lawyers, and we accept only jobs in which the environment is not unreasonably stressful and allows for a balance between home and work life. We are less likely to get the work done at our own expense. We'll change jobs more readily or get less done or get our work done in a longer time. As there are more women in the law, perhaps the percentage of one's life that must be devoted to work in order to advance will decline, and there'll be more of an emphasis on true capability, even if that capability is available for less time."

A 23-year-old, third-year medical student who had just got married talked about women's and men's different ideas about how to spend their time at home. "A wife has to do everything in order for men to come home to relax, be pampered, entertained, and have everything done for them. For us to come home, it means more work. We see ourselves more intrinsically in the household. So we manipulate our hours at work so that we won't completely kill ourselves. But we are more willing to take that time for our families."

She continued:

"The men [in medical school] study all the time. We call them 'The Boys.' Already they are good old boys with all that superficial camaraderie. How hard it is for them to break out of that and have relationships with people! They are consumed by school whereas the women in general aren't. We are interested in other things, dance, knitting, other reading. I accept that medical school means I have to memorize lots of garbage, so I do enough to get by and keep my sanity. Not nearly as many women are caught up in getting honors. We aren't such a glob, traveling as a wolf pack as the men do. We have a lot more individual friendships. But we start out in medical school with more independence than they have. We are being independent when we take time out to have a baby. Most men in school feel they don't have any choices. They *have* to study twenty hours a day. They accept the system. We question it because we don't fit in in the first place."

A 28-year-old civil engineer said the biggest difference between her and the men is that she doesn't have a wife. "They have someone who does all their housework for them. I don't like to do housework, so we pay to have things done. It's tough for me, that day-to-day struggle, and I don't have kids! If I could just console myself to live in a house that looks like a tornado went through it, I could live a balanced life. It means eliminating guilt that some part of your life is going to shambles because you don't have enough time."

Another 28-year-old engineer said she, too, had no one at home to take care of things, so how could she work the overtime the men did?

"The men in my office feel they have to spend their life at the office. They get excited for a little while when they have babies, but then they're right back to living at the office. Fifty percent of them have wives who stay home all the time and take care of their kids. The other fifty percent are married to teachers and nurses. The men I work with have more of their time to devote to work, while a bigger percentage of my time has to go to other things."

## TIME FOR SELF

Finally, as the medical student above noted, the women talked about having more time for themselves. Surprisingly, art often entered into it. It's true that women in general have a greater interest in art than men do in general. When women take vocational interest tests and see high scores on art, they aren't surprised. Most of us say, philosophically, well, yes, I'm very interested in painting or writing or dance or music or photography, but I don't have enough talent to be a professional. (Typically, we dismiss the idea that we could combine these artistic interests with other vocational interests in a job where we actually get paid.)

Consequently, most women set these artistic/creative interests aside, but the need to express them doesn't go away. Women's magazines play on our neglected artistic need with arts and crafts ideas that we are supposed to do in our spare time. They all take more time than "just a few minutes," however, so our closets and drawers are full of bits and pieces of unfinished projects. When these nontraditional women felt frustrated and wanted more time for self, one reason was to finish sewing, ceramic, and home-decorating projects.

"Other interests make life richer," a 45-year-old academic physician told me. "I am impressed by the women I meet how interested they are in many things. We can work out our stresses at home. I find baking a cake, knitting a sweater, even polishing silver, so satisfying. I wonder about the men, in terms of creative activity. It is so important in people's lives. Sometimes the results of medical work are so delayed; some problems are so insoluble. But I love to cook, and I get immediate gratification from it. One time I invented a variation on a cheese cake and brought it in. They couldn't get over it."

But the primary motivation for wanting time for self was to restore mind and body. A really good balancing act has to include selfish time, time just for oneself, time to clear the head, get refreshed, revitalized, at peace again.

Many women lawyers were not happy with law practice from the very start. The law just was not the all-encompassing thing it was to men. "So we are dissatisfied and find it objectionable that our firms want us to sacrifice our personal lives. Firms won't consider parttime work, and it's the rare firm where you only have to work forty hours a week. But being a lawyer is not my whole life. I don't want to work sixty hours a week. I think it's absurd working until seven every night and on weekends unless you have a deadline. I think having a more balanced life is healthier and more productive in that you can pore over something too long. It's better to leave it and return with a fresh view" (Attorney, age 33).

If the women were approaching midlife, they saw the men their age becoming even more money obsessed. "The men my age are desperately making money for their kids to go to college, while I'm thinking, how little do I need to get along?" said a tax attorney. "I just came home from a nine-day backpack vacation, which has got me thinking how much would it be worth to take less and shave an hour off the day? I'm in a worse financial situation than the men in many ways. I haven't done anything about retirement, I have no assets, so the money issue is pretty important to me. But at the same time I think, how much less would I have to work for how much less money?" (Attorney, age 40)

A very articulate broker (age 45) talked about women's natural tendency to be a giver. "We don't really learn well how to take. It is not easy to take or to even know that there is a wellspring inside this female that needs to be filled up. But when we go into this brokerage business, we *have to get something back*. But we give and give and give, because we are trying so hard to get ahead and we get off-balanced, and we don't realize that we are off-balanced. People need exercise or maybe piano lessons or getting involved in being advocates for children on the side. It is very easy to get so into this thing that we give until it burns us out. So we've got to find something that is going to fill the well."

Another broker (age 34) mused, "For every day the market goes down 86 points, there are as many days it goes up 86 points. To have this constant high–low, high–low, you have to learn to balance it. For myself, I do aerobics. I do a lot of physical activities, and I do meditating. I just make my mind stop thinking; I just let it go. You can't hold all this in or you make yourself a completely crazy person."

A woman with a degree in business administration refused to act like a broker in her personal life. She refused to prospect socially.

"I don't pursue my business socially at all. I frankly just like to be me and relax on my social time. I prefer to leave my work at work. Now I am getting my friends' accounts, and these are no blessing. I mean no offense to my friends, but I never asked for their accounts. I am happy to help them, but they seem to be very worried about the smallest dollar amount. When you are handling friends' money, you go to a party and you get nervous because are you going to have to talk about their account? Most men are conditioned to accept that, it is the old boys network mentality. But when I go home I don't act like a stockbroker. I don't want to act like my work role. If somebody didn't know me, they would never guess I am a businesswoman. My work and personal life are very separate. I have a certain work tolerance. If I can't make it, working and living a normal life, then it is not worth it" (Broker, age 31).

The 42-year-old commercial pilot who is also an air-show performer said, "A greater percentage of us postpone moving up to copilot due to other things in our lives, but men would move heaven and earth to move from flight engineer up. Men are more competitive. Men are more oriented strictly toward their jobs. I don't know why that is. I like the job, and it's the career I've always wanted, but I don't subordinate my life to it. For many men, this job is all they've got."

An electronics technician (age 33) has also been a belly dancer for ten years. "I worked here a full year before I would let anyone know about it, because they needed to know *who* I was first, before I'd get, 'There's that belly dancer, that loose female.' So the guys in my shop, who would have laughed about it before, they've been to our shows. We do traditional dancing. They go back and anybody says anything about me, it's up against the wall. I've walked down on a pier in a guy's fatigue jacket, jeans, hardhat, goggles, and some guy from another shop'll shout, 'There's that belly dancer,' and the guys go, 'Yeah, she's ours!' "

## TIME AND TOGETHERNESS

The January 1988 issue of *Psychology Today* published two little articles together about dual-income couples. One by Vincent Bozzi was "Time and Togetherness" and looked at a group of dual-earner couples who were apart something like ten and a half hours a day due to work, commuting, and different schedules. They had only a little over three hours of waking togetherness. But the more time they spent together—eating, talking, and playing—the more satisfying their marriages. Time spent together on housework and childcare didn't affect their marriages, one way or the other. The message was that the more time spent together eating, talking, and playing, the more satisfying a marriage.

The other little article, by Eleanor Grant, "The Housework Gap" (1988), reminded us that full-time employed wives do 70 percent of the housework compared with full-time homemakers who do 83 percent of it. Furthermore, having a high-powered job made no difference. The dual-career, professional women put in just as many hours at home as the dual-income women who held less demanding, straightforward, nine to five jobs.

The logic of these two articles is irresistible: (a) Marriages do not suffer if men do more housework; (b) Marriages get better the more time a couple has to eat, talk, and play together; ergo (c) men should do as much housework as women do so that women will have more time for (b), the stuff happy marriages are made of.

# 8

# NINE TO FIVE? FIVE DAYS
# A WEEK?

---

It's important to get more women into medicine so we won't be degraded for wanting to work nine to five rather than twelve-hour work days. This is why women go into more group practices rather than single practice, so they can have an outside life and time to themselves. (Physician, age 28)

We don't have a pregnancy policy, and we're going to read a lot about that. Right now if a woman gets pregnant she's only 50 percent covered and she can't work. We don't have any light-duty jobs, and you're not supposed to fight fires because the smoke's bad for the fetus. So when women have a stronger say in the union, there'll be leave and light duty. There'll be a place for us. (Firefighter, age 32)

What happens in a little boy's socialization that later makes him passively, stoically, accept employers' ground rules for work? That is, how many hours per week constitute full time, and from what hour in the morning to what hour at night are "the hours" of work?

Joseph Pleck and Jack Sawyer (1974, pp. 125–126) said little boys' socialization helps them accept hierarchies where men higher up control men lower down. From playground rankings boys learn to take orders from those above and give them to those below. On the playground, hierarchy was based on physical strength and skill. On the job, hierarchy is based on mental and social skills. But the outcome is the same. How a man ranks determines what society permits him to do and how much money he gets.

If he is far down that hierarchy, he works as long as and when the organization tells him to work. Furthermore, the company requires that he work as hard as he can, and if he's unhappy over his working conditions, he should remember that they are part of the masculine role. He should take it like a man. To get ahead and make as much money as possible, a man must follow orders. Hierarchy is, as it was in childhood, the natural order of things and, in addition, for his own good.

The alternative to putting families first, as women do, is what men put first, their employers—whatever the organization wants, whatever makes more money. But what makes the organization happy does not necessarily provide greater personal satisfaction or time to share housekeeping and childrearing or time to enjoy life or a long life.

"The company needed overtime engineers at Thanksgiving to push this program. Most guys worked right through Thanksgiving. They're more worried about their jobs than we are. My job isn't the number one priority; my happiness is, and I'd be happier with my family on Thanksgiving than working. I figured the company would just have to understand" (Engineer, age 31).

Are men pitiable pawns of the system? Mary Ingham's *Men* (1985, p. 18) depicts U.K. males as overworked, yet uncomplaining. In spite of the fact that they worked more than 40 hours a week on a regular basis, 85 percent said if given the option of spare time or extra pay, they'd take the pay. They were so wedded to work that they didn't know what they would do with spare time.

Ingham's interviewees also saw nothing wrong with doing the same line of work year in, year out and nothing wrong with spending so little time with their families. Work simply came first. It ruled their lives. They were addicted to work—workaholics. The symptoms were all there, Ingham said, including the most classic one, denying that there was a problem (1985, p. 22).

Women would like men to see that their role is not to make more and more money and to feel like a failure if they lose their jobs. Most of us would like to see them adopt a part breadwinner role and part housekeeper role. We would like to see them work fewer hours on the job and more hours in the home, and we are well aware that the tradeoff is money.

One way to end the cooption and channeling of men in male-dominated jobs is norm reversal. How many of us have fantasized this, reversing the norms so that the standards against which all workers, regardless of sex, are compared are women's standards?

What might women's standards be? What, for example, is our idea of the appropriate length of a typical working day? There would be some flexible range, right? Rigid, single-figure answers like "six hours" or "eight hours" are inappropriate from a woman's point of view.

What is our notion of a career pattern beneficial to society? It is a pattern with breaks and hiatuses and leaves that show we are committed to our families as well as to our careers. Women's broken pattern would be the norm. Unbroken patterns would be regarded as too shortsighted and insufficient to be considered for promotion.

How about women's ideas of a desirable level of job commitment? Work would certainly not be the number one priority. "Totally committed" workers, in our fantasy, would be summoned by personnel managers for heart-to-heart talks about just where this total commitment was leading, and employees with straight and narrow career plans would be periodically reviewed and encouraged to be more flexible in their thinking. An employee who arrived, day in, day out, year in, year out, promptly at eight and who always left at five would be asked how he or she could possibly manage a satisfying family life with that kind of inflexibility.

Such fantasies come from a different set of values than those of men about job success and job satisfaction. They come from recognizing that better working conditions are sometimes of greater value than more dollars for people privileged enough to have jobs.

Women are asking for full employment for all, a shorter working week, a shorter working day, leaves for fathers and mothers to attend to sick children, workplace nurseries and day care, flex time, and parttime. It's a long list.

The last question we asked in the interviews had to do with what will happen as more women enter the occupation. By the time we got to this question, we had spent a lot of time talking about values and attitudes. This may be why here the women identified concrete, structural changes and additions to the workplace, many having to do with time.

Of their five major concerns, their top priority was funding of twenty-four-hour day care, by employer or state, located at work or in the community. They didn't think there was one right way to provide day care. They wanted lots of options. Second, other structural changes they wanted were leaves for family—maternity, paternity, and parental—so that U.S. children could have the kind of care provided in Europe. Third and fourth, they wanted parttime work and job sharing to become fully benefited, legitimate ways to work for both sexes and flex time to be the rule. Finally, they demanded more flexibility at work, a never-ending stream of imaginative ways to make work more humane.

## DAY CARE, DAY CARE, DAY CARE

The chapter I got the most out of in Betty Friedan's (1981) *The Second Stage* was "Reality Test at West Point" (pp. 163–198). She made it clear that there are going to be major new policy arrangements if the army is going to keep its highly and expensively trained women officers. Most of these new arrangements have to do with families. With 8 percent of military women pregnant at any one time, pregnancy is no longer automatic grounds for discharge. Instead, prospective mothers are issued attractive maternity uniforms and are eligible for six weeks' paid post-partum leave.

In addition, the army is facing up to what to do when both parents are in the army, such as assigning both to the same or nearby posts and thinking about who will take care of their children if both parents are ordered to report for battle duty. Individuals no longer will have to solve these problems. The organization, for economic reasons, is going to do so. Still, the most important need in the military, as well as in industry, of workers with children is quality day care.

The women interviewed, in general, believed in sharing the care of their children with outsiders, not just family and friends. Nobody opined that mothers were biologically better at it. No one said that men or other women or communal arrangements simply couldn't compare with the mystique of a real mother.

U.S. day care today is a haphazard, chancy affair. It has a terrible reputation abroad. Among these women, suspicions were strongest among the blue-collar women, although skeptics were definitely in the minority. "Trying to choose between being a Mom and working is kind of hard. My daughter is two and a half now. My mother-in-law watches her. I personally don't want her in a day care with people I don't know. If my mother-in-law couldn't take care of her, I probably would be staying at home" (Shipyard woodcrafter, age 22).

Far more blue-collar women, though, spoke favorably about day care.

"I have a six year old. He's always been in day care. I like my job, I like the way I live, so I'm going to stay working. It hasn't hurt him. By being in a preschool and day care, he's been in since he was four months old, it's really helped us both. His teacher potty trained him. By being exposed to other kids and school early on, it's helped him a lot. I mean I'm totally amazed. He learned to read in kindergarten; he got introduced to computers in kindergarten. It's going to be better for him in the long run, and he's got a lot of friends. Even though there aren't a lot of kids in our neighborhood, I never have to worry on the weekend about him not playing with kids, because he has so many kids to play with during the week. So he can spend the weekend with us" (Metals inspector, age 26).

These nontraditional women were strongly behind institutional, systematic provision for childcare. They see day care as a societal responsibility, not an individual problem. Even one lawyer who didn't believe the government should provide day care thought it definitely should be among the cafeteria of benefits her firm offered.

Another structural change related to kids is covering for other workers when someone has to take care of a sick child. At present, such covering is informal and left to individuals. But organizations should legitimize and systematize it, the women said.

The women physicians talked of formalizing covering for one another. "Women docs support one another because we have similar values. We work out coverage hours so we're not on call all of the time. Work is just another aspect of life and having kids at home puts a strain on being able to enjoy work 100 percent. We need to know our kids are well taken care of. As far as day care goes, I want to buy an older home with a large backyard for my practice. The kids can play there while Mom and Dad are being seen. The employees can bring their children while working, and my kids can be there while I work" (Physician, age 32).

This on-site day care will happen in blue-collar work as well. "There will be more children showing up on the job and more freedom to call or check up on the welfare of your kids in the middle of the day. It's common for office workers to be able to check on their kids. Tradeswomen, too, need time during the day to take care of home things. I can take care of a lot of little problems if I can get to a phone. I see more women's children stopping by and just showing up at work, hanging around for a ride home. In the future, there will be more interaction with families, and I don't think family life will interfere with getting the job done" (Electrician, age 37).

## PARENTAL LEAVES

All of the women interviewed said that maternity leave is bound to get built into our work ethos like paid vacations and health benefits. Maybe because the United States is so retarded in implementing maternity leave, we can leapfrog ahead on paternity leave while undoing what is a national disgrace: We are the only industrialized country in the world that has no statutory maternity leave.

The Economic Policy Council (EPC) is a powerful, American, private-sector think tank that studies major economic problems and makes policy recommendations. Their 1985 study of U.S. family life recommended federal legislation expanding the definition of disability so that women would have the right to ten to twelve weeks' leave at time of birth with some wage replacement, the guarantee of a job at the end of that period, and partially paid parenting leave for either parent for up to six months after birth (Hewlett, 1986, p. 377).

Sweden has a parental leave of nine months at the birth of a child that can be taken by either parent. It replaces 90 percent of the earnings, protects seniority on the job, maintains fringe benefits, and guarantees return to the same or a similar job. Italy gives pregnant women five months leave at 80 percent pay and six more months at 30 percent pay, holds their jobs for them, and gives them two years' credit toward seniority with each birth. France gives women a three-month maternity leave with full pay and two years of unpaid leave, and there is excellent childcare everywhere (Hewlett, 1986, p. 96).

Even Britain, which lags way behind other European Economic Community countries when it comes to parental leave, gives women six weeks paid maternity leave at 90 percent of earnings and the right to return to work up to twenty-nine weeks after birth and to be reemployed no less favorably (Hewlett, 1986, p. 97).

The problem of contemporary American women, said Hewlett, is that compared to women in other advanced countries they receive less maternity leave, less subsidized childcare, less job flexibility, and less money proportional to men (1986, p. 412). Hewlett said that 117 countries, all of the industrialized countries and many poor developing countries, guarantee a woman the right to leave her job for childbirth, job protection while on leave, and a cash benefit to replace all or most of her earnings (p. 96).

The women police officers we talked to are working hard with their departments to draw up new policies and procedures regarding maternity. They are insistent that the leave be parental, that the men have the same benefits as women. "Right now I think it's unfair to the guys that the guys get hassled if they want to take leave when their wives are having a baby. There's a lot of them who want to do that, and they get hassled about it. If you're going to give maternity leave, you've got to give it equally to men and women. It's just as important for them" (Officer, age 38). "Why is it," a 55-year-old assistant police chief asked, "if a child gets sick and both parents are working, it's the woman who has to take time off to care for their child? Why shouldn't men be able to take time off? I think as men and women are more equally distributed on the force, we'll see less of this kind of discrimination."

## PARTTIME AND JOB-SHARING OPTIONS

If we work fifty years full time using the forty-hour week as our standard, do you know how many hours we put in in our lifetime? We work 100,000 hours. How many of us would just as soon put in 50,000 hours? One answer is job sharing at half time, meaning a seventeen- to twenty-hour week. *Job sharing* is two or more employees proportionally sharing hours, benefits, holidays, and salary.

What employers get from job sharing is not having one full timer who is struggling to maintain commitments at home, who gets overtired and is absent more often than parttime job sharers. Job sharers are said to bring in more fresh ideas and enthusiasm and to demonstrate greater commitment when working. There is less job turnover since people don't quit because they can't cope with their other obligations. Also, with computerized payrolling, two sets of contracts and insurance and tax deductions involve no extra cost to employers. Moreover, job sharing can be done in any occupation.

A 40-year-old landscape architect said that our having children *is* the way we are changing her field, because children are the primary reason for parttime work. "In this office we let people work parttime so that that phenomenon of women taking maternity leave, saying they'll come back, and then deciding they don't want to come back, doesn't happen here. We always have two to three parttime employees. Men have not been as open about asking for parttime work as women. But we now have men in the office who take a day off when the kid is sick and can't go to day care, men who will leave work to take their children to the doctor or to attend PTA in the middle of the day. Kids have to benefit from that. The men will now converse about their children where ten years ago, only women did."

She continued: "The more parttime employees we have, the more the way the office operates changes. The men are now dealing with their children and outside commitments. *This has got to make us better designers*, because good design is based on a wide range of interests, on getting out. So men will no longer have to visit playgrounds to observe how to design them, they can watch their own kids. As their wives enter other professions, a whole new world opens up to men. They now have to pay attention to the real world."

As things stand now, parttime work is still seen as something only women do. In the United Kingdom, for example, 90 percent of parttimers are women, and more than 40 percent of the female workforce is parttime compared with only 3 percent of the male work force (Syrett, 1988). In the United States in 1985 two-thirds of the parttimers were women, and 29 percent of the female work force was parttime (McHenry & Small, 1989).

How do we get parttime employment to be attractive to men? Certainly, all the benefits associated with full-time work would have to be guaranteed, for example, seniority, pension and health benefits, equivalent advancement and promotion standards, vacation and leave time, unemployment benefits, and various insurance schemes. Essentially everything offered the full-time worker must be available to parttime workers, at least on a prorated basis.

Still, men will need some convincing. What's this time off for, they ask, besides raising children and cleaning house? Time off is to go to school, get experience at a new job as an intern or trainee, prepare for retirement, pure pleasureable recreation to avoid burnout. Perhaps very stressful jobs should be done only parttime—air traffic controllers and pilots, surgeons and intensive-care nurses, assembly line workers, and police officers.

Parttime work must be made attractive within all occupations, across all employers, to workers of both sexes and all ages. Parttime work simply has too much to offer society in terms of productivity and too much to offer individuals in job satisfaction to be wasted as a viable idea in the workplace.

The physicians always mentioned time. They agreed that it needs to be acceptable to work fewer hours with fewer patients (and naturally, for less pay). They wanted parttime work and shared residencies.

A 47-year-old internist who limits her work to six hours a day five days a week said that many men would like to practice less too and are always asking her how she does it. She does it by living on less income and not incurring a heavy, ongoing debt load. She and the other physicians thought that it was the women who protected patients from the cost-effective mentality of some health maintenance organizations (HMOs) that pressure doctors to see X number of patients per day. One doctor said, "I will always feel more comfortable with more women around. There are traditional ways of doing things in medicine, and it has been women in the past who have changed them. Now HMOs are where we are going, and doctors are caught in the crunch for lower fees and higher costs for equipment. We feel the more time you spend with the patient, the more accurate information you get, and we're not going to let our patients suffer from efficiency."

A physician, age 32, looking for a job-sharing partner, put it this way: "We would each work two and a half days a week. My goal is to spend more time with my family and work less. I have a lot of pressure on me to get everything done so I can spend more time with my child. I love to be a mother and a doctor. I'll cook at night after my child goes to sleep so I can get all the time-consuming stuff out of the way and have more time with my child. I'm not interested in building an empire. I just want to do my best with my child and my work."

Another woman opined that job sharing was the way to hold on to "our greater sense of balance before we came into medicine. An example is the practice of two women I know, two good friends, pediatricians who share their job on the pediatric ward. They share patients, office, nurse, but the total of what the two get paid doesn't equal a full-time person's salary. So the hospital's got a good deal because they also get no benefits" (Physician, age 36).

## FLEX TIME

A 31-year-old electrician compared her previous company to the all-woman company she works for now. "It's more relaxed here. You're not watching the clock; there's not that pressure. In my last big company, your every move was watched. Is she five minutes late? One minute late? People looked at their watches. You really toed the mark. Here the pressures I have, I put on myself. They don't put time pressures on me."

It is not surprising to find women objecting very much to the male view of work as done in big slabs of time, often nine to five, five days a week. They also object to men's seeing full-time work as forty hours a week. Women want our ideas about time implemented in male-dominated jobs.

Do we think differently about time than men? Anne Schaef, in *Women's Reality* (1981, p. 100), said that men always use, and believe only in, clock time. Time is numbers on the clock and calendar, and time is what those numbers measure. This must be why male employees are so preoccupied with how many minutes are allotted for tea breaks and lunch and changing clothes and why male managers are so preoccupied with employees being early or late or on time. Minutes to men are money, that's all.

Women obviously use clock time too, but, Schaef said, we also use process time during which things happen and we get things done, but in which the concepts early, late, and on time, have little meaning. Because relationships are of primary concern to us, worrying about being on time sometimes can be counterproductive (1981, pp. 101–104). How important is time when a child needs to be listened to? Or when a patient needs to be diagnosed? Or when a client is trying to explain what he wants built or what her investment goals are? Women find it easier than men to switch gears and use process time instead of clock time depending on what the situation calls for.

Flex time was universally endorsed across all occupations by the women interviewed. Because it generally refers to putting in the traditional hours required for full-time employment, the forty-hour week, flex time will probably be the most acceptable of our ideas to traditional men.

A 22-year-old woodcrafter devoted to her craft wanted more time with her 2½-year-old daughter. "I'd work ten hours a day four days a week, if I could. If they were more flexible here, they'd have a lot happier people. A lot more women would work here, for one thing. I'm basically pinned here five days a week. If we had flex time and flex hours, too, like to be able to start earlier in the morning and get out earlier, it would break up the monotony. We wouldn't have to take so much leave either, during business hours time, to take care of transactions, trying to catch a place open for whatever reason."

The women engineers mentioned flex time in every interview. They are all pressing for it. A structural engineer (age 34), for example, whose greatest job satisfaction is interacting with other people said, "I'm more sensitive to the way people feel, allowing them more freedom to do the work, boosting their image of themselves, more willing to trust their flex time hours, their working ability."

Another engineer (age 33) who runs her own shop thinks flex time and parttime are great. "You can work forty-eight hours or twenty-six. That's okay, but when we're really busy, it doesn't make any difference who you are; we all have to work. I use consensus decisions to run my company. It will come to that everywhere as people become less willing to work long hours. We see our employees as people and *ask* when we need them to work weekends, not demand it. We're more socially aware, know how to get consensus, and are just more flexible about how work gets done."

A 32-year-old chemical engineer thinks that if you give people more freedom, productivity goes up. "It's not important to me that people work eight to five with one hour for lunch. I want them to work eighty hours every two weeks and get the work accomplished. I emphasize getting the work done. I don't care when they come in or whether they work straight through lunch. I'm for flex time; some of my people work nine hours a day for eight days, plus a day of eight hours, and take the tenth day off. I think women would tend to want people to work in a more relaxed atmosphere."

This woman's sensitivity to mind and body rhythms also makes for better management. She continued: "If more women in engineering means more people with my attitude, then I think there'll be a positive change in hours. If people are more productive in the A.M., then work in the A.M. If they're more productive in the P.M., then work in the P.M."

## FLEXING THE SYSTEM

I like this January 6, 1988, *London Times* (p. 16) headline: "Women Bosses Would Reduce Stress at Work." The author, John Spicer, reported that women bosses are good for workers' health because women are better at coping with change than men. So we teach employees how to cope with change. We encourage them to take more control over their work and give them more freedom to handle responsibilities their own way. The autocratic, male style of management, Spicer said, costs the United Kingdom billions of pounds a year.

With more women practicing law there will be an inevitable shift in the time commitment required of attorneys. Since time is money in the law, this means firms' accepting and validating getting less productivity and less money out of each employee in the short term. Because women are not willing to sacrifice the rest of life for the law, men will, as well, have flex time, alternative working environments, and day care for their children—and it will happen like this.

Half of the attorneys at one small firm are women. Half of each sex can be described as work centered, the other family centered. How has this greater family orientation in the men come about? "In general, more women are interested in going home at night, while more men are so ambitious they forget why they're working so hard. So it has been a problem for women if you couldn't devote your entire life to your profession. The great thing here is that one of the partners works parttime so that she can be home at five to feed her kids. *Because one of the bosses does it*, it's permitted for everyone" (Attorney, age 35).

She continued: "I'd like to see people's attitudes lighten up a bit. This is something women can do. We say there's something wrong if you don't have time to smile at your secretary or be civil to others or have time for your family. Bad things can happen. Balance means understanding that and not taking yourself so seriously. Go home and see your kids if they need you. Do the work tomorrow. We need more people like my boss in positions of power."

Although another attorney was less sanguine about changing the traditional structure of the mega law firms in the foreseeable future, still, "if there were a way to make $100,000 and not have that structure, women would definitely go for it. But the purpose of these firms is to generate enormous amounts of money, jillions from the people below for the partners above. A small number of people make money off the efforts of many below. Having more women in these firms gives the young men a support group without their even knowing it. Maybe things would change if the men heard more often, 'Enough is enough; I'm leaving' " (Attorney, age 40).

Men not only need more options at work; they need more options about whether or not to work, more options about changing careers, more options about quitting if they hate their jobs so much. I stated in Chapter 5 that it may be a long time before women can get men to think about changing careers completely. One tradeswoman sighed and said that getting men to change was a slow process, and she thought that it mainly stemmed from the fact that

"Men can't say, 'I'm going to quit and go find someone to take care of me.' Now, women really can't either, but we learned this idea way back, this notion that I can find some man to take care of me, this copout, this notion that you can put it on autopilot; you can cruise instead of drive. So we've always had this option. Now if you think you've got one option, you start thinking of other options, better options. But men haven't had the luxury of this idea of being able to kick back and say, 'I don't have to do this.' They feel they're stuck with their breadwinner, take-care-of-the-family role. But if men could be more equal, if they could say, 'I'll let someone else take care of me,' then they'd start to have all the other kinds of choices women have" (Electrician, age 31).

I like that. I've always been irked by defenders of the traditional full-time housewife saying this is a choice we have. These same people are also saying that men do not have that choice. Why shouldn't both sexes have it? Why should it be an option just for women?

Many of the women interviewed had had a previous career—housewife, nurse, secretary, art teacher, and so on. But they changed their minds and decided to do something really radical, a man's job. With that idea came a lot of other radical ideas about work such as why should any job last a lifetime? Maybe most jobs are only good for a few years and then people should move on to something else.

Can the men who work with this 45-year-old electroplater learn how to make a really big change? She decided when she began her blue-collar job that ten years would be enough, and when it was up she would do something different, a new challenge. "It is funny how it worked out; they didn't know my goal, but when the time came, they offered me the job of planner. So I'll stay with the company in planning. I was getting stagnant, just like I expected. I wanted to learn something new. I think everybody gets stagnant, but men just go on doing the same thing for forty years."

## RATTLING THE GILDED CAGE

"Rattling the Gilded Cage" was the title of a 1986 *Time* article by Richard Lacayo. Young lawyers of both sexes were balking at the gargantuan size of the firms they worked for and the dreary dregs of work they were assigned. Hence they were leaving in droves.

To keep their younger associates, megafirms with more than 200 attorneys had adopted a number of structural alterations they could have learned from the women interviewed here. Each young person had a partner assigned to her or him to act as a buddy and mentor. Young people were given full responsibility for handling less complex cases. They could apprentice several specialties before choosing the one best suited to them. They were put on committees that recommended raises, bonuses, and promotions, to give them a sense of participating in management. These structural changes, designed to improve the workplace environment and job satisfaction, had finally been recognized as more important to keeping people than simply throwing more money at them.

# 9

# NOT LIVING WITH STRESS

---

My first three years in the brokerage I worked very intensely, long hours, lots of pressure from management, lots of stress headaches. At the end of three years, 20 percent of us were still around, and every year there are less and less. But I finally realized it really wasn't worth all that. My best was going to be the best I could do. It's my life and I'm not going to succumb to being the puppet they want. So I am no longer driven, producing as much as they would like. But I'm happy. I never want to do that dancing as fast as I can again. (Broker, age 45)

An important plank in the Berkeley Men's Center Manifesto is to "end destructive competitive relationships between men" (Pleck & Sawyer, 1974, p. 174). This collective of men refuses to compete to live up to the "leader of men" image and rejects the idea of being sole breadwinners for families and profit makers for companies.

Because our interviews so strongly linked on-the-job competitiveness with stress, we need to ask ourselves how men learn to become so competitive on the job and so addicted to that job that they are willing to die for it. Ruth Hartley (1974, p. 10) told us that for little boys, being able to play many competitive games—baseball, basketball, football—is a crucial part of being masculine. When they are men, boys say, masculinity means having a good business head and making money to support a family. Parents instill adult competitiveness by praising little boys for their athletic skills and fighting ability and by punishing them for being a sissy and backing away from competition.

Joseph Pleck and Jack Sawyer (1974, p. 74) also said that male socialization includes being taught they must get ahead and must compete
with other males for society's rewards. Male culture teaches men to
compare themselves continually with other men and to use men higher
up the hierarchy as a standard of what they should be able to do. It is
other men's regard that men are after; it is other men that they use as
the judge of whether they are a success or failure.

Finally, Phillip Hodson's (1984, pp. 139–140) big pitch to men to become more like women (more emotionally dependent and sharing of
their feelings) is based on men's need to reduce the stress of all this
competition. Because men are out of touch with their emotions, they
don't take care of their work-related stress problems and consequently
die seven to eight years ahead of women.

Hodson noted that being out of work seriously damages men's health
(unemployment increases suicide, crime, and mental illness) but having
work also endangers men's health (1984, p. 93). Far too many men find
work addictive, a kind of drug that makes them defer the gratifications
of home life and family for the alleged rewards of hard work. Hodson
devoted the second half of his chapter called "Work Kills—Official" to
steps men can take to overcome their "morbid compulsion" to compete
as their parents taught them as little boys (pp. 100–107).

Once again, early sex-role socialization plays a large part in creating
a difference in the adult behavior of men and women. But what else
might be related to differences in the way women and men respond to
stress at work? Stress is also related to the amount of control people
feel they have over their lives. Job stress goes up the poorer the working conditions, the lower the pay, the less desirable the hours (shift
work), and the more isolated one feels in dealing with abuse and
aggression.

It's ironic that women live seven years longer than men, when we're
the ones stuck in dead-end, low-pay service and clerical jobs; we're the
people glued to video display terminals and trapped behind sewing machines doing piecework. Then we go home to another full-time job where
the pay is really poor!

What may be important is that women don't perceive they lack control on the job in the same way that men do. From their sex-role socialization men believe that they have to work, they have to put up
with poor working conditions, and they are saddled with supporting a
family. An unskilled, single-parent woman perhaps doesn't feel as
forced to take any one of her options. They're not great options, but
they do mean she has some choice, some control. She can go on welfare, take an undesirable job, or find other people to support her and
her children. Men are not taught that they have these options too and

perhaps don't see that they in fact do. Maybe this is the source of their greater job stress.

Our ten groups of women had a range of job stress from the low levels of the engineers and landscape architects to the high levels endured by the police and firefighters. But they all had an advantage over male colleagues in that they thought they had a high degree of control over their lives. Even more than unskilled, single-parent women, they believed they had choices and options. Second, they understood how stress affects mind and body, they believed in communicating feelings and emotions, and they defended their right to talk about stress. Third, objectively, they had more social support than did the men who, generally, had only their wives; the women had friends, relatives, and female coworkers to turn to.

Each woman we talked with had developed, consciously, a set of coping behaviors and a set of healthy attitudes for reducing stress in her life. Without exception, each valued health over job. You might ask, who doesn't? Men don't, the women said.

There are five topics in this chapter. The most important one concerns the women's rejection of competition. They were competitive with themselves but not with coworkers. The second topic is not of the same magnitude as avoiding competition, but they said *not* avoiding tears alleviated their stress. Third, especially in the skilled crafts, the women's greater concern for health and safety was making work less stressful for their male colleagues as well. Fourth, related to their awareness of their bodies' reactions to fumes, noise, and weather extremes, they took care of themselves by taking time off when they needed to. Finally, if things got too bad, they were more ready to quit than were the men. They weren't afraid of change, even of changing jobs completely, if it meant more life satisfaction.

## REJECTING COMPETITION

It was rare to hear a woman say that the women in her occupation were as competitive as the men. Although the women had been competitive in school, had been competitive continually to prove themselves and get promoted, they still said they weren't as competitive as men and didn't believe in competition.

A 30-year-old commercial electrician said: "Competitiveness? I'm appalled by it. I don't think it's a good work atmosphere, I really don't. It's harmful saying 'I'm better than you.' It's harmful to your progress, and it endangers people's lives and properties, taking shortcuts. I'm glad to be out of heavy-duty construction now, because they're all keyed to competition. Those competitive work attitudes and ethics lower the quality of their work."

The biggest thing wrong with competition, they said, was that competition was stressful. The landscape architects said that the men were more stressed than the women because they thought they had to keep up a professional image. The women pursued the field in a more human vein; they were there to enjoy it. "We don't have to prove ourselves. We let our hair down, let our audacity have free reign. Men always have to be so professional and businesslike in front of other men, proving their worth. They are so crazy about their images. I just see them as insecure. Underneath they're all concerned about image. In some cases, they're more ego than flesh, always worried about what other people think about them. It's awful" (Landscape architect, age 42).

The women firefighters were astonished at the competition underlying male interaction. Before the women joined them, the men had contests about everything, which appalled the women, such as which man could eat the most. The men, they said, enjoyed competing no matter what the contest, which the women simply could not understand. "It's not as bad now, but they used to bet they could do crazy things. They used to bet they could climb around our tables. When there was nothing to do around the station, they would pull out the table we eat at and climb around the edge without falling off it, completely around the table, just to see who could do it—crazy things. So they're really very competitive" (Firefighter, age 32).

Firefighting drills, for the men, are a "natural" occasion to call forth competition. The women's attitude, however, is that we can do the work, and we don't care who can do this or that fastest. They simply refuse to compete. "One guy in particular is so competitive, he wants to race me to the hose. In my opinion, he can have it; I'm not going to race him for it, and it's like that all the time with him. In actual firefighting, on fireground tactics, the men are more competitive with each other. I want to work as a team, whereas they would rather do it on their own" (Firefighter, age 28).

"A 36-year-old police sergeant said that women competed only over things that were really important. What point was there in competing about physical strength, for example, when it doesn't matter anyway? "I went to arrest a six-foot, seven-inch drunk who had hurt the last officer who had arrested him, and I said, 'Look, John, I have to arrest you, and there isn't a backup car for me, and you could probably hurt me if you wanted. It's a pretty moot point; you're a lot bigger than I am. But, uh, eventually there is going to be a whole lot of people here, so I'd really appreciate it if you'd just get in the car, and it would make it a lot easier for me.' I think that would be very hard for a male officer to say. I never compete with a suspect, whereas the guys get in pissing contests with their suspects; they really do!"

Besides being stressful, the women said, another thing wrong with competitiveness was that it destroyed trust between coworkers, the very trust one needed to combat stress. Competition set men against other men and women and sometimes a woman against another women. A carpenter (age 36) said she had worked only once with a woman. "A friend of mine. They paired us together, and we became very competitive. It was really sick. We got into racing. It was my first job as a journeyman, and I had to prove I was knowledgeable. It was really terrible. I finally had to quit the job. Before I became a carpenter I worked well with women, and I was shocked that this happened, and I've never had the chance to work with another woman since."

Most women brokers are uncomfortable about inner-office rivalry. I don't think they liked being winners any more than they resented being losers. No, losing was clearly more painful. A 29-year-old broker hated the posted production list. "I know I've only been in the business two years and that jerk at the top has been around for twenty years, and he's got $35 million in assets to control. But still I don't like it when I am at the bottom. Women sometimes have trouble dealing with the hierarchy. We haven't been taught the gamesmanship that goes with this." The expectation always was that they should continue to produce more and more, more than other brokers, more than one's previous record. The women found this win–lose mentality tiresome.

A lot of women said they were only in competition with themselves. One landscape architect, age 30, who subscribed to this philosophy said that feeling in control was what's important, not job position or title. "The men are more interested in what makes them money and establishes them as successful, and for myself I don't care about the money. I pursue my work through my love and concern for the land. I am really oversensitive, and it definitely comes out in my work. I care; it means a lot to me. I do not have the male landscape architect's attitude of 'Go for it. Whip it out,' that male hard attitude of competition and push."

An internally motivated stockbroker (age 32) said she only has to be number one in her own mind.

"My main competitor is my inner self that says, 'I'll bet you can't do it.' I have always competed mainly with myself, even when I was swimming on my college team. I was always pleased if I could beat my time. The thing I hate the most in this business is they rank you with all the other brokers in the business. But I have my own goals and my own rankings, and I don't like budget goals or yearly goals. It is not my goal to be climbing the corporate ladder, but we've got our Chairmans Council, which is the top ten percent of the brokers in the firm.

I'm the only woman in the firm to have made it there, and I like to think of myself as worthy. Those plaques on the wall? They're mainly to remind myself that I'm okay. I say to myself, 'I'm just going to do the best I know I can do' or I'd feel like I was driving myself crazy."

A 36-year-old physician said her boss used to reduce her to tears by saying she wasn't like the men. "I felt so up against a wall, so lacking control. So I decided to divorce myself emotionally from the clinic. I now approach it strictly as a business deal. Here is what I get out of it, here is what you get out of it, and here is what the clinic gets out of it. This is working. I actually consulted an attorney to accomplish this; attorneys are good at making cases, and I was making a case. She helped me with this. I don't feel so frustrated and angry anymore. But I'm thinking about what would be even better for me, a small group practice that is fifty–fifty or even female dominated, rather than this large group of men."

"I just don't like competing," said a 37-year-old electrician. "There have been times when that has shown up real strong, how competitive men are, and I refuse to compete with them. For example, residential trim work is a highly competitive thing. You will have thirty apartments that are identical, and you will have six in a crew, and everyone will take their own apartment and see who can get done first. The men will do a slam-bang job, but then they have to go back and fix everything, to do it neat and tidy. Then they redo it, and I end up finishing first because mine is done right to start with. I am real fast, but I refuse to compete."

## GREATER ACCEPTANCE OF TEARS

"When I first went to school, if the boys tried to push me around, I'd haul off and sock them," said a 55-year-old legislator. "I got in more trouble. I was made to sit in the corner to control my temper, which I finally learned to do. So when I get angry now, I cry instead, because it is not nice to shout. Crying's my only outlet. It is just the way I've been conditioned. It's far better than shouting, 'You so and so.' Then I'm perceived as out of control."

With more women entering nontraditional jobs, society can expect more weeping at work. In spite of the fact that women know it is considered "unbusinesslike" and "unprofessional," in our earlier lives we were not punished for crying when we were stressed. The emotional release of crying can be so gratifying that crying becomes its own reward. How many of us seek out tearjerking movies so we can release the tears and tension inside us?

On the whole, most women see little wrong with crying, whereas men, generally, see everything wrong with crying. For men, crying at work is the ultimate no-no. It means that the crier is weak and manipulative, behaving inappropriately, out of control, disrupting the office, and making everyone feel awkward because the crier is "acting like a baby."

What do babies need? They need a physical response, a hug or touch, something nonverbal, intimate, and deeply comforting. What man wants to do that for someone else at work?

What criers need is simply to be allowed to cry, because crying is its own reward. It is a great stress reducer. Still, with men in control of performance evaluations and promotions, should we or should we not cry at work?

Women tend not to overreact when someone cries at work. We figure, rightly, it's only going to last a few minutes. While the crier is blowing his or her nose, we can use the time to think back and figure out what may have triggered this reaction. Car problems? Kid problems? Girlfriend problems? Then we forget it. But if it is work related, maybe we should do something about it.

Several women talked about crying with clients. The vets said women get asked to do more euthanasias, because owners know they are going to cry and that women vets will accept it and know how to handle it.

"I work with a lot of women who have gone through a divorce or whose husbands have died," related a broker (age 32), "and the male in the family handled all the finances. So it is easy for me to relate to that female client. Sharing my own emotions has helped me more than it has hindered me. They know I am not an impersonal cold sort who just thinks about business. I share my life experiences, too, and it helps them. I've been through a divorce, and when I could see those little tears getting ready to roll, I've broken down and said, 'Hey, I have to admit this; I've been there too.' "

A 30-year-old captain in the fire service recalled that in her recruit class there was a very outgoing, expressive woman, who was working hard pulling hose with tears rolling down her face. "The instructors didn't know what to do. So they sent me over to see if it was something major. So I went over and said, 'Mary, is there something wrong?' And she said, 'No, I just hurt.' I walked back and said, 'She just hurts,' and they said, 'Well, there's nothing in the book that says you can't cry. She's doing her job, so what can we do? We can't knock her down for it.' There was a realization there that came to those men that were evaluating us that, well, she's crying; we don't like it, we're uncomfortable with it, but she's doing her job and it's not affecting her performance, so what do we do? Our emotions are a real issue and are having a positive effect because we are saying, 'Yes, stuff affects us,' and that brings us back to the need for all of us to talk about stress."

A 32-year-old geriatrician said she cried with her patients and felt it was a very female thing to do. She remembered an experience she had years before. "The patient had leukemia. She came in Christmas Eve with a large clot under her tongue, her mouth was in effect closing up. She would die very soon. I admitted her, and we decided that we would, with her permission, IV heroin, which basically meant that it would be acting as the final push, so to speak. Her family was in the room, and we watched her die quite peacefully, and we cried together. That experience will always be with me."

A GP, age 36, said early on that she wanted to meet other people's professional expectations of her and had worried about whether crying with patients was appropriate. "Now I think it's a valid way to relate with the patient in reasonable situations. It's good to share when you're touched, also letting other people you work with know your emotions— anger, frustration, crying."

## ADVOCATES FOR BETTER HEALTH AND SAFETY

From the first weeks of their apprenticeship, tradeswomen are fresh and alert and attuned to the physical nature of their environment, the sights, sounds, smells, around them. They continue to monitor how their various body parts react to stress and strain. But although they first keep these feelings and thoughts to themselves, as they gain confidence, they speak their reactions aloud: "This is terrible! God, I hurt! We shouldn't be breathing this stuff! I'm calling an inspector!"

Women expressing how they feel, informally, openly, honestly, about work conditions are models for men as to how they can express their feelings as well. A 34-year-old electrician who always wears her mask said, "You can hardly breath in those clouds of dust. Masks are available for everybody, but the men won't put them on. It's a macho thing with them, like handling hot power rather than taking one minute to switch it off. They are less safety conscious. I'm just waiting for one of them to follow my example and wear a hard hat, earplugs, and a mask. Showing my weakness, talking about health, should make it easier for men to take care of themselves. I've gotten a lot freer in my feelings. Before I'd just take it. Now I say, 'This is awful' or 'I hate this,' and if I can't lift something, I don't strain myself. I say I need help. So here, too, I think men might be more likely now to ask for help."

The women said there are significant differences between them and the men on safety issues. Many women will risk their jobs rather than compromise health and safety. "On one job I was on, they were operating an unsafe crane after somebody already died from it. I kept demanding that they fix it and warning everybody. The crane operator wouldn't do anything, the supervisor wouldn't do anything, so I called the inspectors anonymously. They came out and said they'd shut down the job site unless we stopped using the crane. It was fixed within a week. The men were very angry, and they suspected me, but I didn't get in trouble" (Carpenter, age 30).

The women thought older workers shouldn't have to do very heavy work but should be allowed to supervise and use their heads. That's what *they* were going to do when they reached middle age.

"Women in the trades look more to, 'What am I going to do when I'm too old to walk up that ladder and carry that pipe?' We think also about all that noxious dust, the fumes, the dirt and dust you expose your body to for that long, the metal shavings, fiber glass, cement dust. We tend to look at the future and say at age 50, I'd like to be in another branch of the electrical trades where I use my brain more. I'm serious enough about my trade to want to keep doing it, but I don't want to subject my body to these physical conditions when I'm older. Guys have the attitude that I'm going to do this until I die. They just follow a path and don't veer from it, on track; you do this and you die doing this. Men are still into those culturally bound male–female social roles, where they're expected to act certain ways" (Electrician, age 31).

One woman said:

"Once an old carpenter told me, 'I'm glad women are getting into this field because it will calm things down and make people more reasonable. Maybe they'll sack cement in thirty-pound sacks instead of sixty.' Maybe he'd noticed that I look for easier ways to do things than mule work. Like I use a bigger pry bar or a piece of machinery or stack up the lumber and use a forklift rather than carry one piece at a time. We *are* safer on the job than the men. There's a whole lot wrapped up in competition among the men. Women are more cautious with their bodies. We shouldn't have to risk our life or our health to work. I ask for help carrying things that the men just heave around by themselves. What's wrong with asking for help? Some men don't tie on when they're up high, but the women I know always do. Men push their bodies farther. It's okay to have limits and ask for help" (Carpenter, age 34).

The women were unanimous that women carpenters are more careful on the job, trying to keep accidents from happening, trying to protect themselves with fume masks, safety glasses, and ear protectors, checking ladders to be sure they are in good condition. A cabinetmaker (age 30) said: "When I started working at this one place I couldn't believe those people weren't wearing respirators with replaceable filters for dust, chemical mists, gases. They were using those little paper 3M things that are garbage because they don't fit my face and they don't protect you from chemical mist. I'm not sure I was responsible, but maybe they looked at me and decided I wasn't crazy, because five months later a salesman came around, and everyone bought a respirator and hearing protectors."

One woman complained that their equipment is never attended to until it breaks. She keeps suggesting routine maintenance, but in the meantime, "I keep calling the inspectors. Right now I have some samples of asbestos I'm going to have checked out. One time they wanted me to work standing on top of a hose with concrete pumping through it, after it had already broken loose and thrown concrete in this guy's eyes. So I called OSHA [Occupational Safety and Health Administration] and the inspector would only let them pump concrete on weekends when the rest of us were out of the way. I got fired for that" (Electrician, age 34).

A construction electrician (age 32) shook her head about men's greater mechanical and electrical knowledge, yet lesser respect for safety.

"They have this good background knowledge whereas mine is in sewing and drawing, this and that and the other thing. But in spite of their knowledge, guys do stupid things, even if they've been in the trade a long time. Yesterday this senior journeyman didn't bring a high pot tester with him, which is for testing high voltage lines. You never assume that the power has been turned off. So what does he do? He throws a piece of metal at the high voltage lines, face to face, to see if it shorts out. If the thing had been hot, it would have blown all three of us right off the roof: 26,000 volts and he throws a thing across it to see if it's hot? That's sheer stupidity, and that guy's been an electrician for forty years. Two hours later this other guy climbs up this big steel structure that supports the high voltage lines to disconnect them with no safety belt on—twenty-two feet off the top of the roof. All these safety violations have got to be reported, and if I get in trouble for it, that's okay."

Employers, usually, are the source of health and safety violations, however, and the men don't protest because they are worried about losing their jobs. The woman above continued:

"There are so few jobs, and they're worried about job security. I was working on this big department store, and the temperature was in the teens. I had so many layers on I could move my arms up and down, but I couldn't bend my elbows. I was fine for about the first forty-five minutes, and then you got so cold that you couldn't warm up until you left the job. You couldn't really produce under conditions like that. Our dry shack had two little space heaters, each one had one element working. They didn't even cut the frost, and the guys were complaining about how freezing cold it was in there. So when the foreman came around, I asked if we could get some heaters that worked properly. He said if I was cold I could go sit in the office trailer, and all of them just sat there and shoved their sandwiches in their mouths. They wouldn't support me and say, 'She's right. We need better heaters. We can't all go up to the office trailer to warm up.' "

## TAKING TIME OFF

Family responsibilities are as much a man's as a woman's, which means that men should take more time off for families but also because it reduces job stress. Even driving kids to Little League, doctor's visits, shopping for school clothes, and parent–teacher conferences gives men something different to worry about than work.

Books about men in midlife make particularly depressing reading. So many men are unhappy, grinding along, doing work they feel they have to do, coming home to supper, television, and bed. At midlife, routine stresses are harder to cope with, and the prospect for men is that they are going to have to go on for many more years, feeling hopeless and helpless. Many middle-aged men respond by trying to work even harder and accept indignities younger people won't tolerate. Older men worry about money, losing their jobs, how fast society is changing, all of which makes them feel even less in control of their own destinies.

In contrast, a 30-year-old attorney for an old, prestigious firm has a prescription for burnout I expect she will take with her to the end of her career. When she feels too stressed, she takes time off. "When I can get the balance right, it's wonderful. I love the kind of work I do, the people I work with; it's a wonderful firm to work for. But when I work more than I want and things get out of perspective, it gets to the point where I don't like working. So I try to balance it back out. I take extended vacations. I need them for my health and stability. I just tell the partners I have to go and I go."

This taking time off to get back a feeling of control over one's life starts early in women's lives, whereas it rarely starts at all in men's lives. An engineer who had just turned 30 said she uses her time completely differently from the men. "They come in early and stay late and accomplish less than I do. I take care of my self to be more productive. I don't go to coffee for forty-five minutes every day, but if I need a long lunch to be more productive, I will. It sounds like I'm antisocial, but I don't want to listen to them complain. I'm not going to spend time worrying about unimportant things. I focus on what's important and just Xerox other stuff to be read later. I balance my life better than they do. They think only about careers and retirement. The women I know have no concept of retirement. They never say, well, in ten years I'll be vested, so I better stay here."

A landscape architect, age 45, thinks that her generation is more work centered and juggles more than the younger generation who don't seem as work oriented. "I don't mean they are less ambitious, but they do seem to have found cleverer ways to balance things than we did ... and at less personal cost. Lots of young women specifically want to practice out of their homes, which is one way to achieve balance. Now the men in my age group are asking, why am I here and who am I? We women are lucky. We start going through this self-examination much earlier, so we're pretty good at it by now and good at changing jobs to keep balanced."

A 45-year-old broker told me that a year previously she had realized her goal of making it in seven years after starting late, after her family was raised. "At that point I decided to lay back, because what's been important to me was proving to myself that I could do this. But the pressure to produce never lets up. There's always a big push from January 1 to April 15 to sell more IRAs. I dread it every year because I figure I'm going to do the same those months as I always do. So I took off this January on a two-week cruise to celebrate our twenty-fifth wedding anniversary. Well, that's unheard of—until now."

"Men do more overtime, go for more money than women. Women ask to be laid off after a while," said a 30-year-old carpenter. "We like to make good money and get time off too. We never thought we could make so much money, but the work is hard. It's cold and miserable, and you get so tired you just come home, shower, and go to bed. It's sad, though, that the men are so unimpressed with their wages and don't think that they make good money. They should have that satisfaction."

## OUR GREATER READINESS TO QUIT

Britain's number one television newsanchor was a woman named Sue Lawley. She was so good that the system kept dumping more and more assignments on her to the point where she finally said, I quit. She had four children and a husband who was only home on weekends, and finally, she had a midlife crisis reminiscent of Gail Sheehy's in *Passages* (1976, pp. 2–10). Confronting death in friends and strangers helped her see that she was so caught up in clock watching, deadlines, lists, and timetables, that she wasn't really living. She had never deserted her job; she had never neglected her children or kept her house anyway other than pin-neat. She had neglected one person, however—herself. So in May 1988, she quit (Grove, 1988a), and I'll bet that every women who read about Sue Lawley understood, but probably very few men did.

"Even a very competitive, aggressive woman lawyer recognizes there are other things in life besides her job. Lots of men lawyers are consumed by their jobs," said an ex-teacher, now lawyer. "We don't get consumed. I have a male friend, a sensitive, neat guy, who is watching his life slipping by as he works seventy hours a week. He will have his name on that partners' list, if he lives past forty. In contrast, I have a woman friend who had a job with the most prestigious firm in town, but she asked herself one day, why am I so miserable? Because she was totally sacrificing herself to a job where she was expected to work more than seventy hours a week. So she quit" (Attorney, age 40).

One reason men die younger than women is that (unless made redundant) they are expected to work at the time of life when they are the most worn out, the frailest, the sickest. Maybe having to work through this time is the thing that kills men a year after retirement, not the stress of the actual change. Age affects our ability to cope with stress, that is, the older we get, the less easy it is. How much of men's premature dying is because of a sex-role expectation to work when they are too old for the aggravation?

There are all kinds of laws around the world having to do with the age at which women and men can retire, start drawing social security, and receive a pension. In no instance is the age at which the women can stop working above that of men. Why is this? If 55 is right for us, or 62 or 65, why shouldn't that also be right for men?

Another factor influencing stress is how much we think we are loved and appreciated. If you know your boss can hardly wait for you to retire, when you are feeling unloved, unsupported, and unappreciated at work, a failure in comparison to your earlier years, this puts even more stress on an older worker. Next to needing a spouse's love, we need our employer's love. How awful for men who see no out but to keep hanging in there, knowing they aren't pleasing the boss as they used to, afraid of being laid off, and not allowed by law to retire gracefully at a more humane time in life.

Women have the attitude advantage I discussed at the beginning of this chapter. We don't *feel* we're forced to stay in a situation that is no longer satisfying, and if we do stay and work just as long as the men, our mindset is that if things get bad enough, we'll quit and get on with something else. This different point of view gives women a tremendous advantage over men in dealing with stress. We feel that we are in control, that we have options, that we do not have to work if it becomes unbearable—this is our attitude.

Our attitude is built on the residue from years past when it was completely okay for us to leave our career at any point from midtraining to preretirement but not okay for men. Even today we get social support and approval when we quit, particularly when we have children at home or if our job is male dominated and thus thought to be more stressful for a woman. Men deserve the same support when they feel they've had enough.

A 37-year-old engineer who didn't like teaching and switched said that guys will stay forever in a job they hate. "Guys become engineers for the money. Women become engineers because it's interesting. I'm still going to school, working on a master's, so that I can be aware of newer stuff that's coming out. The men just want to put in 30 years and retire. Whether they do it well is beside the point. We are interested in the profession and want to do our best. If not, we wouldn't be in it. We'd get out of it."

A firefighter, age 28, said that if it came to having happiness or having money, she'd quit. "I'd rather have the happiness; the men would rather have the money. If it came down to where I was truly unhappy here and it was messing up my homelife, I would quit. The money wouldn't keep me here even though it's a big part of why I'm here. Some of the men would stay at it and divorce first. I think you find that in any job. I'm more willing to quit. My pride might take hold, but I don't think it would. Men are more likely to just sit around for the rest of their career and cuss about it the whole time and be unhappy, whereas if I'm unhappy, I'll change."

Many blue-collar women simply walked off jobs if the health and safety practices were poor. They wouldn't put up with it. "Being our own bosses, we get to take the time to do all the safety things. Some bosses don't allow time for this. If I worked for such a boss, I'd quit. Nobody can pay me enough to hurt myself. I'll never break my back for money. It's always been easy for me to quit jobs. Most men have a hard time with the idea that they might be out of work, and that makes them put up with unsafe, unhealthy working conditions" (Carpenter who coowns remodeling business, age 31).

In middle age, the physical stress of blue-collar jobs may cause some women to quit. "I don't want to be puttering around anymore on the outside of a ship when I'm fifty," said a 36-year-old electrician. "For my job I climb around anywhere from 150 to 200 feet in the air standing on a guard rail. I just can't picture myself at fifty years old doing that. I'd like to get into a job where I can learn some more. I'd like planning; that's still blue collar. Basically, you order the material for the jobs. There'd be no money difference, just a change of learning process and a change of scenery."

## LESS STRESSED BECAUSE WE'RE LESS COMMITTED?

I don't want to create the wrong impression. I don't want women's greater readiness to quit to be misinterpreted as lack of commitment to work. My point is that we are not committed to work in the same way that men are.

But women are extremely committed to work. The statistics to prove it are summarized in Barbara S. Deckard's 1983 book, *The Women's Movement*. Deckard (pp. 94–95) documented that women are not absent more often and do not quit jobs more often than men. We have equal absenteeism and turnover rates, in spite of dropping out to have children and taking care of all of the housework, when three factors are controlled for: skill level, age, and length of service to employer.

Aggregate statistics may show that we quit our jobs more often but only because so many of us are in low-level jobs where work conditions and pay are so poor and turnover for both men and women is very high.

If women and men are compared at similar job levels and under similar circumstances, however, they have the same attendance and turnover records, said Deckard (p. 95).

This proof of equal commitment shouldn't hide the important sex difference this chapter is about: Men's commitment to work is borne of conditioning and socialization that make them think they have no options but to stay at the same grindstone until they die. Women aren't as willing to pay that price in stress and years of living.

# IV

# *Skillful at Organizing*

---

Many women have a remarkable ability to do many things at one time. Yet has anyone really written about it, directly? It just seems to be something we know and recognize throughout women's literature.

It is behind the way we behave with friends, talking about a myriad of topics and keeping track of past shared confidences, as Susie Orbach and Luise Eichenbaum described in *Bittersweet* (1987, p. 16). It is also behind Doris Lessing's depiction, in *The Diaries of Jane Somers* (1983, p. 65), of a conversation between two sisters. One is a housewife, one a career woman. They have nothing in common, except a fascination with organizing large-scale projects. Knowing "how it all works" made them like one another after all.

Women who talk about our organizing ability tend to connect it with the socialized housewife role. The most grotesque example of this is Margaret Thatcher, who said she is good at running the country because she is a good housewife. After a chapter devoted to this theme, "Doing Many Things at One Time," its natural successor follows, the chapter "Women's Managerial Potential."

The interesting thing is that very few of the women interviewed had taken even one course in business administration. Only a handful ran their own business. They are *not* organizational women. But they had all developed organizational skills from their early sex-role socialization.

What writers should one mention of the many who have written about women's managerial potential? "Feminine rhetoric" is how Sheryl Pearson depicted women's management style in her chapter in Barbara Forisha and Barbara Oldman's *Outsiders on the Inside* (1981, pp. 62–68). This feminine style is characterized by respectful downward communication, humanized feedback, collaborative problem-solving skills, listening skills, ways of talking that avoid conflict and promote integration, and respect for different points of view. It comes from women's private sphere, home, and how we are taught to manage people in it.

*Women's Work, Men's Work* by Virginia Novarra (1980, p. 51) describes women's managing less academically. When women manage, Novarra said, we are accessible, unstuffy, informal, direct in getting to the point, spontaneous, averse to wrangling, sympathetic, and not long-winded or pompous.

Elizabeth Nickles and Laura Ashcroft's *The Coming Matriarchy* (1981, pp. 206–207) referred to women's style, as do many other writers, as "Beta leadership style." Women, they said, use power as a means, rather than an end goal. Power is for the good of the group, not the individual. Good management means sensitivity to those not in power and creating a work environment that fosters growth and learning. Beta power cares more about the quality of work life and uses flexible schedules, job sharing, permanent parttime work, and decentralization of authority. No more chief executive officer (CEO) at the top of the hierarchy making decisions.

The chapter devoted to women's managerial potential then leads naturally to the last chapter in Part IV concerning women's different ideas about power. The first theorists to mention are four who inspired *Women Changing Work*. Women are socialized to be more democratic, egalitarian, and cooperative, said Adrienne Rich, Arlie Hochschild, Aleta Wallach, and Florence Howe in their chapters in Howe's *Women and the Power to Change* (1975). Thus Rich spoke of dehierarchizing the male-dominated workplace. In her view, the best way to equalize the position of women in these pyramids based on sex, age, color, and class is to establish childcare centers. These facilities should be available to all within the organization and staffed by women and men, old and young, parents and nonparents (1975, pp. 36–37).

"Why should women go to law school?" asked Aleta Wallach (1975). Her answer was, so that they could get *power* and thus change the laws that men have made which dictate women's debased status (p. 99). Women lawyers need power to humanize the basic institutions of society according to women's nurturant values (p. 123).

However, said Florence Howe (1975), women are not out to reduce men's power as we gain power. This view of power as finite and as a commodity is men's view (p. 131). Women have an alternative view of power based on sisterhood, which involves first gaining power and control over one's own life and then using power to achieve political goals (p. 139). Interestingly, Howe predicted that it would take several decades before women in nontraditional careers such as medicine, engineering, and architecture would have enough power to significantly change those professions (p. 169).

For Arlie Hochschild (1975, pp. 78–79), bringing women's nurturant values into the workplace also meant replacing men's meritocracy with a more democratic, cooperative structure. It was Hochschild who called for leavening the ethos of making it with the ethos of caretaking. It was she who called for women to have meaningful careers but not on the system's terms. Instead, women should institutionalize a balance between competition and cooperation and between doing well and doing good.

Anne Schaef, too, in *Women's Reality* (1981) said that women don't define power as a limited commodity. Domination and control over others is the male definition; for us power is personal power, people being empowered (pp. 124–126). When we help another person have greater control over her life, we don't lose power or control. We create more power. When women manage and organize people, our goal is that power, resources, ideas, and credit for successes be shared collectively.

Judith Bardwick in *In Transition* (1979, p. 58) predicted that women's supportive, humanistic work style will some day be the norm. She wrote about work changing through our encouraging cooperation and discouraging competition. Women must, however, in the short run compete with men for leadership positions. Only by getting quantum numbers of women in powerful roles can we increase other peoples' self-security and self-respect to the point where they have personal power and control of their lives.

Much of the "Leading with Our Kind of Power" chapter is devoted to the state legislators who confirm Jeane Kirkpatrick's earlier findings reported in *Political Woman* (1974, pp. 143–157). Kirkpatrick's women described government in terms of solving social problems. They didn't have a marketplace concept of government where competition and self-interest reigned. Their concept of government was the public service conception within which constituents were most important because *you* were representing *them*.

I think this lack of separation between the goals of Kirkpatrick's legislators and their constituents mirrors the lack of separation for women between the public and private spheres. Traditionally, to men belonged the public sphere, to us the private sphere. But it is the men who have wanted to keep the spheres and men and women divided. For women, today at least, the division makes no sense.

Women's political concerns overlap the public and private. For us, all of the following are political decisions: domestic violence, day care, abortion, rape, the homeless, food stamps, infant and maternal health, sex discrimination, divorce, prostitution, care for the elderly, pornography, and pay equity, as well as masculine subjects such as business and industry, transportation, taxes, natural resources, defense, and war.

Janet Flammang has edited a volume called *Political Women* (1984), which testifies, chapter after chapter, to what she called women's "politics of connectedness" (pp. 11–13), meaning that the personal is political and the political is personal. We can't separate abstract on-paper solutions from the reality of individuals' daily lives. For women, there is no distinction between public and private, work and home, one's government and one's community. This dichotomy of men's has got to go.

But can we change men and work with our different notions of power? Elizabeth Janeway (1985) is optimistic. Through the three "powers of the weak," we can get those few men who are terrified by other men's notions of power to bargain with us. Some men, she said, want our talent, energy, and intelligence (pp. 333–336). What are the three powers of the weak? First, there is a distrust of men's definition of power and a trust in our own; second, there is bonding with others through which we gain self-confidence and a sense of control over our lives; and third, there is joint action together, inside and outside of the patriarchal structure (pp. 330–332).

# 10

# DOING MANY THINGS AT ONE TIME

I can balance a multitude of projects and priorities. Like any housewife, I am used to doing sixteen things at the same time. I can change
diapers, knit, read the *Christian Science Monitor*, write a letter to my
mother, read to the kids, watch TV. I automatically do as many
things as I can. My husband can only do one thing at a time. It would
never occur to him to do two things at once. (Landscape architect,
age 42)

I considered calling this chapter "Why Mothers Make Great Landscape
Architects" because of the above remark. This landscape architect currently works parttime as the marketing coordinator for a medium-sized
architectural firm. She told me that architects have to keep at least six
projects going at once. As a housewife she already has her brain programmed for several ongoing projects, so it's easy to keep track of deadlines, meetings, checklists, and approvals. However, landscape architects
weren't the only women able to do many things at one time. It turned
out to be a certifiable sex difference in all ten occupations.

American and British women alike continue to hone this ability as we
face up to governmental philosophies that dictate that more and more
caring will be done at home, by us. We couldn't take it on if we weren't
programmed to think about, plan, organize, reorganize, and carry out
several activities simultaneously.

The ability to do many things at one time is another skill that comes
from the homemaking role, as did the service orientation to clients, our
nurturant attitude toward coworkers, and our attempt to balance career

and homemaking. Women learn it as part of our socialization for managing the house and the children. We develop a knack for switching tracks swiftly and for monitoring chaotic sets of circumstances (Burr, 1987, p. 107).

A firefighter (age 28) said that women's ability to do a lot of different things at one time really stood out in the fire station. "The men tend to have a one-track mind. A lot of times we can have three or four things going on at one time and keep track of them, whereas they need to do one thing at a time. It's just a different way to do things. There is quite a bit of paperwork here, and we're more efficient, more organized about it. I don't know if that's because we've done it for so many generations or what. It's just like in the home. You might be cooking dinner, but you put a load of wash in, you're cleaning something else, and if you have children, you're thinking about them. Our mind is just geared that way."

Our minds get geared that way. But how do men's minds get geared so that it seldom occurs to them to do two things at once? Little boys start out with just as many and as varied interests as little girls. Why not? But by the time they are 33 or so, British men told Mary Ingham (1985, pp. 9–10), the male role simply consists of how they earn their money and what they spend it on. Apart from watching football on Saturday afternoons, washing the car, and tackling do-it-yourself projects on Sunday afternoons, men's only interest was their work. Indeed, their work made them put off and cancel interviews and to meet Ingham only after office hours because they were "invariably up to their eyes in work." The thing that she really didn't understand was that these men so willingly accepted the very real burden of supporting several people and showed no resentment of the way work intruded into their personal lives. They didn't even notice that they worked such long hours.

By the time, then, that men are 35, they are modeling themselves after their one-track-mind fathers, urged on by a consumer-obsessed society that urges them to buy more and more. As for the fact that the women in their lives can do many things at once while they can only do one, I expect very few men have ever noticed. It's a sex difference they aren't even aware of.

Juggling for little girls starts by absorbing how our mothers do it and then practicing under their tutelage. A 39-year-old stockbroker said that "we have balanced different aspects of our lives, even as girls. We helped our mothers at home, did our homework, helped the teacher, sold cookies for scouts, babysat for neighborhood women, had our hobbies, practiced the piano. Females have always juggled different tasks. So as grownups we are better equipped to organize the volumes of information a broker must handle, from clients, the market, transaction legalities.

There is so much information coming in, there is so much room for disorganization, which is why brokers are required to have [female] sales assistants."

A 30-year-old engineer notices the difference in her parents to this day. "Women engineers are much better organizers and planners, that's one thing women bring to their work. But that's not limited to engineers. When I look at my Mother! My Dad gets up, goes to work, that's it. My Mother, in a given day [she rattled off a string of activities], she's accomplished so much more. We're better organizers, better long-range planners. My mind automatically starts working on other problems in meetings. I let it go ahead and do problem solving. Men don't do that. But I hear from other women that the notes they make in meetings are from this kind of thinking."

There are five topics in this chapter. First, successfully juggling meant that the women wanted to get the full picture first. Where were they headed? How does this project start, what happens in the middle, what does the end look like? Second, the women sometimes wanted more time to do a job because of other peripheral, complicating activities. Third, off the job, the women had more going on in their lives, more hobbies and commitments, of a much greater variety than men's sports. Fourth, homemaking had taught them organizational skills that made them good at managing and balancing several projects and the people involved in them at work. Finally, they were not interested in playing God and doing it all alone, because it was also fun to organize helpers.

## LIKING TO SEE THE FULL PICTURE

Liking to see the full picture was expressed in a variety of ways. It was tied up with the women getting up in the morning and planning how they were going to get everything that must be done squeezed in somehow. They consulted the calendar. They needed a general idea of the week as well—and the month and the year. If you manage a home and family, you must be a long-range planner.

"We were brought up to take care of other people, to manage things around the house, to see the beginning and end of various processes," said a 45-year-old emergency room physician. "This gives us a broader understanding of patients' needs. So in the doctor's office we're thinking, 'How did this start? How will what happens here affect patients in the future?' We think of before and after, and we feel responsible for the patient's family, the whole idea being that we are used to managing households and always juggling many things of a varied nature. Why hasn't this occurred to more corporations? Any women who is in my age group not only has mastered her education, career, the household arts, entertaining, cleaning, and cooking but a whole lot of different things we do in addition to keep intellectually alive and aware."

Even if the women hired others to help out at home, they were prepared to do any job themselves. No task was too demeaning. Similarly at work, they knew how to type, file, and run the office machines. They knew the location of people's offices and where supplies were hidden.

Women brokers had learned the whole picture of the brokerage office, and they were willing in a pinch to do everything. "Seventy-five percent of the women know exactly what happens when they hand in money. They know what is going to happen and what to expect. Seventy-five percent of the men don't; they are dependent on their assistants. They don't *care* what happens. They just want to do the orders. They leave it to their assistants to know how the system works. They focus their attention on making money. Women brokers are more willing to step in and do the work. If they need help and the assistant is not there, they go and do it, whereas men will lay it down and come back to it when the assistant returns" (Broker, age 27).

Landscape architects used their knowledge of the informal, inner workings of huge bureaucracies to cut through red tape, rules, and regulations to get jobs done fast. "Working for a government agency, you have to have tolerance and malleability if you're trying to use power from the bottom. My manager gives me jobs that must be finished in a day. When he needs to get something done quickly, all those signoffs et cetera, the best time you can get is a day. I don't use standard procedures. I use cookies, coffee, and calls. I run around, sit around, and stand around. It's just straight manipulation, but it is not demeaning. You have to know the personnel, all the secretaries. Then he gets calls from the top. 'Who the hell's this woman? All this woman's projects are emergencies. Call her off' " (Landscape architect, age 39).

"A 45-year-old undercover agent gave more attention to detail but at the same time was more interested in background and collateral issues than the men were,

"because if an investigation is a long-range thing, it dominoes. You can miss important things in the beginning, so I tend to take a broad view. I'm patient, and I have the ability to wait things out, to allow a situation to define itself and suggest its own resolution. I don't have that 'I want it now' syndrome. One time we had a search warrant to get this company's records. There were records specific to the events we were interested in but other records broader in context. I gathered up everything, stuff that went way beyond our investigation. The guys said, 'Why do you want all that? What are you going to do with those?' Well, we took those boxes years ago, and we're still dealing with the fallout from those other records, other leads. We would not have had the opportunity to go back and get them. My thinking was, 'If he did this on a particular day, he's done the same things on other days.' "

I talked to a 34-year-old woman just starting a carpentry apprenticeship who said she can already see that she looks at things from a different angle then male apprentices do. The difference isn't simply that she has a more positive attitude toward learning. The different angle also has to do with being unwilling to do something until she understands it. "If they tell me what we're going to build, I picture what they're going to do, the shapes, and how they're going to do it. I try to take my time, look at it, make sure I know what I'm doing. I'm not afraid to ask them if I don't understand. I don't want to start something if I don't know what I'm doing and what it's going to look like when it's done."

An electrician, age 30, said her trade fits in with her college major, environmental studies. "The thing I get out of my trade is the beauty of a nice, complete, solid electrical system. It's like an ecosystem. If you do it right, it's neat to see the nice balance you have going. I don't think about what I'm doing. I think about the total picture, about having a balanced system. I really have a desire to do quality work, to make a solid, totally coherent, perfectly done job."

"It could be cultural, it could be our upbringing," mused a 40-year-old shipyard mechanic.

"We were trained to manage a house, and working isn't that much different. You still have to do your job as efficiently as possible, and you're looking at the finished project, where men have a tendency to be concerned with what they're doing at the moment. They don't care where it came from or where it's going. My male coworkers as a rule just don't seem to take that extra time, those few extra seconds to maybe make sure that things are more or less organized on paper or in their heads before they start the job. They just kind of barrel in and then, whoops! We are more apt to research. We see that we're starting to get into trouble and stop and ask questions. My male coworkers would rather finish the job and worry about whether it's right or wrong afterwards, and we joke about this. The guys are not aware of it."

The engineers said their connection with a life beyond the drawing board made them better engineers. "A person's productivity depends on whether they are conceptual, and the women here have a better ability to conceptualize, to know where the project is at the beginning and where we want to go and what steps it will take to get there. That relates to our ability to see the broad picture, to the fact that there is more to our lives. We also have a better appreciation of the aesthetic visual product, how the product will look. A lot of women engineers are like that. The value of being able to conceptualize before you fill in the details is invaluable in engineering" (Engineer, age 33).

Perhaps the best application of seeing the full picture comes from the chair of a state legislative committee who developed the idea of an ongoing agenda from year to year based on major issues.

"Instead of each session reacting to the problems in that session, we have continuing broad issues. Before, when you came into session, if the big problem was unemployment compensation, that is what you dealt with that session. There was no overall planning. We have taken various issues and have packaged them. We women did this; we packaged them for the floor. If you had several bills dealing with children's issues, they all come out of several committees, and so we wait until several of them are in and we try to get them moving at the same time, and we spend a day or two dealing with children's issues. It makes it so much easier, first of all, to understand the issues and have some continuity. The press love it and we do. Members come to me all the time and say, 'Can't we do an issue package on this thing?' We are motivated by wanting to accomplish something on issues, and we want to make these into categories and get them orderly. We like organization and focus" (State representative, age 56).

## TIME TO DO IT MY WAY

Chapter 7 discussed time versus money. There we saw how women wanted more time for family, domestic responsibilities, and personal revitalization. Here it has to do with wanting more time on the job, rather than more money, so that our job satisfaction on a day-to-day basis is higher.

Some women interviewed wanted more time on the job because they wanted to go about working differently from the standard male way. It wasn't that they were slow or inefficient. It's that they didn't like the pace of men's work, the clock watching, the emphasis on rigid schedules. This need surfaced as well in Chapter 8. The women thought they could do a better job, and a more fulfilling job, if they could determine their own schedules. They would get the job done by whatever final deadline was set, but in the meantime they wanted the freedom to choose their own pace.

A 30-year-old carpenter wouldn't trade more money—which she could have earned in a large production shop—for the freedom and control she had doing custom work in a small shop. "I don't let my wage get me down because I love what I'm doing. I know I'm worth more than I'm making here, but I'd be miserable and the men here would too. It's very satisfying working on one-of-a-kind pieces. But the men are a lot more vocal and think they're being taken advantage of. They want more money now. I'm a lot more patient."

Another carpenter, age 31, said she knew right away that most union jobs were not for her.

"I don't need men's competitiveness. If I worked with all men, I'd continually have to prove myself. I admit that I do some things differently than other carpenters, and I sometimes do things slower. If I worked with men, I'd have to feel bad about that. I don't like to be defensive and on guard. Because I work with women, I'm able to get down to business and enjoy myself. If there were more women carpenters, the pace of this business would slow down. There'd be a lot more room for sharing and being friends. There would be time to ask people how they're feeling. Having a bad day distracts people from their work. If you talk to them and get it off their chest, they can be safer and more productive. Those are the kinds of things women pay attention to."

The brokers believed that all brokers should be spending more company time caring about and being involved in "community things." They did not mean the company pressuring everyone to donate to the United Way campaign so that the company could brag that they got 100 percent compliance. "We should give more to the community and hopefully receive something back. I don't think we do enough of that. Maybe we don't always have to grow more and get bigger and bigger, and we should focus on what we are good at, and that is giving personal service. So we should not be so big that we can't afford to care about the community" (Broker, age 32).

## HAVING MANY AND VARIED INTERESTS

When men do allow themselves time for recreation, it almost always has to do with sports—active, spectator, or, at least, televised. Women, on the contrary, feel free to have any interest men traditionally have had, in addition to all our own traditional interests. How many women now bicycle, run, or play softball? How many women now take care of their own cars? How many women figure out do-it-yourself projects on their own without even thinking of asking for help? How many women calculate the family income tax and take vacations alone?

A 30-year-old second-year medical student noticed that fewer men in medical school were interested in psychosocial issues. "In terms of extra projects and political groups, these are all female dominated. There may be fifteen percent men, the rest women. I think it's because we have always done many things at the same time. I would like to see medicine go towards making less money and spending more time with patients. I was an art major before going into this and happened to get interested in medicine by working in a hospital in recreation rehabilitation. My husband is an artist. We make time for each other. My dream is to practice medicine internationally. I've been talking to a group of people who would like to set up a group practice where we could take off every three years and do volunteer work in other countries."

A 34-year-old landscape architect who owns her firm keeps her mind loose by pursuing interests other than occupational ones. "The problem with landscape architects is that they become narrow and introverted, so I am heavily involved in an arts commission, and also by starting my own business, I have more time to write and pursue that edge between art and landscape architecture. When I am 90 years old, I want to be able to look back and say I have explored and pursued with great intensity all the concerns I have and that I have not led my life following a wave of some corporation."

To me the most fascinating arena for observing male–female sex differences in interests is the blue-collar world. It is true that many of the women who joined the trades in the 1970s because of the women's movement were college graduates weary of secretarial and teaching jobs. They brought with them the broad, cultural interests college is designed to instill. Thus to find them drawing comparisons between their hobbies and recreation and those of the men isn't surprising. But when tradeswomen from blue-collar families complain that the men are too boring because they don't have much to talk about—just the job, football, and bars—higher education has to be seen as only part of this sex difference.

A carpenter–mason, age 31, with three years of college in accounting said that women were more concerned about being a whole person. "Most of the men have work and their family and that's all. All the women carpenters I know have a whole other life outside of work. I was having lunch recently with the women in my shop and one man. We were talking about all our activities, who was knitting or crocheting what, who was doing sports, who was taking this class or that class. The man was floored. He said, 'You do all those things? How?' I think this impacts the work we do because if you feel whole, if you feel good about yourself, that makes you a better worker. If you can give your all in activities you enjoy, you can give your all at work."

A 34-year-old electrician with a bachelor's degree in fine arts met me at an apartment house she manages in addition to her regular job. She keeps in shape with aerobics and Kung-Fu. She tutors refugees in English. "Basically I got into it for the constant learning. It's interesting to learn new things along the way, and there are a lot of evening classes offered. I also like to have control of my time. I can work a certain number of months and then get laid off or quit. I like to do other things. So I don't want to work overtime. I like my eight hours and that's it. I save my money, and I will make a trip to Brazil this next year. I went to China a couple of years ago and Europe seven years ago."

What about craftswomen from blue-collar backgrounds? Some of them have always had many interests. "I like doing things, I like to keep busy," said a 36-year-old electrician. "I have rented three stalls in malls, little areas you can rent. I've got gifts, bells, crystal, figurines, combs, jewelry, silver, some used items. It cost about $15,000 to buy the stock and the shelving. I have my own display areas, and I don't have any overhead. The mall supplies the sales people, so I don't have to be there, but eventually I want my own place where I can sell my crocheting and crafts items. Oh, no, I have no intention of giving up my job!"

For others, the job itself gave them exposure to the varied interests highly educated women enjoyed. They adopted life-styles that went beyond the old blue-collar expectation that women stayed at home and were only interested in the home.

One 39-year-old crane operator, for example, thought her mind finally started working when she became a single parent and had to learn a trade. To help her get more confidence, she took her first class since high school, a human effectiveness class at the shipyard at lunch time. "They teach you that you can do anything you put your mind to. So I keep taking classes, and I read a lot too now. I never used to read at all. There are so many things you can learn about yourself from reading, things you've done with your kids wrong. I think of myself a lot more highly now than I used to, and I try to do more things, expand. Before, I'd sit home all the time, but now I do so many things, I'm never home."

## ORGANIZATIONAL SKILLS

A physician talked about her children, her practice, the articles she writes, her research. "You have to be very organized to work full time as a doctor and have a family. Compared to the men I know, I'm very organized but nothing like my friend who went into practice with some men and they decided to build the office themselves. She not only participated in designing the building, but once it was built, she was the only one who could go in and organize everything. The men were absolutely incompetent" (Physician, age 43).

*Women at the Top* (1977, p. 18) by Joan Wheeler-Bennett is based on questionnaires and interviews with sixty-five British women, all married with families, who held high-level jobs in a variety of occupations including law, medicine, and science. One reason they were successful was economic, that is, they had the money to buy other women's labor to clean their houses and look after their children. They could never have worked at all but for these women, because they all subscribed to the belief that a woman's most important job in life is to look after her husband and children.

Another reason they were successful, however, was their ability to organize. Their jobs were not organizational, as I have indicated. They were psychiatrists, television producers, university lecturers, and architects. But organization on a personal level was necessary for them to hold jobs; priorities had to be sorted out, they said, and they were good at that (Wheeler-Bennett, 1977, pp. 33–34). They developed an unusual talent for organization, both at work in relation to staff and at home in relation to children, husbands, and helpers (p. 57).

It is clear, reading Wheeler-Bennett, that it was at home that these women learned to balance, delegate, keep lists, and set priorities. It was at home they learned to be well rounded, versatile, balanced, and many sided. It was at home that they absolutely had to keep things in perspective and be utterly flexible. How very easy, then, to take all this organizational skill and apply it at work.

Flexibility and the ability to juggle were also what the legislators who started politics after childrearing said they brought from home.

"Consequently, we are more organized and we are better at balancing, and we always do two things at once. Most of us had to do that to get here. Well, you don't go out and do a single errand! You pile things up, and you do everything when you go out. You get people to help, and you organize your life the best you can, and I know almost no man does that. It is simply because we have always had to do so many other things at once, rather than concentrate on one thing. So we are better organized and better able to handle variety. We don't need the kind of supports that men need. We are better able to take care of our own lives, our families' lives, *and* the legislature. This is the distinct female experience that we bring here. We are in the middle of a fight now over who will be the speaker. Two men are involved. The one thing that all the women agree on, no matter what side we're on, is that both the candidates are totally disorganized" (State representative, age 58).

Another legislator (age 56) said that the interesting thing to her was that most women never have the luxury of concentrating on one thing, like the corporate manager who has a mission and shuts everything else out. "We have never had the opportunity to do that. I recall shoving food into the baby's mouth sitting in the high chair, keeping the other two toddlers from killing each other and keeping the mush from going over on the stove, and reading my packet for my League meeting that was going to go on that night. We are really suited for this arena because you don't have much chance to focus on one thing at a time. You have to be aware of so many things at once. Most of us bring that with us."

"So," said another 49-year-old state representative, "I stuff those myself (point to large pile of mailers), answer the phone, cook a meal, and organize at the same time. Men have got to get somebody else to do everything—hire consultants, rent campaign offices, get a mail house, overkill with it. My senator constantly tells me he has got to have $50,000 to run for office. He asked me, 'How much did you spend for the primary?' 'Four thousand.' 'How did you do it for so little?' Why don't they let us take over the budgeting process for the state? We could cut the budget by at least a billion and still do everything the money's going for now."

Women in the skilled trades, attracted to working with things and with their hands, just like the men, were also noticeably more adept at organizing men and machines. They said maybe it came from being a mother, both the organization and the compassion. Their husbands accused them of having too many things going all at once, but they retorted that they wouldn't be happy any other way.

An electrician (age 34) said she keeps finding herself managing. "They keep asking me to do it. Like on Friday the foreman had to leave, so he put me in charge of locking up, seeing that all the trucks were in the yard and everything squared away. I try to get along with every person. The manager has to get along. The men *do* want women electricians to succeed. They really do want me to succeed. It makes them happy. They'd like me to be a foreman."

"I didn't get into the trade to get into management, but I can see me falling into it just by watching how things happen," sighed a 40-year-old shipyard mechanic. "I know if *he* can do it, I can do it. I have a teaching kind of aptitude, which is the same thing as managing, handling people. I'm seeing things fall that way. You go out to do a job and you organize it out of self-defense. Well, somebody's got to do it. Nobody's doing it, so I end up doing it. Somehow I get the job done even though other people do parts of it. We've got to get the job done and I'm good at planning."

## NO GODDESS SYNDROME

Rosemary Burr in *Female Tycoons* (1987, p. 67) said that a lot of male tycoons suffer from what she called "The God Syndrome." They want to do their jobs all by themselves. They aren't willing to share the responsibility. Gods like to go it alone. But it takes a lot of time.

Women tycoons, on the other hand, not only have to run the business but also have to look after staff, customers, husband, housekeeper, nanny, children, one's social life, the children's social life, the nanny's social life, and the price of groceries and laundry. They also do a lot of charity work, devote whole weekends to children's activities, and make time for themselves. So they can't afford to play goddess or have a syndrome.

For their three basic jobs, businesswomen tycoons hire at least three helpmates: a secretary, a housekeeper, and a nanny (Burr, 1987, p. 97). Then with "extremely good organization," "split second timing," and "attention to detail" through itineraries, lists, and posted priorities, they do just fine.

To help them get their jobs done, the brokers we interviewed often shared responsibility with money managers. They said men brokers loathed money managers because they took away control and money. "Men like to pick stocks. They like to have big egos up there. But I learned that if I spend a year opening an account with a pension and profit-sharing plan for a million dollars, I can then turn it over to a money manager. That is all he does. He puts transactions through. He makes those decisions. If he doesn't make good decisions, then I fire him. A male broker has a real tough time using managers whereas we women went right to it. We never had the control, for the most part, anyway. So it is easier for us to turn it over. But men have boundaries, territory, and, God forbid, they should give up any of it" (Broker, age 45).

To help them get their jobs done, women engineers gracefully accepted their complete dependence on their support staff, whereas men, in a sense, fought it. The men held on to activities that didn't require engineering degrees, whereas the women thought that other people, with a little appropriate training, could do those things and free themselves for higher level work. "I need a draftsman as much as he needs me. All the ideas I have aren't worth one iota unless they can be put on paper. It doesn't matter how many wonderful creative designs I have because no one is ever going to see them unless they do their part, use their skills. They need me and I need them, and I don't feel superior to them. That's probably why they put other people's work aside to work on mine. It's a very nice feeling" (Engineer, age 30).

## NO TIME FOR BLAME

Anne Schaef's *Women's Reality* (1981, p. 136) contains an interesting example of women's ability to do many things at one time and be organized without having an organizational chart or accountability-blame system.

Schaef consulted, maybe annually because the problem was perennial, with a school personnel office that had a staff of eleven women and one man. The office functioned smoothly except for the fact that the man lasted only one year. Each year they had to get another one. The man in charge would always be disturbed by the office's "lack of organization." In spite of the fact that everything got done, well and on time, he would say that they couldn't run an office that way because they had to decide who is accountable for this and who is responsible for that. The women always asked "Why?" and proceeded to frustrate his ideas about organization. So at the end of a year of trying to get the women to accept some formal accountability-responsibility system, he'd move on.

You have to reckon that the eleven women had a very efficient, informal, unaccountable, everyone-is-responsible-for-everything system going, or *they* would have been fired. What they needed was a woman boss who understood that responsibility to them meant the ability to respond and get the job done. It didn't matter that much who did what, because they had the attitude, we're all capable and willing to do the different tasks in a project. "Doesn't matter" probably isn't strong enough. Sometimes women believe it's *better* if we're all capable and willing to do any of the different tasks in a project.

You have to feel sorry for male supervisors wedded to the white male system, though, when they're trying to institute the responsibility-blame concept to a group of women to whom it just doesn't make sense.

# 11

# WOMEN'S MANAGERIAL POTENTIAL

---

I've worked with two female officers, and they have a less authoritarian approach. Everything seems to get done, and the people who work under them, they probably enjoy it because they still get the message across. But it's not like, "You can step on me and I'll do anything you say." The way they give an order or ask for something to be done is more polite, and people appreciate that because they feel like they're being treated with a little bit more respect. (Firefighter, age 32)

From Helen Franks' 1984 book, *Goodbye Tarzan*, I remember Eric, a social scientist who admitted that he felt lost in departmental meetings in which women predominated. He missed the way men did business, in a logical, direct, straight-line fashion, one thing at a time. These women, incomprehendingly, were absorbing hosts of seemingly unrelated material into their planning; yet somehow decisions got made and the work completed in the time available (p. 176).

I didn't expect sex differences in management or leadership style to come up in a big way in the interviews because I wasn't interviewing managers. I thought perhaps the legislators or an aspiring chief of police might comment on women's different management style, but that would be all. I was in for a surprise.

What happened, across the board, in all ten occupations, was that women, given the opportunity, relished managing and organizing. They were drawn to organizing people, data, and things, in spite of the fact that organizing was not what they were hired for. Without formal train-ing, without MBAs, they interacted spontaneously with coworkers in a style that is certainly more Beta than Alpha.

As Betty Friedan described these two management styles in *The Second Stage* (1981, p. 244), the feminine Beta style is the opposite of the mas-culine Alpha style. The Alpha style means being authoritarian, hierar-chical, competitive, and controlling and has clear win–lose solutions. The Beta style is relational, supportive, consensus building, tolerant of di-versity and ambiguity, sharing, and open to change.

The employers of these nontraditional women clearly wanted them to take on management activities. But they did not necessarily want to pay the women for it or promote them for it. In fact, I think the em-ployers were blatantly coopting the women's capabilities. What is im-portant here, though, is that their bosses recognized that the women had this capability and valued it.

What I found is similar to what Betty Friedan, Rosemary Burr, and Leah Hertz reported. In both the United States and the United King-dom, according to Hertz' *The Business Amazons* (1986), successful women business owners practice a totally feminine style of management, that of the "matriarchal boss." Throughout her book, the women interviewed drew parallels between running companies and families. Quite simply, the company was like a family, the employees like one's children.

Hertz' millionaire business owners had a soft, interpersonal manage-ment style. They paid employees well and took a very personal interest in their lives and welfare. They took a personal interest because they wanted harmonious relationships at work, just as a mother wants har-mony at home. They did not worry about money; they worried about people. When they expanded their businesses, they said they did it for their workers (1986, p. 250).

Rosemary Burr's (1987) British "female tycoons" treated staff the same sympathetic way, although Burr called it "paternalistic." They convinced others to follow, rather than pull rank. They placed great stress on a pleasant working environment. They tried to conciliate and talk things through. They did not have a "them versus us" attitude toward em-ployees but promoted a team approach and tried to see problems from the staff's point of view (pp. 104–105).

There are six topics in this chapter. "Women's intuition" about people was the first aspect to the management style the women told me about. They depended on it to match the right people with the right jobs. Second, they gave people more praise than men typically do. Third, they gave orders in a nonconfrontational, polite, and motivating way. Fourth, the women said, they were more sensitive to the needs of the people at the bottom of the hierarchy, and fifth, they sought consensus on just about everything. Finally, they may not have played football or baseball in high school, but they were all for teamwork based on mutual trust.

## INTUITIVE ABILITY ABOUT PEOPLE

We believe, the women said, in letting each person do what he or she is best at. They delighted in finding out what everyone's skills were and then finding the niche that was going to make each person happy and productive. The legislators said that the most efficient way to solve problems was practicing a philosophy of "I'll do what you want me to, *not* because you are the official leader but because this is your area of expertise, and then I expect *you* to do what *I* say when it is *my* area of expertise."

A 30-year-old electrician noticed that women bosses paid more attention to workers as individuals. "They're more interested in individuals' strong and weak points. That's what good management is all about, making the crew more efficient by taking everyone's individuality into account. Women also see the best partnerships by listening to how people get along. We are also more patient and accepting when people show their inconsistencies. We don't say, 'You've made a big mistake; you're dumb,' that's not our way. We're more patient with people's deficiencies."

A 28-year-old civil engineer works for a firm with 200 engineers, 20 of whom are women. Not one woman had yet been made head of a technical department, so she thought that the greatest impact of more women would be their breaking through as managers. "And women managers are more concerned about people's personal preferences in work, whether this person would rather work on this project or that. They'll pay more attention to the individual. I would like to work on more treatment-type projects, where you design the secondary treatment for a sewer plant. It takes more creativity; it's more involved, takes more thought than pump stations and pipelines, where it's this is the way you do it, this diameter, this slope. But my present boss keeps giving me pipelines even though I've told him I'd like a change."

Here is an example of the way an engineer (age 33) recognized another woman's managerial talent. "I have delegated to my second in command the supervision of all the design engineers. It's a way in which her people skills can work. She does regular reviews, is accessible, knows when to tell me about a problem. She talks to people who are complaining and finds out both sides of the problem, from below and above in management. She is very good dealing with the people and knowing what to do to solve the problem. Not only does she listen, but she also cares about the people reporting to her."

Women's intuitive ability about people was especially valued by management in meetings. The women got more out of meetings by turning on their feeling, clinical side. An electrical engineer's boss, when they had left a group, would close the door and say, " ' Well, what'd you think of that meeting? Did you see anything we need to check on? Any potential problems?' That's because I read those meetings. It's so-called women's intuition, and it's valued by my boss. Men have it, too, but they just don't pay attention to it. I pay attention to people's feelings; I watch what they're doing. These guys aren't direct; they're not coming out and saying things, or they're not understanding what's being said and not admitting it. I really enjoy gently pulling someone back who is being very technical, very theoretical, and everyone's getting mad at him and they don't agree with him, and he's so off in a fog he doesn't even know it" (Engineer, age 30).

These women engineers were very proud of their intuitive skills. They saw them as essential to getting work done. One energetic woman has dropped all her inhibitions about questioning how well projects are being coordinated. "If you stay on top of things 'til you're half way through, you get a feel for who does what well and who the airheads are you'll have to cover for. Or if we have a problem, I say, 'How can we get this person to feel good about their situation?' For example, in our structural department we used to make new graduates just out of school do shop drawings for three years. That's terrible! They need interesting things to do like everyone else, but no one but me sensed it was a problem" (Civil engineer, age 28).

Sometimes the women's sensitivity told them not to go for the "best" match. A metals engineer (age 31) said she was in charge because she met deadlines and was good at picking people for different parts of projects. "I had this upset man, and I let him do higher level work than I *thought* he could. Because he was so frustrated I gave him a chance, versus giving it to someone I *knew* could do it better. My common sense said not to, but my heart said give him a chance. It's working out. I have to dog him a little. He's happy though, and that's half the battle. If someone is happy, they will work better."

## PRAISING PUBLICLY

Praise is a very important management tool. Which is another reason why women make good managers. Women know how children need praise to thrive and grow and risk trying harder. We know how we need praise as adults to thrive and grow and risk trying harder. Knowing these facts about the power of praise, women are generous with it.

The women gave more praise than male colleagues did, downward, straight across to their peers, and upward to their bosses. They were constantly watching for competence so that they could reinforce it. The men felt differently about giving praise. The women said, in the men's minds a competent performance simply did not deserve praise. You had to be very good to rate a nod and a "well done."

On the other hand, the men adored being praised and didn't mind it for only an adequate performance. They basked in being commended and couldn't win enough prizes and awards. It didn't seem to matter how prominent a man was; he couldn't get enough praise. The more prominent he was, the less he gave praise to other people. Do men think they lose something if they praise another person?

A 34-year-old engineer gave this example of how awkward men were at giving praise. "Human relations is engineering's weakest link. We could certainly teach the men how to deal with people. Engineers are terrible at it. At last Monday's meeting this principal is saying that this project by Joe is outstanding, a really good job, and then he asks a guy where Joe is and Joe is standing right there, and the principal didn't even know who he was, so this praise fell flat. Instead of feeling a pat on the back, the guy was insulted."

A police sergeant, age 36, said her experiences as a mother using praise have helped her be a good supervisor. "My guys get gold stars on their good reports. It's silly and they laugh and they chuckle about it, but they save them. *They save them*! And they like it—stars, smiling faces, all the things that you say to a child that says you've done well. As a mother, I'm aware of the need for that, and a lot of male supervisors are slow to compliment. They're slow to say, 'You did good,' you know, and they are slow to say, 'You're important around here. I need you. You're an important part of this team.' It's easier for me to say, 'I'm not a whole 100 percent officer who can do absolutely everything just as well as everybody else. I have strengths but I need you to fill in the blanks.' "

## KINDLY GIVING ORDERS

"I'm gentler than other supervisors; I show more respect; that's what the people I've supervised have said," related a tradeswoman. "For example, a job came up and we needed laborers, so I called down to the union hall for them. They sent over four guys over 60 and one guy just back from a broken thumb. Most men would have laid them off on the spot. But I thought, 'Okay, we're going to do this.' The overseer was mad. He had wanted to hire nonunion teenagers, but I wouldn't. These older laborers were grateful and very determined to do a good job, and they worked very hard" (Carpenter, age 34).

Here is another female "weakness" that needs to be set straight. What goes into our giving orders kindly? It includes a nonconfrontational style. The landscape architects were loathe to throw their weight around with contractors. "I am more likely to say, 'If we do it this way, such and such will be better, don't you agree?' Less direct is more humane. Most contractors are men in their 50s, and they all have daughters. I am willing to manipulate that fatherly kind of feeling they have, the attitude they have toward their daughters. So I say, 'If we do this, then . . .' and not 'Do this!' " (Landscape architect, age 40)

A polite style is also part of it. A firefighter, age 32, always gets her work done, and her crew gets its work done when she is in charge, but the men tell her she's too nice. "If it was a guy that did it, they wouldn't think he was easy; they would just think he's okay. There's the opposite type, the marine leader who gets the job done because he will kill them if they don't. That's still kind of their ideal style, which is nowhere near what I would ever do. It's easier for me to ask them to do it than order them. If you order them, they're going to be real brats about it. They're responsible people, and they don't like having you tell them. So it would be worse if I tried that style . . . besides I did once and it didn't work!"

An involving style is also important. Rather than tell people what to do, some women used a lead position to train and teach subordinates to make crucial decisions. "I'm in charge on the aid car, and I've noticed that I and the other women explain things more and ask someone to do things, not tell them. Our discipline is never harsh or cruel. When I need to make a decision, I'll always say, 'Well, what do you think? Do you agree that we should do it this way?' And it's not to make sure I'm right. It's to see that we both agree on doing these things, even though I am in charge and we could do it my way. I've worked with people who just say, 'We're sending him to the hospital,' whereas we might not need to. So I'm always asking, 'Do you agree with this?' " (Firefighter, age 28)

A motivating style is involved. Many of the women so disliked the idea of bossing other people around that they literally could not do it. They defended not giving orders by saying that motivation went up the more freedom you gave people. A 32-year-old engineer who has supervised for two years said, "I'm not real strong on riding herd. I let them decide and help them, but I don't want to tell them how to do their work."

As progressive organizations admit that there is more than one effective style of managing, women will be more willing to be a boss. A 39-year-old state trooper was changing her thinking about promotion. "I've never liked the idea of supervising people. I don't like to be 'a boss' or 'bossy.' But I've got enough maturity now within the job, and I think I've got enough experience that there are things that I could help people with, and a lot of the sergeant's job is to help people, not to just boss them and be responsible for them but to show them different ways to do things and also to let them go ahead and make their own mistakes."

The main point of giving orders kindly is that it makes for a relaxed, supportive work environment. A civil engineer (age 28) who works for a huge consulting firm was aghast watching how men treated secretaries as "just someone there to type their letters. They never talk to them. It's just, 'Do this, do that.' I talk to them about clothes, haircuts, what they did over the weekend, and this helps; it makes them more willing to do something for me when I'm in a hurry. It gives them better feelings than if someone's always ordering them about."

So why do men behave this way? Men are overly fond of hierarchy, the women said, whereas they had their doubts about hierarchical relationships and sometimes refused to obey the rules of the game. A 50-year-old electrician who urged the men to change their cruel treatment of apprentices also had this to say about hierarchy. "Well, you have to obey the rules or you will get hurt. But the chain of command is silly because sometimes the person in the lead position doesn't have his wits about him, and yet that's the way life is out there in a man's world—sort of like the military. I have no time for the military chain of command and 'Thou shalt not speak to someone below.' I've never had to defy anyone, but I say to myself, 'I'm going to talk to anyone I like.' "

## SENSITIVITY TO SUBORDINATES' NEEDS

One of my favorite interviews was with a 24-year-old army helicopter pilot who graduated from West Point. Her goal is to fly 747s, and she's going about the career of airline pilot in the traditional male way through military training. Now I know the academy teaches officers to look out for the interests of their people, but she had that extra ounce of sensitivity to the needs of her men.

"If they have a question, I will come back the same day with an answer. I'm there to protect them. I work *for* them. They come first, and I try to help them in their professional life and personal life. Nothing irritates me more than an officer who blows off at an enlisted guy. The enlisted guys come first. In the field I wait for them to eat; then I eat. Everyone likes to have someone above who is thoughtful, who will intercede. My warrant officers are happy to work for me because I step right in there and get my guys as many flights as possible. I tell them, 'You'll make it. I'll see to it that you're PIC (pilot in charge) of an aircraft.' They don't have the career options I do. So even though I'm dying to qualify for PIC as soon as I can, I give up my opportunities for them."

Rosemary Burr's *Female Tycoons* (1987, p. 105) drew a big distinction between women and men business owners' attitudes toward employees. The women owners' attitude was "give them all the facts." The women wanted no barriers between their employees and themselves. So they put no barriers up, and if the employees did, the women calculatingly dissolved them. The women wanted to be approachable. They wanted to work out solutions on the factory floor, together. Rather than dictating to staff how it will be, they wanted people to understand why they were being asked to perform in a certain way.

Part of the "no us versus them" philosophy is exquisite sensitivity to employee needs. One female tycoon sensed an employee was no longer happy in her work. She took the employee aside and discovered she was upset because her schedule now didn't allow her to see her child off to school. So this boss arranged for a car to pick up this mother and bring her to work after she had seen her child off to school. The boss's husband said it never would have occurred to him to do such a thing, and that if it had, he would have rejected the idea (Burr, 1987, p. 104).

One of these U.K. women entrepreneurs' strengths was their ability to see problems from the staff's point of view. When there are more women managers, personal problems, such as the one above, will be dealt with more individually and some, like childcare, more systematically. "They are going to have to put in daycare centers. I'm not kidding, without question. With women making as much as they are in this business, you are going to see a lot more women having children, and they are going to have to pay attention to our needs. We had a lawsuit in this office over sexual harassment, and all the swearing stopped. Males are more careful about what they say and where they say it. That cleaned up the language and some of the actions in many of our offices" (Broker, age 34).

A minor managerial theme is that women believe more than men that if you take care of your people, they will take care of you. "This is the first year that Shearson has ever given bonuses to their salaried people. It is incredible how pleased they are. Another nice thing, for example, at Bill Gates' Microsoft, is the beautiful grounds they have, and they pay for sitters and the kids are happy when they pick them up. You *know* it helps. But the main way managers can take care of their people is salary. I used to feel so bad years ago that the assistants didn't make much money. I'd take all the guilt home; I'd feel so bad. But us bleeding hearts can only do so much. It's got to come from management" (Broker, age 33).

The brokers said that more women in their field would also affect who gets to be manager. Currently, the decision is guided by men's rules: Whoever makes the most money wins and gets to be manager. The broker above said: "We women would say that doesn't make any sense. We would say whoever makes the most money doesn't matter. We need the *best manager*. Typically, too, the lowest jobs in brokerage firms have extremely low pay, no chance for promotion, no chance for bonuses. Yet these people make us run, and we see the value of that. With women in management that is the first thing we would change. We would look at our sisters and understand what they are contributing. To me that is the whole problem with society. Here are these people, as you go out tonight, working their butts off for their six dollars an hour and have three children at home and no husband. They have to be here! Yeah, I think women managers would change things like that."

Firefighters and brokers alike thought that as more women come into their organizations and stay on the job longer, they will move into the higher echelons of management and that then things will really change. In the area of firefighter pensions,

"A lot of men are under the old pension plan and don't want to understand the complexities of the new pension plan. All they know is that the new plan is bad, and they're glad *they* are not part of it, and they object to maternity leave because they think it wouldn't apply to them. So when I talk to them about maternity leave and light duty, I point out the long-term effect for men of having light duty for various health reasons, and I get them to realize how many men are under this new, inadequate plan that nothing's being done about. Get them to see we've got to get back to basics, that we need to look out for *all* our brother and sister firefighters. A good manager can take women's issues and make them issues for both sexes" (Firefighter, age 33).

## COMPROMISE AND CONCILIATION

The legislators described themselves as practical, realistic, and well prepared so that they don't waste anybody's time. "The women, if they have to, can sit down and do it themselves. Men can't, because somebody else organizes them; somebody else does their typing; they don't want to put in the time it takes to be well prepared. Women have a much better sense about when a group is ready to make a decision, what is going to work and what is not. Men are more interested in what kind of game playing they can do to get it their way. Somebody has got to lose, and somebody has got to win is their solution to almost everything" (State representative, age 49).

A 33-year-old engineer talked about her management team that schedules and plans work on all projects. "There are two managers I would label as difficult; they easily have an opinion and are difficult to sway. I try not to back them into a corner, try not to stonewall them, but try to go around, give them room so it's okay to slide sideways. I like to avoid conflict, and they aren't afraid of conflict. I'll back off and try for compromise and consensus even if it takes more time. Sometimes they get their way; sometimes I'm not willing to argue about it. I own 51 percent of the stock, but I try not to pull rank often. It can feel difficult for them to work here if they feel they've lost control or don't have a say."

Many of the women were known for their problem-solving ability. "One of the things I am asked to do constantly," a 55-year-old legislator said, "is resolve problems. When people get in trouble and they can't figure out how to get out of it, I'll say 'Why don't we do this and that,' and they say, 'Yeah, that'll work,' and we go ahead and resolve it. They look to me if they want to resolve it. If they don't want to resolve it, they stay as far away as possible because I'll try to solve it. I don't type well, and I'll never be a Miss America, but I can solve problems. If something doesn't work, I keep thinking to myself, 'How can I make it work?' There is no one-two-three formula for solving problems. But nearly always you start with things you know will work, with consensus, and work from areas of agreement. Pretty soon the areas of disagreement have been resolved, or they aren't important anymore. Problem solving is one of the reasons I enjoy state office so much. I truly, thoroughly enjoy it."

A 41-year-old veterinarian compared herself to her partner: "Women feel they need consensus for everything, while men say take it or leave it. Women don't want any hurt feelings or people feeling bad for days. The big difference between me and my partner if we have problems reaching a decision is that he becomes the authority and dictates what will happen, while I say, 'Okay, you people come to a decision and we'll come to one, and then we'll talk again until we all agree.' It's hard to let control out of your hands, but it is very important to do so."

A software engineer, age 29, said she was the one always going to classes on how to get people to produce more based on how you treat them. "There's no interest in dealing with people in the guys, no interest in management. If you're a manager, people are your business, not technology, and in working with people I always try to get along, try to resolve conflict. For example, I was working with this guy, and my solution was unacceptable to him and he got mad about it and at me. I was upset. I like to think I can get along with everybody, so I try to keep relationships in good working order. So I've tried to work it out with him, and although the problem's not resolved, he's not mad anymore and we're working together again."

## TEAMWORK

What did Rosemary Burr's (1987) female tycoons say about teamwork? They thought it was the natural result of knowing not only your strengths but your weaknesses. You had to put together a team (p. 68). It was stupid to try to do it all on your own. They couldn't manage their homes without depending on other people, so how could they run a multimillion-pound enterprise without a team? The team, like a family, needed to know about profits and reinvestments and the way the company was going. Their automatic response to problems was to talk it out (p. 105).

The foundation of teamwork is trust. A 33-year-old movie-theater owner said she trusted her employees completely and they knew it. "I always let them know I am not protecting anything in the theater from anyone. They know where the money is. They keep their own records of loans. There are no controls. I don't check up to see if anyone's taking candy bars. I get an amazing amount of loyalty from the people who work out front. Other owners act like there is a big difference between the people downstairs and the people upstairs. I keep everyone up on everything and everyone involved in everything. They feel like they're important because they are important. It's now broken down so much there is no designated manager anymore. The boundaries are gone, and everyone can perform all the functions."

The engineers interviewed claimed that practically every woman had her eye on a management position. Less than half of the men did. The women wanted to manage not just because it's a promotion but to exercise their people skills. "Women would rather manage a project than be immersed in technical detail. All the women would like to manage! Some men just want to be responsible for their own work only and don't even want to be on a team, let alone run one" (Engineer, age 30).

When the landscape architects and engineers looked at projects, they tended to think, first, who is this project going to help in the community, and second, how will people working on it benefit?

"And three, are we going to get consensus so we'll be working as a team? I'm a real team builder working with people who got into engineering to get away from people! I created all the training sessions for our section. Sat down with the boss; what subjects did he want to cover? Got everybody's voice, got everyone to buy into the idea. What do *you* want to get out of more training? Another time I was in sewer utilities and management wanted to buy a new computer for the field staff. I was to make up the justification for the purchase. But they hadn't even asked the field staff what they wanted the computer to do! So I created a survey and had all the field people fill it out and compiled a draft, and they all read the draft and signed it and felt included in the project. Otherwise that computer would have sat in the corner gathering dust for a very long time" (Engineer, age 28).

## HOW TO BE A GOOD MANAGER

Think how you feel about the following: In her 1986 how-to book, *Climbing the Ladder*, Janet MacDonald offered advice to the ambitious woman manager. Her advice squares with much of what the nontraditional women told me. Here, paraphrased, are some of MacDonald's main points (pp. 99–108).

Look for things to praise people for and praise them in public because people not only like to be appreciated, it's better if everyone else hears it.

Team efforts deserve special praise, words like "You did a great job, team," followed up by cream cakes at break time or flowers or thank you notes.

Emphasize your counseling role. Go around first thing in the morning and see if there are any personal problems that need to be sorted out.

Let people work flexible hours where "the larks come in early and the owls come in late," and everybody will be happier.

Know where each of your staff lives, what their spouses' names are, and what their spouses' chief hobbies are.

What's your reaction—admiration and approval? Disgust and a sneer? If it sounds unbelievable and Pollyannish, isn't that because we're used to male-norm how-to-manage books? What manager is going to reward with cream cakes and flowers? What man is going to learn the husbands' names of the women in his department, or what his male employees' personal problems are?

Women's style of managing is different. It comes from our culture. It's about time that how-to books validated our managerial potential, potential that comes from learning how, and expecting to, manage a family and a home, potential that proved itself here in the most difficult management situation for a woman, the male-dominated workplace.

# 12

# LEADING WITH OUR KIND
# OF POWER

This guy who ran against me raised money from all over the country saying I was too liberal to represent this district, that I supported baby murderers and gays and all that other hot stuff. But I knew there were a lot of people out there who agreed with me and who were proud that I stand up and say, "This is what I really believe." It is important to be out there standing up for your people. The women's organizations really saved me. They doorbelled, telephoned, sent money. They just really were there for me, and you know what happened? Seventy-one percent of the people voted for me. That is real validation. (State legislator, age 49)

A stereotype that seems to have had its day is that women are apolitical, inept at organizing, naive in bargaining collectively, and not interested in affiliating with trade unions or political clubs. This leaves me wondering at the strength of the desire to organize and manage found in these nontraditional women.

I know I have to step back and remind myself that women are at the top of very few companies and countries. I have to ask if women might not be good at running things only on a small scale, within microcosms, such as their homes and their jobs.

What I believe is that the main reason women are not managing the world at the highest levels is that men do not want us to. So far they have had their way. American women learned a bitter lesson with the Equal Rights Amendment (ERA). The ERA reminded us that male-created political power is in the hands of a few, that even if an overwhelming majority of people polled say they want something, it won't happen if the men in control do not want it to. Because men have the money to get what they want.

But women have also been limited because of unrealistic fears that we weren't emotionally as tough as men and because of realistic fears based on the high cost of going to court, both emotional and financial. We have also lacked political support from men coworkers and unions for our grievances and aspirations and lacked emotional support from men at home who see our organizing activities as taking more time away from them. So we are left with a lack of practice using women's brand of power and style of organizing, which truly revolutionizes society when it gains ascendency (see the end of this chapter regarding women governing differently).

In the meantime, some good has come out of the bad. The good thing about defeats like the ERA is that they make us even more democratic, more inclined toward the underdog. They tilt women even further to the side of the neglected and unheard and powerless. Defeat also has strengthened our alternative notions about power, one of the most important of which is that the personal is political.

In the context of this project, the wage gap between the sexes women see as personal and political. So are sex discrimination and sexual harassment. So, too, were working conditions, the physical environment, hours, health and safety provisions, and individual control on the job far more personal and political for the women interviewed than for their male coworkers. In every occupation, from medicine to stockbroking, from engineering to firefighting, the women saw the workplace and what happened to workers as political.

A 30-year-old structural engineer said that the engineers who let the *Challenger* go up knew it shouldn't have been launched but that they were afraid to say anything. "It may have helped if a woman was there. *I* 'd have called the press. I would have risked my job before I'd let the *Challenger* go off unsafely."

" 'If you vote this way, you can have X amount for your next campaign,' or 'I can help you with this or that other thing.' The minute, the very minute someone says this," said a legislator, age 55, "I make it public. It not only protects me, it stops it! Otherwise the pressure just grows and grows and gets bigger."

"Women have a more humane way of looking at work. It's not worth lives to build a bridge. Life and health are more important than work. I think there's an official policy that the company expects to lose one life for every one million profit. That's okay with them. It's not okay with me" (Electrician, age 32).

These are just three examples of these women's other notions of power and politics on the job. Now here are some thoughts about women's alternative definitions of power.

Jeane Kirkpatrick (1974, p. 143) reported that the women legislators she studied did not see politics as a zero sum game where one person's advantage is another's disadvantage. This is exactly what the women said here about how Washington State's male and female legislators differ. For men legislators, the most important principle is keeping their party in power; political power is a battleground, a marketplace, a zero sum game. But for Washington State's women legislators, political power means primarily serving the public; the goal of government is to solve social problems and create public good.

Some Washington State male legislators brag that power is their life-blood. They use their vote to cut deals, dole out porkbarrel projects to supporters, and redistrict to get rid of opponents. They use power to reward friends and punish enemies. Accumulating a fortune in dollars can get you in trouble, but no one goes to jail for accumulating too much power. The women's reaction to this kind of politician is, "Power corrupts and absolute power corrupts absolutely."

However, the women reported, shaking their heads, if they wanted to do things to benefit others and distribute resources fairly, they needed power. They needed to be in the majority. They wished they could do good using women's definition of power, but it couldn't happen right away.

In the meantime, they said, we must get men's power, the zero sum power men create and compete for. As long as the legislature is male dominated, the only way for us to insure that resources are distributed justly is to have enough of male power to make sure they are, and that means holding leadership positions within our parties and state government.

We have been powerless too long, they said, so now it is important that we come out and say that we want power, power-as-control, so that we can make life better for the unemployed, elderly, poor and disadvantaged, disenfranchised, and handicapped.

The most difficult lesson for women to learn, in their opinion, is to accept the fact that men are not going to give away their kind of power. So we have to take it. These women were up against the fact that if they wanted power, they were going to have to wrest it away from men, and that was going to be uncomfortable.

But when they had it, they could set the agenda and get critical issues through, because they would be the committee chairs who controlled totally what happened in committees. They could hear a bill or not. They could push it for a vote or not push it. Leadership positions are essential for women to get important issues through.

The five sections that follow start with the women's different way of playing hardball. They didn't lie, cheat, or steal. They did their homework and battered the opposition with facts. Second, because their ideal was government by consensus, they tried to get everyone to contribute to solutions, especially when they were leaders. Third, getting people to cooperate involves the skills mothers use to get teamwork in the home. Family members must support and help one another. Fourth, one of mother's tasks in all of this is to make sure that all the children get something. There will be no losers, and there will be no fighting. Finally, when women are present in critical masses, they democratize big institutions. They don't like hierarchy because it is anticonsensus, interferes with getting the job done, and sours relationships. But mainly, when women are there in critical numbers, they can lead with a different kind of power.

## PLAYING HARDBALL OUR WAY

Research on women politicians' distinctive contributions to politics has been summarized in Vicky Randall's (1987) *Women and Politics.* Randall tended to dismiss such differences because of their unfortunate origins, that is, in roles that men have assigned to women and in women's relative lack of power. But although the origins of our values and approaches may be regrettable, if the results are desirable, why should we deny these results?

What Randall reported (pp. 152–154) is that women politicians do their homework with extreme conscientiousness. They see politics as problem solving rather than a power struggle. They are resistant to lobbyists and open to constituents who attest that women are more approachable and sympathetic. Women spend more time representing their constituents' interests than playing the specialist who makes policy.

Other differences, according to Randall, are that women politicians are more liberal than men and universally concentrate on health, welfare, education, consumer affairs, and women's issues. In doing so, however, women don't speak up and initiate as much as men do.

Jeane Kirkpatrick (1974, p. 211), who is not known for her prowomen's movement ideology, believes that problem-solving women "come close to being the ideal legislators for a democratic society." Not socialized to greedy self-interest and private ambition, uninterested in the bribes of lobbyists, and able to balance a family and a private life with public service, women problem solvers can concentrate on seeking the public good.

So it is with a certain sadness that women do learn to play hardball. What does it mean to play hardball—lying, cheating, and stealing to get ahead? Or less serious forms of lying, cheating, and stealing such as taking credit for other people's work, exaggerating your own abilities, and blaming others for your mistakes? Women rarely commit even these minor offenses even when 90 percent of the people around them are playing rough.

So even when women say they are playing hardball, it isn't anything like the men's version.

"Most women learn how to do it. There are times that you have to withhold your vote to let them know they just can't walk into my door and expect me to be easy. You have to let them know in their own way. A colleague who thought this might be her last year changed her mind last month. She decided, 'I'm good at this. I've got to be here. They need more people like me, so I'll learn how to play hardball so I can stay in it, make progress and break through these barriers.' We hope it doesn't change us; we hope it is a temporary thing to get us through the barriers so that we can operate the way we would really like to operate. My friend decided she had to develop this skill of not being available when they want it. Men just can't get out of this win-lose game-playing thing, so for now I guess we'll have to play it" (State representative, age 49).

She continued that it hurts

"in our guts that we have to play hardball, but it's the only game the old boys understand. To move into leadership we have to stand up and be tough. But creating a tough image is a form of hardball that is easier for us because it doesn't involve being unfair to someone else. It's extremely difficult for us because we want to get the job done and hate all that wasted time, energy, and maneuvering. We are much more logical and have a better feel for how things are going to affect people. That will never leave us. We are much more sensitive to what a piece of legislation will do to the public at large. We are much more sensitive to the broader issues, children's issues, school issues. There are a lot of things men just can't understand until they become a househusband, I guess, involved in the daily struggle for life."

Thus women's form of hardball depends on doing research and marshalling objective facts as well as dealing with frankness and toughness mixed with modesty.

A seasoned, 58-year-old legislator described the following as "playing rough." There was a committee assignment she wanted and for which she had the right credentials, and the party bosses gave it to someone who neither wanted it nor had the background. This angered her.

"So here's where my attention to detail comes in. I analyzed the positions our party and the other party held, each member, and I color coded them. Guess what? The good old boys, whoever had been there the longest, they all had the power. Not only did they have the powerful committees, they had the best of everything, and everybody else was out in the fringes. Nobody had ever sat down and looked at it. You know, it is such stupidity to give it all to a few people, because if they don't get elected, you've lost all that knowledge. You don't have anyone trained. It wasn't the smart way to do it. We didn't have the best people in the right places. It was a good project. I think it helped everybody, and it wasn't based on gender. That isn't why I did it. I did it because tenure shouldn't be the deciding thing, giving a position to somebody who has been there forever who knows zilch. That is not good for anybody. It was a fun discovery. My little color dots were so pictorial, and it changed everything, and I didn't do a thing out loud—no big fuss or anything. Everyone went, 'Ahhh,' except the ones who knew."

A new legislator, age forty-five had to learn to play hardball when given a party leadership role.

"All of a sudden I am the point person. I mean I am the Mouth. It is a role that I don't really visualize myself in. It amazes me that I am in that position sometimes. It is that my colleagues trust me to treat them fairly, and they respect my honesty. I don't lead the floor fight on every issue, but it is my responsibility to see that it gets done. I don't particularly want to grandstand myself. I wouldn't mind being Speaker; I wouldn't mind being Governor. I think of myself as aggressive in that there are some things that are absolutely important to get done. I'm aggressive because if I feel that I am being cut out, I have no qualms at all about making a place for myself. I just go right to it. I jump right in and say, 'Hey, what's going on here? Why wasn't I consulted?' I don't do that in a confrontive way. Criminy! I don't say, 'You Goddamn whatever...' when I go in. My colleagues approach people that way. I would just matter-of-factly approach people and say, 'What has happened here? I don't understand. Why was I left out?' I am very gentle with the hard hit."

To learn hardball the women of both parties got together to teach one another the ropes and to try out ideas in a supportive environment. I don't think anyone even referred to the meetings as a caucus, the women's caucus. But the men saw it that way, as a power play. "I saw a lot of eye opening on the part of men because we were going to meet, network. We set up regular times. They got so nervous it was incredible; it was unreal. We weren't plotting and planning anything diabolical, but we were meeting regularly. They said, 'What if *we* did that!' and we said, 'Well, you do! You guys do it all the time.' But they had not experienced women doing it. Most women have had to pick it up on their own, but the men have always taken care of one another."

She continued: "We are learning the importance of helping other women up the ladder, of educating them to subtleties. We don't need to be loners or tag along after the men or try to fit into the men's group. We are learning that we can help one another and strengthen ourselves in the process, and there is an important bit of information for women to realize; there is strength in numbers. We don't have to each learn everything. We can learn from our sister legislators" (State representative, age 58).

## BUILDING CONSENSUS

Marilyn Ferguson in her 1982 book *The Aquarian Conspiracy* talked about how women's caring form of power can change the political scene. She juxtaposed two lists of assumptions, one list behind old male power politics and one list for our new paradigm of power politics. Prominent in the new list is the idea of consensus—government as consensus, change that grows out of consensus. Consensus means power *with* others, a win–win orientation, a dynamic relationship between leaders and followers, with each affecting the other, and a horizontal distribution of power as opposed to monolithic, centralized power (p. 229).

Ferguson said that wherever this American social transformation is taking place, there are far more women to be found than you'd expect. She said that when women represented only 8 percent of the physicians, for example, they constituted one-third of the founding members of a new holistic medical organization. Furthermore, the men in these organizations emulated women's empathic leadership style. Women, Ferguson believes, with cultural permission to be flexible, affiliative, and cooperative, are redefining what it means to be a leader (1982, p. 249).

Here are two legislators' ideas about building consensus. One legislator (age 58) said:

"Women are generally more patient working with groups. They are accustomed to being peacemakers, and compromising, and trying to get something done, and trying to keep everybody reasonably happy, because they have to do that at home. I have told many groups of women that we are socialized to be good legislators. Anyone who can keep her husband and her kids at peace with one another has been well trained for the legislature. I think those things all work for us. We are the peacemakers; we set the tone for our homes. If the woman is angry and hostile, then the whole family is. If the woman keeps things running smoothly, then things go that way in the house, and men are used to stomping their feet and having women go, 'Now, now, dear.' That is typical, trying to make things go smooth, looking for what really matters. 'Now if we include that piece of legislation, then this person can maybe tolerate part of it, and we can get this taken care of.' We should have lots more women down here. I think it would make a big difference, and I think women, as a general statement, tend to have more integrity, and we sure as hell need that down here."

The other legislator (age 56) said: "We like to talk through issues. I want to say, 'Look, what if . . .' and toss ideas out and discuss it. We bring that desire to share and toss ideas back and forth. Problem solving and sharing ideas is something we do very well. It is healthy for a legislative arena, not like days past when the leader pulled out of his pocket just exactly what he wanted you to vote on a bill, and you did it. We are far more consensus builders and that is to the benefit of the public."

She continued:

"Maybe it is because I raised six children, but I know that I am more into building consensus than arriving at a conclusion and trying to impose my position on other people. I am also less needful to have personal recognition. I am willing to share that with others when we get the job done. In a way I think I am viewed as being too nice, that I can't be tough enough, and that is not true. I can be tougher than hell and am and have been. As a committee chair I have to keep people from killing each other, keep discussion and debate going, and building consensus. These are skills I learned as a teacher and in my home life raising a family. People acknowledge that and have given me great praise for not being abrasive and being fair. I guess I'd underscore that word *fair*. I believe that we women have a real need to be fair, to hear both sides of any issue."

Here are more of her thoughts:

"I like to throw ideas and bounce them off with a group. Nothing pleases me more than to have somebody come out with an idea that I wanted to come out and give them credit for it. I have a political philosophy, and it is: I make it tough for them to be mean to me. My leadership style is very direct and very positive. I get results and I do it quickly. But I do it in a manner that I do not have people angry at me because I forced them to do something they didn't want to do. I build it around 'Get compromise.' You almost always make some progress. Another old adage is 'Nothing will ever be attempted if all possible problems must first be solved.' As long as we are making progress, I don't have to see the end product, right up front. There comes a time sometimes where you have to get very rough. I feel very uncomfortable with that, but I have done it when I had to. You have to say, 'I'm calling in my chits; I need your vote,' and occasionally you have to say, 'This is it, buddy.' "

## GETTING PEOPLE TO COOPERATE

Society teaches boys to be competitive and girls to be cooperative. But this latter fact about girls is often overlooked, especially by men who see only our lack of competitiveness and not the many forms of cooperation women use to get the job done.

The uncooperative situation at work most frequently mentioned by the women was the meeting. They hated meetings. They said meetings could be a big waste of time. Here was this group that could work so well together and get so much done, but instead the men just sat around and criticized each other. It was not "I'll help you and you help me so we'll all succeed." Instead, the men's attitude was "I'll do my part and that's all and I could care less about *our* succeeding." The women admitted they were too generous about what they gave to other people's projects in this situation.

A civil engineer, age 28, looked around her at meetings, and all she could see were dollars ticking away on the clock. "When there's no agenda, no proposed outcome, it totally infuriates me. So I do the secretarial chores so I can control the agenda and get the hell out of there. I say, 'What are we here to decide? What do you want to cover in the next hour? Anyone else? Okay, we have these three things to accomplish and here is the agenda.' Otherwise meetings are totally political and aren't meant to get any results."

Concerning the women's misplaced generosity in groups, they said they were more willing than men to take responsibility for the whole group on a project and also more willing to help when men were in charge than vice versa.

The women said that they felt, more than the men, that the company was like a big family, and helping coworkers was like helping family members. The men puzzled them. The men were happy to take the women's supportive assistance because it made them look good, but they wouldn't reciprocate. "So what should we do?" they asked me. "Stop helping them? We don't want to stop helping, but it doesn't make sense if they won't help us in return."

A 30-year-old carpenter said that the major difference between her and the men in the shop was that if she had someone helping her, she wanted them involved in the whole process, not just doing the dregs. "If we're going to share in work, we're going to share in the responsibility too. See, one person has the blueprints and figures out how the joints go together. If he's gone to all that work, he wants to do that part, the major part. He gives people who are available simple things to do that they can't mess up. He lets them sand or put glue on. But the way I do it is I divide it up and give each person a major part of the project. I trust their skills for the major things. Everyone hates to help. 'Here's this stack of doors; sand 'em.' I shouldn't have to do all their dirty work, so they shouldn't have to do all of mine."

A 35-year-old electrician likewise saw a way to do a supervisory kind of job different than men did it. "I had the lead-off position with two guys working for me, but we worked as a team. I didn't consider myself any different, because if there was something to be done and my two guys were busy, I went and did the job. I just can't sit around and let somebody else do all the work when I know they're already busy, and to keep the job going, sometimes I just sat down and drew up the drawings of the electronic system we were installing and sent them to the design department and said, 'This is what we've really got here on the waterfront, and it is not on your prints.' You have to see what needs to be done and go ahead and do it."

A carpenter, age 45, said that women hadn't as much experience being leaders and were apt to follow the only role models they had, men, until they had more confidence and could change their approach and "be more human, less domineering. My company now is all women, and the difference is that we all work alongside each other; there's no big split between bosses and workers. The woman in charge at the project isn't a *boss*; she's just someone who's spent more time looking at the project. We ask for opinions all the time, and it's safe for us to give ideas and feedback. As a worker I have more control and feel I really understand the project as a whole. You feel equal with the other workers when your opinions and work are valued. The work gets done better, and we can take pride in it when it's not us against them. We take turns being boss. I don't like being boss, but it's a good learning experience."

Women stockbrokers found the team approach to working on investment decisions a very interesting process.

"I use the team approach where I'll have attorneys, accountants, the wife, mother, whoever wants to be involved, and we will be looking at my plan and making group decisions about should we do more tax free, more taxable; should they retire with ten-year forward averaging? should they do an IRA? I do more group decision making involving more individuals in the plan than everybody else. Maybe the other brokers are afraid the CPA is going to squelch the deal, but I encourage group decision making. I am more willing to leverage my time and bring other people in because I don't always have to be the one who calls the shots. I don't lose anything by bringing others in. In fact, these people bring me more clients. So I love it when they say, 'I'm bringing my accountant' "(Broker, age 29).

A 55-year-old assistant police chief talks about when she was acting chief:

"When I was acting chief, I was accessible. Police chiefs, even in small departments, can be arrogant! But I enjoyed working closely with my guys. I felt like we were a team, relying on each other. I didn't put distance between myself and my line officers. Every Friday I had what I called a bitch session. It was not mandatory, but my guys came willingly. It was a time when we got everything out on the table and talked it over. I don't know how many officers have told me that they like the approach I take to situations. But we're taught that from the beginning—be sensitive to male needs, aren't we? I also think the men aren't threatened by me. I don't try to compete with them. I curl my hair, I wear my makeup. I never resent a fellow officer opening the door for me. I hope that other women entering the field don't lose that. They can do the job without becoming masculine."

A 22-year-old apprentice air-conditioning mechanic had to do a stint in the shipyard planning department.

"Before when my group needed help, a planner would come to our shop, and the shop's attitude was, 'You make more money than we do, so you figure it out for yourself.' So when I was a planner, it woke me up real good. The crew had the same attitude toward me: 'Figure it out for yourself.' So I slapped the papers on the desk, and I said, 'Listen. Either you help me or I'm going to plan this job the way I want, and you're gonna suffer because you're gonna do the job,' and it was like a lightbulb. 'Oh, yeah, we'd like to help you,' and I told them, 'You don't help those guys when they come out because you're envious of them. So they have to plan a job to the best of their ability and then you gripe and moan because it isn't the way you want it. But you wouldn't give them any input. So the next time one of these guys comes out, think twice before you turn them away.' "

## THE WIN–WIN SOLUTION

The legislators said they tried to solve problems not by winning but by putting everyone in a win–win situation. Some said they learned how from doing volunteer work in the community where you had no power over others, and you had to get everyone to be a part of the solution. They said compromise was what political solutions were all about and that there weren't a lot of black and white solutions out there. They just wanted to get the job done. The men were more concerned with how well they were playing the game, and for some men, unless they *alone* win, it doesn't count as a win.

All the women lawyers talked about their preference for "alternative dispute resolutions." What this means is that, like the legislators, they prefer there be no clear-cut winner and loser. Most said it is far better if nothing ever goes to trial. "At trials no one gets what they want. Trials are *not* the best way for all parties to get something out of the process. There is rarely a true right and a true wrong. Because women care more about people as people than as legal cases, they find ways not to go to court. Women biologically and culturally are geared to raise families. In disputes in the family, you want all of your children to get something. You are used to dividing the pie up" (Attorney, age 33).

So here are the peacemakers complaining that their employers want results where their side wins and the other side loses. But "as a result of the feminine perspective my natural inclination is to negotiate, not clobber the other person. One of the things that I value in my relationships is satisfaction in both people involved, both getting rewards. So when I approach legal problems, I try for a solution in which both parties feel they've gotten what they want. My employers, in contrast, want results where we win and they lose. My boss's boss's attitude is, 'Well, let's go in there and beat them up.' He feels most successful when someone leaves his office feeling whipped. I'm always tempted to apologize for his behavior" (Attorney, age 29).

The male behavior that the women found the most difficult to imitate was aggression. These women are tough and assertive. They weren't hired for their reserve and timidity. Yet too much aggression could spoil their day. "I don't like other lawyers to harass me on the telephone. It affects my psyche and my outlook. After many years of practice I yell right back, but inside it makes me feel bad. I started out doing litigation—intellectually, a wasteland. Maybe this is where the woman's point of view comes in. I would have had to have the killer instinct, where you achieve your end at all costs. I think it's more interesting to put together a deal and have everyone go away happy, so that's why I specialize in taxes" (Attorney, age 35).

It was so nice to have women colleagues who demonstrated the best in female behaviors to counterbalance aggression. "We have a new woman plaintiff attorney in our firm who has a really strong advocacy stance. Her enthusiasm for what she can do for clients is infectious and so different from the how-can-we-screw-the-other-guy attitude. We've taken on a case we really want to do, age discrimination—cab drivers being told on their sixty-fourth birthday, bye-bye. It's fun to be able to focus on more liberal cases, on more caring things, that can change the world" (Attorney, age 40).

The lawyers agreed that the law is not an efficient way to resolve disputes and that women will change that in time. "It's silly, expensive, unwieldy, lengthy, emotionally wrenching. In this state the judiciary is not very good, and that means there is very little predictability to the whole process. The law is not consistent, not predictable, not according to rules. You could take the same case to ten different judges and get ten different results. There are maybe five out of forty judges who can stay with you all the way. So we need more women trial court judges. Women jurors are much tougher than men jurors. They have much less patience and compassion if they get an inkling that someone is not playing by the rules. Women in the judiciary would be that way too" (Attorney, age 31).

In the meantime, they said, women in the courtroom were better able to deal with clients and less able to deal with judges and other lawyers who are still mostly men. But women see through what's going on. It's a game that doesn't help anybody. Trials are a way for lawyers to earn money and massage their egos. Women lawyers resist male lawyers' behavior—the bluff, drama, and condescension—and they savor explaining legal problems in normal terms to juries.

A 30-year-old lawyer talked about how she looked forward to the day when there would be less posturing of attorneys with their colleagues, fewer tactical maneuvers designed to freak out other attorneys by intimidation.

"I can't stand the mentality of clients' being able to say, 'My lawyer's tougher than your lawyer.' I don't believe in using *any* means against the other team. At meetings, one-on-one, in court and out of court, women are less likely to intentionally embarrass someone. I just like to make my points subtly, do the best possible job I can, and make sure nobody gets the better of me. My style at the beginning of cases is to cooperate with opposing counsel especially on schedule. Why fight over things that aren't worth the energy, procedural things rather than the issues? I don't take a hardnosed position right off the bat. I'm courteous; I cooperate. It's always in the client's best interest to settle; that's something you classify as a 'good' result for the client. It's always a crapshoot to go to trial. My cases rarely go to trial, maybe once every two years."

## THE DEMOCRATIZATION OF BIG INSTITUTIONS

Women's presence can democratize big institutions such as a state legislature.

"Women have never had so much power as today, and because women are very vocal and because we can go to the press, you have more democracy in the total institution. The women are demanding more of a voice, less 'going along to get along.' Because we have been demanding to be a part of it, there is a growing together of men and women legislators and less difference in the way they operate. Women have made it possible for the institution to be more democratized. But I can tell you one institution that will really change with more women, and that is the Congress of the United States. They are still doing things the old boys way. If you had a woman speaker, I bet you would know where the money was going. Right now they have no idea" (State representative, age 62).

Women legislators didn't go along with the idea of a boss man and doing what they're told. They liked being their own boss. They also weren't very impressed with hierarchies or systems where you went through too many hoops to get anything accomplished. "We recognize the necessity of hierarchy, but I have never felt any more deferential toward the governor than toward the newest member of the House. I don't let hierarchy interfere with relationships. You have to have a spokesman, you have to assign responsibility, but I have never seen a woman feel intimidated by somebody's title in the political realm. Every other woman politician probably feels the same way. We carry over the ease and freedom of feeling equal from unstructured women's groups, so we feel equal regardless of a person's title" (State representative, age 55).

The women said that they were afraid of backlash when their numbers rose to, say, 20 percent, but it hadn't happened with over 30 percent of Washington's House women and sixteen percent of the Senate. Because of the high quality of women legislators, the men clearly respected their judgment and ability as much as they did that of male colleagues. There has also been a sex shift among lobbyists. Women lobbyists were described as true professionals, as persuasive and skilled and numerous as men lobbyists. They represented all kinds of groups, including male-dominated organizations such as land developers and builders, pulp and paper companies, and banks.

On the floor and off the floor, the legislature is no longer a white male structure.

"When we finally have women in positions of power in the legislature, then you'll really see some changes. Up to now, it has been considered appropriate for women to work on minority type issues, affirmative action, social issues, but when it comes to banking, insurance, corporations, and pensions, then no one has thought women could do it. That has always been my objection to the leadership in the House, in agencies, and in the government. Important committees are chaired by white men; the leadership are white men; when the governor wants to talk with someone about something to do with economics, it's going to be a man. Eventually, that will change. Decisions that affect everybody will be made by everybody" (State representative, age 58).

## WOULD WOMEN GOVERN DIFFERENTLY?

Geneva Overholser asked in the *New York Times* of June 15, 1987, if women would govern differently. For the most part, women have behaved no differently from men in political office, she said. But would that be true if the number of women in high office better reflected our share of the population? Would we then govern politics differently?

She used Norway as her example. She told us that Norway's prime minister is a woman, and of seventeen Cabinet ministers, seven are women. The Labor party's members of Parliament are more than 40 percent women, and the same holds in the party's ruling National Board. The difference women have made is that when huge spending cuts had to be made when North Sea oil prices fell, childcare subsidies went up and paid parental leave went from sixteen to eighteen weeks. The government continued to emphasize support for women and children.

Just as we found these nontraditional women transforming the social atmosphere of work to make it more homelike, the atmosphere of the Norwegian Cabinet had changed to the point where the defense minister felt comfortable excusing himself to go pick up his son at nursery school.

Overholser said that Norway offers an attractive taste of the future where, in governing, women emphasize compassion and interdependence, congruent public and private values, and a definition of power as consensus rather than will.

# 13

# REFORMING MEN

---

The dolls in the corner over there are anatomically correct, and we
use them for interviewing sex-abuse victims. But we also use this
room to occupy children whose parents are being interviewed or are
busy with something. It's gradually become a space that's frequently
utilized by employees' children. My own children are frequent visitors to the workplace, and what has evolved from that is the guys'
children are visitors more often. I think that's a significant change.
I don't think you'd see children in many other police stations, but
here it happens a lot. (Police sergeant, age 36)

"Women in the Workplace are Reshaping the Economy" read the 1985
headline by Stephen Dunphy. But have women reshaped, or are women
reshaping, the men they work beside? What evidence do we have beyond
the experiences of the women we have come to know in this book that
men are becoming more like women in their values, motives, and behaviors?

Certainly, there are reported failures. To me one of the saddest was
observed at the University of Arizona. There Susan Aiken, Karen Anderson, Myra Dinnerstein, Judy Lensink, and Patricia MacCorquodale
mounted a four-year program to integrate Women's Studies into the
general curriculum. Their project, *Changing our Minds* (1988), was directed at the male faculty. But in the end, only a quarter of the forty-
two men who participated had experienced serious intellectual or personal change. Another quarter agreed to add some material about
women to their courses. But half of the men remained unchanged
(p. 139).

Apparently, these scholarly, thoughtful, highly educated, very intelligent men could not transcend male sex-role socialization. They put the women in the role of school marms coming after little boys with a ruler; they ignored and labeled female and inferior any man who voiced a feminist position (pp. 144–152).

Why then, how then, could the nontraditional women in our research have succeeded? I think there were two reasons. (1) They were hired for one purpose: to do a job. That was their top priority, not changing men. There was no frontal assault, no immediate challenge to men's ways of doing the job. (2) What got changed first in male employers and coworkers alike were behaviors. Changes in their attitudes followed (although, in some cases, new behaviors are in place, and incompatible, inconsistent attitudes still linger).

The workplace aspects that Dunphy attributed to the influx of women during the previous decade were three big ones—economic growth, low inflation, and expanding jobs—broad, dramatic, national states of affairs, not the stuff of this book or of this chapter.

I am going to give you some evidence of the kinds of changes women have made in men's day-to-day lives at work, some small changes, some large, but all profound. I'm going to steer clear of the changes many male liberationists want—greater emotional expressiveness, the restored capacity to relate to children, dependency, and vulnerability. These are personal changes. But male liberationists also talk about being freed of the traditional masculine pursuit of power, prestige, and profit (Pleck & Sawyer, 1974, pp. 1–2). It is professional, workplace changes that I focus on here.

This chapter is testimony, then, to the fact that women have changed work, the workplace, and their male colleagues. If you think that this can't be traced to women's influence or that this trend doesn't necessarily have anything to do with women coming into the work force, I can only say that I don't think men got these ideas by themselves.

Here are examples that fit each of the previous chapters to illustrate how men's work lives have been reformed by the dramatic increase of women in the work force, by the women's movement, and by the movement of women toward change.

## THE HELPING ATTITUDE

Are women really more empathic than men? More nurturant than men? Carol Tavris and Carole Wade (1984) said on both counts that "it depends." As far as empathy is concerned, they concluded from their review of the research literature that whether men are as empathic as women depends on the situation and the people involved (pp. 60–61). As far as nurturance goes, Tavris and Wade said the evidence is mixed.

Certainly, adult men appear as altruistic and willing to help others as adult women, and fathers observed with their newborns in the hospital were just as adept at handling them as mothers (pp. 69–70).

The problem for men as far as both of these personality characteristics are concerned is that society has encouraged and reinforced empathy and nurturance in women while sometimes even punishing men for being sensitive and caring, because it wasn't "manly."

Thus it isn't surprising that in the first half of this century men were attracted to police ranks because they could play a tough, macho role controlling crime while women were attracted to the police because they could play a social service role. But as the number of women officers has gradually increased to more than ten percent and as the role of the police has become more community and service oriented, a new breed of male cop has appeared, part blue knight, part social worker.

Men and women today have the same motives for becoming police officers. Just to cite one study of several that support this change, Ralph Weisheit (1987) did research among Illinois State troopers and found that service to others and security for oneself were the top motivators for both sexes. Among officers 30 years old and younger there were no differences between the women and the men in their motivation for policing. To be of service is now just as important to men cops as it is to women cops.

The other thing men can do today with their nurturant motives that was not as acceptable twenty years ago is to enter occupations that have been nontraditional for them. In contrast to women who experience many disadvantages when they are token members in male jobs, men experience advantages when they are token members in female jobs such as nursing (Ott, 1989).

One example is Trevor Clay, a British nurse who, when interviewed, was the general secretary of the Royal College of Nursing (with 270,000 members). He said that when he was in training he was totally spoiled by his fellow students who were all women. I think he has been spoiled by them ever since. Everywhere he was employed he was heralded as the first male, and he seems to have been put in charge very often. Now, even though only 10 percent of nurses are men, the union spokesperson for the whole profession is a man, and male nurses make up 50 percent of nursing administrators (Grove, 1988b).

## CAREFUL LISTENING

A 28-year-old firefighter said that during her first year there were two men who didn't speak a word to her the entire time.

"I decided that this one guy did not know how to speak to a woman. He couldn't hold a conversation with me. I worked with him for over a year. I'd sit down, and he'd answer my questions, but he couldn't turn around and talk back. This had been his home away from home where he could cuss and swear and didn't have to listen to women. With this other guy, I don't know why, if it was our personalities or what, but we just weren't getting along very well. I'd ask him, 'What's the matter? Have I done something to offend you?' I brought it up and asked him, whereas he would never have asked me, and even as it was, he said, 'No, why would you think that?' and I had to turn around and say, 'Well, we can't even talk to each other without being argumentative or without a lot of tension in the air.' We'd talk for a little bit, and I'd say, 'Geez, I feel like I've offended you again.' He opened up gradually, and things got a lot better over the year."

Phillip Hodson (1984, pp. 25–26), in his explanation of how boys learn to be "masculine," said it takes only nine years to teach a boy the art of "nonspeak." By nine, Hodson said, girls have skills at introducing themselves, asking personal questions, sharing their own motives and anxieties, and discussing problems. By nine boys have none of these skills and are, instead, embarrassed, timid, and incompetent in relationships. Girls will reveal three times as much about themselves to a stranger of the same sex as boys will. Boys focus instead on doing, on making things, and on talking about the technical side of games and play activities. The boys had learned to keep themselves to themselves.

By nine, Hodson said, boys have learned to be incurious about other people; they aren't inclined to conversation; they aren't interested in discovering more about other people. They have already learned nonspeak and nonlisten.

No wonder, then, that one of the benefits of the women's movement for men has been the consciousness-raising (C-R) group. I know, very few men participate in them. But what I'd like to pass on here is one man's formula for success, one person's ideas of how men can unlearn the nonspeak of early childhood and learn careful listening, which has vocational as well as personal applications.

Paul Hornacek (1977, pp. 125–129) said that a men's C-R group cannot follow the leaderless format of women's C-R groups. Instead, men's groups must have structure, lots of structure. Only through structure will there be no competition, no misuse of aggression, which make groups self-destruct.

Hornacek's antisexist C-R group has about six to eight men. Meetings are conducted regularly once a week. Each meeting lasts for a predesignated time, usually three hours. The meetings start on time and require full attendance at every meeting. Time is divided into discussion and analysis, criticism and self-criticism, and equal time (say fifteen minutes) for each participant to speak.

The group uses an experienced facilitator and a pact of strict confidentiality. Topics are selected by group preference the week before.

During the session the topic is addressed by each person until it is exhausted. All topics must relate to the socialization of males and females that lead to the perpetuation of sexist behaviors. Speakers must use "I" and talk only from personal experience. No one is to interrupt the speaker. No one is to confront or challenge the speaker. Listeners are to give their full attention to the speaker and try to understand what he is saying. Questions are raised only during the discussion period.

After several months of meeting in this way, the group must search for a larger purpose, that is, for political activities against sexism. These activities occur in addition to the on going C-R meetings, so that the men make the personal political, as feminists do. But the very important personal day-to-day benefit that the men can take back to the factory or office is the ability to listen without interrupting and to understand other people's points of view.

## NO US VERSUS THEM

*The Third Wave* (1980) by futurist Alvin Toffler describes the global civilization that is evolving rapidly all around us. I went immediately to Toffler's index to see what he might have given women credit for; he didn't give the women's movement credit for any of it, but I read his book anyway. Here is some of what Toffler said men are gaining at work from the "demassification" of our society, that is, the breakup of traditional mass production.

Men will no longer work in dirty, noisy, dangerous factories. Instead, they will work in quiet, spacious facilities such as Hewlett-Packard in Colorado Springs, where their desks are decorated with flowers and plants, where they wear ordinary street clothes so there are no visible distinctions in rank among workers, and where they choose their own working hours (pp. 195–197).

This last gain, flex time (set in motion by a woman economist in Germany in 1965), Toffler considers already achieved. Men can now work parttime or at night (pp. 262–266). At work there will no longer be just one "bottom line," profit. There will be many bottom lines—social, environmental, informational, political, and ethical (pp. 257–260).

Men no longer have to be sole breadwinners. Instead, they can choose to live alone, remain single and adopt a child, or live in a very large aggregate family. (Indeed, Toffler devotes an entire chapter to the wide variety of "families of the future" open to men, pp. 224–242.)

Men's personalities can be, indeed must be, androgynous, for the worker of tomorrow must have a personality that is sensitively tuned in to the people around him, adaptable, questioning of authority, desirous of work that is socially responsible, versatile, and, above all, balanced. Men gain women's "subjectivity," women men's "objectivity." Men no longer judge themselves solely on how much money they make and what they own. What they do is also of value (pp. 401–405).

## THE NURTURANT APPROACH

One of the best examples of greater numbers of women leading to a more caring attitude toward workers is the change in how medical residents are trained. The norm used to be 120 hours of work a week, 36 sleepless hours at a stretch, and 18 hours straight in the emergency room. But now the norm is 80 hours a week, no more than 24 consecutive hours of work, and a 12-hour limit on emergency-room shifts (Case, 1989).

Women residents say, though, that these new standards have not gone far enough. They continue to speak out and say that the present system is horrible and that it is impossible to learn or make proper decisions about patients when you are exhausted. Women physicians and groups such as Physicians for Social Responsibility will keep pressing for a forty-hour work week, not just to safeguard patient care but so that doctors have free time to recover from this stressful job, to socialize with spouse and family and friends, and to take care of errands and study (Case, 1989).

## RESPECT FOR DIFFERENCES

How much discretion do employers have in dictating standards of dress and manners of employees in terms of sexual identity? Men as well as women benefited from the Supreme Court's upholding a woman accountant's contention that her firm had to prove that sex discrimination played no part in their decision not to promote her. After all, the firm admitted she was the top ranked of all associates and brought in the most business. But, they said, she was too abrasive and aggressive; she was just too unfeminine to be a partner. So they had warned her to walk more femininely, talk more femininely, dress more femininely, have her hair styled, and go to charm school. So, she said, because Price Waterhouse had told her she was too unfeminine, they would now have to prove in court that there was no sex bias in not promoting her (Landau, 1989).

Jack Landau, who reported the story, asked if a male accountant, told to talk more masculinely and dress more masculinely, could also accuse his supervisor of operating on illegal sex stereotypes of men? Why not? My guess is that most men would come to that conclusion. So the Supreme Court has given both men and women greater freedom from the boss's ideas of what is proper masculine and feminine dress, personal demeanor, and manners. Although most men probably aren't keen to show up in dresses and makeup, they might welcome being able to let up on the aggression and abrasiveness. Living up to other people's sex stereotypes to get promoted has got to be the ultimate insult to a person who is already doing what the company wants most, making them lots of money.

What this ruling perhaps has spared men is being on committees charged with guidelines for what men are forbidden to wear. Michael Korda (1974, pp. 70–71) recounted how a friend of his who worked for a large corporation in New York City had been assigned the task of defining for senior management what a woman's trouser suit was, as opposed to just trousers. They were about to set a policy that permitted only trouser suits but no slacks or jeans. The women were all wearing trousers anyway in defiance of current policy, so it was really an exercise in saving men's faces. Korda thought the image of three middle-aged men leafing through *Vogue*, *Glamour*, and *Harper's Bazaar* to draft this fashion memo was hilarious. But even more hilarious was the fact that by the end of that year (late 1960s) not only were the women wearing hot pants and braless T-shirts, but the men had discarded their ties for turtlenecks and had exchanged their Brooks Brothers shoes for shoes previously seen only on pimps.

## BRIGHTENING THE BLUE-COLLAR WORLD

Surely one of the cheeriest *London Guardian* articles I have ever read was about eight shipyard workers made redundant when their town's 600-year-old tradition of shipbuilding came to an end (Ward, 1989). These were men whose fathers had told them they would have a job for life. These were men who had left school at age fifteen or sixteen to become apprentice shipwrights. They had responded to a display on teaching jobs set up in their canteen shortly before their jobs were eliminated. Now they were becoming elementary schoolteachers in a town, we are told, where real men don't push baby carriages.

The men had enrolled in a special ten-week "access course" to prepare for a four-year bachelor of education program. They were staying up all night writing essays and doing homework in politics, economics, sociology, and mathematics and then spending the afternoon assisting in the local primary school. Their instructors were impressed by their commitment, seriousness, and industry. I was impressed by their photograph in the classroom. In place of the rough-clothes image of the blue-collar worker were tidy, trimmed men in soft cotton shirts and trousers, looking every bit the teacher.

These men were probably surprised that their parents and spouses turned out to be so supportive, but they were, to such an extent that the men were not worrying about how they were going to finance their college education. After all, there was no point in competing for the few marine-related jobs left on the river when the nation had a teacher-shortage crisis that was worsening. So these blue-collar craftsmen were breaking with stereotypes and tradition and training for a woman's job with a reliable future.

## THE BALANCING ACT

The "Daddy Track" seems to have started in the early 1980s. Phillip Hodson was reporting in 1984 that young executives were no longer tempted by high cash bonuses and were refusing to work weekends so that they could be with their children, even that they were turning down unwanted postings to advance their careers in favor of advancing family life (p. 106).

But an article by feminist Felice Schwartz in the January–February 1989 issue of *Harvard Business Review*, by ignoring that men are parents too, has produced nationwide protests—from men! The popular press came to dub Schwartz' proposal that corporations have two tracks for women (career only versus career and family), the "Mommy Track." But guys said that balancing career and family is a Dads' issue too.

Working fathers are now jumping into the thick of the debate. They don't want to be forgotten when corporate managers redesign careers. They are tired of the old attitude that deprives men of sharing the joy of active childrearing. They are fed up with the corporate culture that sees families as a woman's issue not a man's issue, and they are making their opinions known in employees surveys. Thirty percent of Du Pont Company men, for example, now say they want more flexible working hours after the birth of a child (Reynolds, 1989).

More San Francisco Bay area men prefer the Daddy Track than the "High Flier" track. Given the option of a career with more flexible hours versus one with more promotions, 47 percent wanted flexible hours, and 42 percent wanted the promotions. (Among women, 62 percent went for the hours, versus 29 percent for the promotions.) Men were quoted as saying that flexible hours were just as important to them as salary and that when they could not find a job with flexible hours, they took lower paying jobs closer to home so that if anything happened to their children, they could get home quickly. Being there for their kids counted for more than making more money (McLeod & McCabe, 1989).

Apparently, men are coming closer to this 36-year-old police sergeant's definition of success. "I was raised to believe if I had a successful marriage and happy children, then I was a success, and anything else is gravy. If I am a successful career woman, that's just frosting on the cake. But for a man, it's the other way around. First, they must be

successful economically, a success in business, and only second have a
healthy marriage and a couple of kids to leave the world, and it takes
him into his fifties, if then, to realize that his marriage and those kids
are *really* his important contribution to the world, and everything else
is frosting."

## NINE TO FIVE? FIVE DAYS A WEEK?

"Flexibility in Hours Works for Men Too" reads the headline (Syrett,
1988). The wide variety of forms of parttime work that women have
created are now in place to meet, as well, men's needs *not* to work full
time.

What are the advantages of parttime work for men? In addition to
the obvious one, being better able to raise a family, men can undertake
further or higher education. Physically or mentally handicapped men
unable to work full time can now work, and parttime work can be one's
semiretirement or an excellent way to prepare for retirement (Syrett,
1988).

Other advantages of parttime work cited by Susan McHenry and Linda
Small (1989) are the perks companies offer, such as complete dental and
medical benefits provided by the Shaklees Corporation of San Francisco.
Job sharing, one form of parttime work, has the perk of total flexibility
when teams are allowed to divide their hours any way they choose—
alternating hours or days or even weeks as the Rolscreen Company of
Pella, Iowa, permits (Rolscreen also picks up the full medical benefit
package for parttime workers).

## NOT LIVING WITH STRESS

A *Seattle Times* article by Marsha King (1989) quotes several women
firefighters as concerned about the fact that 25 percent of firefighters
can't do the job. According to the department's physical fitness specialist,
whom King interviewed, 25 percent of the force, male and female, are
not fit enough. Nationwide, he said, this 25 percent figure holds.

A major cause of unfitness is the aging firefighter whose strength is
declining or who has medical problems. What Seattle's chief examiner
of the Public Safety Civil Service Commission wants is an ongoing testing
of individual strength. Ongoing testing would mean that firefighters
would stay in condition. They would thus not be a risk to themselves or
others. The women I interviewed were all in favor of regular physical-
fitness training so that they and the men could do the job, prevent
injuries, and avoid heart conditions.

What male firefighters have gained from the influx of women into the service is a serious look at exactly what the fitness standards should be for this physically demanding job. Where there have not been performance review systems after training, in the field, there will be now. Where strength standards have not been enforced throughout a firefighter's career, they will be now, because even the strongest firefighters can deteriorate to beyond what is acceptable.

The same recommendations have been made in the police service as a result of the men's concern for women's strength. Fitness experts have recommended that departments develop individualized programs tailored to each officer's needs and interests. The documented benefits of continued fitness for the police are reduced incidence of coronary heart disease, slowing of the aging process, increased longevity, reduced injuries on and off duty, decreased worker's compensation, decreased worker absenteeism, and financial savings to employers (Charles, 1983).

## DOING MANY THINGS AT ONE TIME

By finding self-fulfillment primarily in the home and family, men will learn to have as many and as varied interests as women do and to enjoy taking more time with tasks so that they can "do it my way." As men no longer find their identity in the narrow interests of the organization, as they struggle for wholeness and satisfying human relationships, they may even learn to do many things at one time, as women do.

Betty Friedan's chapter, "The Quiet Movement of American Men," in her book *The Second Stage* (1981), declares that many men have already changed their identity as a result of the women's movement. Friedan wrote about an airline pilot and a bank president who have become schoolteachers in order, as one of them put it, to do something "worthwhile from a human point of view." She said that young executives now refuse to accept transfers or extra assignments that would lead to big promotions, and men of all ages now work parttime, to find their self-fulfillment in their families (pp. 133–137).

Friedan said there is a move on among executives to leave big cities and to work in smaller towns for less money because the quality of life is better there. This same concern became a union demand in contract negotiations with AT&T in 1980. As important as increases in pay and pensions to AT&T workers was a better quality of work life (p. 139). To Friedan it seems that men now seek new life patterns as much as women do and, as a result, that corporations will have to change as men insist on their right to a humane and meaningful work environment (pp. 158–160).

Friedan ended her chapter by quoting a West Point man who doesn't want men to be role models for women, even in the army. He said men are jealous of women's feelings and closeness to life, of women's ability to see the world as a realistic gray and not in the black and white terms men use. He wants women not to imitate men but to stay as they are, as new role models for men (p. 161).

## WOMEN'S MANAGERIAL POTENTIAL

Tom "In Search of Excellence" Peters (1989), syndicated columnist, asked readers to think back over his column during the past year and to catalog the requirements he said management needed to survive in the 1990s. Those requirements were (1) replacing hierarchy with bound- aryless networks, (2) power sharing and the empowerment of all em- ployees, (3) employee teams without cop–supervisors that had responsibility for quality of work life as well as product quality, (4) no more adversarial relationship between customers and company, (5) con- tinuing education for all employees, (6) lifelong relationships with cus- tomers, (7) "soft," service-added attributes for all products, and (8) constant change and fluidity as the norm. Then he said, "Do you get it yet, fellas?" Because these survival traits read like a "portfolio of women's inclinations and natural talents."

What men gain from Peters' recital is a chance to get ready for the year 2000 by learning women's style of leadership. This means empha- sizing intimacy and affiliation rather than the individual ego, valuing relationships and connections, using power not to dominate and control but to put egalitarian relationships in place of the hierarchy, and leaving behind seeing the organization as an extension of the battlefield where political maneuvering, empire building, and the game itself take prec- edence over getting the job done.

Peter's final line is to the effect that the United States' greater emphasis on women in management already had given the United States a strong competitive advantage in the emerging, global economy (men's bottom line again, ironically).

## LEADING WITH OUR KIND OF POWER

Tavris and Wade (1984, p. 30) listed a number of "masculine" qualities admired in men, a list everyone is familiar with by now. Men have been admired who were very aggressive and competitive, very independent and not at all emotional, very self-confident, and very dominant. In Great Britain, as far as politicians are concerned, "very insulting" should be added to the list.

For Americans who might think that most British citizens are dignified, well-mannered, and polite, it comes as a great shock to learn that the men in the House of Commons are chauvinistic and routinely shout obscene and cruel insults to their fellow members of Parliament (MPs)

(Abdela, 1989). Men MPs behave toward one another like rude school-boys, sometimes even like drunken gang members in a pub, and just like rowdy schoolboys, they reserve their most appalling abuse for women. They called a woman MP debating abortion legislation a *slag* (whore). Their treatment of a Conservative woman cabinet minister be-fore a committee was described as "the nearest thing to a public hanging."

Women MPs are doing what they can to put a stop to this juvenile, stupid, counterproductive, bizarre behavior. Abdela reported that phys-ical abuse (bottom pinching) has died out and that the women feel gen-eral House decorum has improved. The Labor party women believe they have made strides with their male colleagues, and the Conservative women could undoubtedly make more progress if Margaret Thatcher didn't commonly join in to prove she can insult with the best of the men.

## CONCLUDING REMARKS

There's the old joke about men and women when they marry, how he hopes she'll never change and how she hopes he will change, and how they are both bound to be disappointed. My hope is that this book can help in some small way to change men.

How many other women have tried through writing? Hundreds? Thousands? Just what kind of message does it take? Why, for example, wasn't Marilyn French's (1985) brilliant chapter "Men under Patriarchy" sufficiently convincing? In it she tried to get men to see patriarchy as the source of their mistrust and competitiveness vis-à-vis other men, the stunted relationships they have inside and outside of their families, and the repression of their emotions (pp. 323–324).

It is the male system, French said, that deprives men of valuing and enjoying pleasure, love, sharing, and community (1985, p. 297). It is the male system that manipulates men, in return for money and security, to conform, fit in, have the correct attitude, obey and defer to the hi-erarchy, and be blindly loyal to the organization, hoping against hope they will not be betrayed (pp. 315–317).

*Women Changing Work* is another tack taken in that long line of feminist discourse that says to men, there is another, better way to be. It is another reminder to men that those in control of our economy and politics press the idealized male image on them to maintain the status quo. It is a reminder that women see more clearly than men the alternatives, op-tions, and choices men really have. We are saying, "Listen to us. Use us as models for work based in service, nurturance, balance, and empow-erment. Use us as models for making the political personal and the personal political. Why can't it be "women *and* men changing work?"

# REFERENCES

Abdela, Lesley. (1989, June 30). The House of common behaviour. *London Times*, p. 11.

Adams, Jane. (1979). *Women on top*. New York: Hawthorn Books.

Adams, Margaret. (1971). The compassion trap. In Vivian Gornick & Barbara K. Moran (Eds.), *Woman in sexist society* (pp. 555–575). New York: Basic Books.

Aiken, Susan H., Anderson, Karen, Dinnerstein, Myra, Lensink, Judy N., & MacCorquodale, Patricia (Eds.). (1988). *Changing our minds*. Albany: State University of New York Press.

Arditti, Rita. (1979). Feminism and science. In Rita Arditti, Pat Brennan, & Steve Cavrak (Eds.), *Science and liberation* (pp. 350–368). Boston: South End Press.

Bardwick, Judith M. (1979). *In transition*. New York: Holt, Rinehart, & Winston.

Becraft, Carolyn. (1989, July 10). Women do belong in the military. *Navy Times*, pp. 47–51.

Bernard, Jessie. (1981). *The female world*. New York: Free Press.

Bozzi, Vincent. (1988, January). Time and togetherness. *Psychology Today*, p. 10.

Breakwell, Glynis. (1985). *The quiet rebel*. London: Century.

Brownmiller, Susan. (1984). *Femininity*. New York: Linden Press.

Burr, Rosemary. (1987). *Female tycoons*. London: Rosters.

Case, Frederick. (1989, February 26). New look at how we train doctors. *Seattle Times*, p. K1.

Chafetz, Janet S. (1978). *Masculine/feminine or human?* (2nd ed.). Itasca, IL: F. E. Peacock.

Charles, Michael T. (1983). Police training: A contemporary approach. *Journal of Police Science and Administration, 11*, 252–263.

Chodorow, Nancy. (1978). *The reproduction of mothering*. Berkeley: University of California Press.

Cline, Sally, & Spender, Dale. (1987). *Reflecting men*. New York: Henry Holt.

Deckard, Barbara S. (1983). *The women's movement: Political, socioeconomic, and psychological issues* (3rd ed.). New York: Harper and Row.

Dunphy, Stephen H. (1985, January 27). Women in the workplace are reshaping the economy. *Seattle Times*, p. C1.

Fein, Robert A. (1974). Men and young children. In Joseph H. Pleck & Jack Sawyer (Eds.), *Men and masculinity* (pp. 54–62). Englewood Cliffs, NJ: Prentice-Hall.

Ferguson, Marilyn. (1982). *The aquarian conspiracy*. London: Granada.

Ferree, Myra M. (1987). She works hard for a living: Gender and class on the job. In Beth B. Hess & Myra M. Ferree (Eds.), *Analyzing gender* (pp. 322–347). New York: Sage.

Flammang, Janet A. (Ed.). (1984). *Political women*. Beverly Hills, CA: Sage.

Franks, Helen. (1984). *Goodbye Tarzan: Men after feminism*. London: George Allen & Unwin.

French, Marilyn. (1985). *Beyond power: On women, men, and morals*. New York: Ballantine.

Friedan, Betty. (1981). *The second stage*. New York: Summit Books.

Gallese, Liz R. (1985). *Women like us*. New York: William Morrow.

Gelb, Joyce. (1989). *Feminism and politics: A comparative perspective*. Berkeley: University of California Press.

Giele, Janet Z. (1978). *Women and the future: Changing sex roles in modern America*. New York: Free Press.

Gilligan, Carol. (1982). *In a different voice*. Cambridge, MA: Harvard University Press.

Gould, Robert E. (1974). Measuring masculinity by the size of a paycheck. In Joseph H. Pleck & Jack Sawyer (Eds.), *Men and masculinity* (pp. 96–100). Englewood Cliffs, NJ: Prentice-Hall.

Grant, Eleanor. (1988, January). The housework gap. *Psychology Today*, p. 10.

Grove, Valerie. (1988, May 15a). Beating the clock, quitting the jungle. *London Sunday Times*, p. B5.

Grove, Valerie. (1988, May 29b). Wards full of fans cheer a man in a woman's world. *London Sunday Times*, p. B5.

Halcomb, Ruth. (1979). *Women making it*. New York: Ballantine.

Hartley, Ruth E. (1974). Sex-role pressures and the socialization of the male child. In Joseph H. Pleck & Jack Sawyer (Eds.), *Men and masculinity* (pp. 7–13). Englewood Cliffs, NJ: Prentice-Hall.

Heilbrun, Carolyn G. (1979). *Reinventing womanhood*. New York: W. W. Norton.

Hennig, Margaret, & Jardim, Anne. (1977). *The managerial woman*. New York: Pocket Books.

Hertz, Leah. (1986). *The business amazons*. London: Andre Deutsch.

Hewlett, Sylvia A. (1986). *A lesser life*. New York: William Morrow.

Hochschild, Arlie R. (1975). Inside the clockwork of male careers. In Florence Howe (Ed.), *Women and the power to change* (pp. 47–88). New York: McGraw-Hill.

Hodson, Phillip. (1984). *Men: An investigation into the emotional male*. London: Ariel Books (BBC).

Hornacek, Paul C. (1977). Anti-sexist consciousness-raising groups for men. In

Jon Snodgrass (Ed.), *A book of readings for men against sexism* (pp. 123–129). Albion, CA: Times Change Press.

Howe, Florence. (1975). Women and the power to change. In Florence Howe (Ed.), *Women and the power to change* (pp. 127–171). New York: McGraw-Hill.

Hunt, Pauline. (1984). Workers side by side: Women and the trade union movement. In Janet Siltanen & Michelle Stanworth (Eds.), *Women and the public sphere* (pp. 47–53). London: Hutchinson.

Ingham, Mary. (1985). *Men: The male myth exposed.* London: Century.

Janeway, Elizabeth. (1982). *Cross-sections from a decade of change.* New York: William Morrow.

Janeway, Elizabeth. (1985). Women and the uses of power. In Hester Eisenstein & Alice Jardine (Eds.), *The future of difference* (pp. 327–344). New Brunswick, NJ: Rutgers University Press.

Jones, Liane. (1987). *Flying high: The woman's way to the top.* London: Fontana.

Josefowitz, Natasha. (1983). Paths to power in high technology organizations. In Jan Zimmerman (Ed.), *The technological woman: Interfacing with tomorrow* (pp. 191–200). New York: Praeger.

Kanter, Rosabeth M. (1977). *Men and women in the corporation.* New York: Basic Books.

King, Marsha. (1989, February 5). On the hot seat. *Seattle Times,* pp. K1–K3.

Kirkpatrick, Jeane J. (1974). *Political woman.* New York: Basic Books.

Kohn, Alfie. (1988, February). Girl talk, guy talk. *Psychology Today,* pp. 65–66.

Korda, Michael. (1974). *Male chauvinism: How it works.* London: Barrie & Jenkins.

Lacayo, Richard. (1986, August 11). Rattling the gilded cage. *Time,* p. 39.

Landau, Jack C. (1989, May 15). Court backs women on issue of sex stereotypes. *Seattle Times,* p. A8.

Lenz, Elinor, & Myerhoff, Barbara. (1985). *The feminization of America.* Los Angeles: Jeremy Tarcher.

Lessing, Doris. (1983). *The diaries of Jane Somers.* Harmondsworth, Eng.: Penguin Books.

Lipman-Blumen, Jean. (1983). Emerging patterns of female leadership in formal organizations. In Matina Horner, Carol C. Nadelson, & Malkah T. Notman (Eds.), *The challenge of change* (pp. 61–91). New York: Plenum Press.

MacDonald, Janet W. (1986). *Climbing the ladder.* London: Methuen.

McHenry, Susan, & Small, Linda L. (1989, March). Does part-time pay off? *Ms. Magazine,* pp. 88, 90–94.

McLeod, Ramon G., & McCabe, Michael. (1989, June 1). Bay workers want a "parent track." *San Francisco Chronicle,* pp. A1, A6.

Marshall, Judi. (1984). *Women managers: Travellers in a male world.* Chichester, Eng.: John Wiley.

Miller, Jean B. (1976). *Toward a new psychology of women.* Boston: Beacon Press.

Nickles, Elizabeth, & Ashcroft, Laura. (1981). *The coming matriarchy.* New York: Seaview Books.

Nieva, Veronica F., & Gutek, Barbara A. (1981). *Women and work.* New York: Praeger.

Novarra, Virginia. (1980). *Women's work, men's work.* London: Marion Boyars.

Number of women in state legislatures increases yearly. (1987, October). *State Legislatures, 13* (No. 9), p. 7.

Orbach, Susie, & Eichenbaum, Luise. (1987). *Bittersweet*. London: Century.

Ott, E. Marlies. (1989). Effects of the male-female ratio at work: Policewomen and male nurses. *Psychology of Women Quarterly, 13*, 41–57.

Overholser, Geneva. (1987, June 15). Would women govern differently? *New York Times*, p. 20.

Pearson, Sheryl S. (1981). Rhetoric and organizational change: New applications of feminine style. In Barbara L. Forisha & Barbara H. Oldman (Eds.), *Outsiders on the inside* (pp. 55–74). Englewood Cliffs, NJ: Prentice-Hall.

Peters, Tom. (1989, April 11). Listen up, guys: Women fit profile of execs of future. *Seattle Post-Intelligencer*, p. B6.

Pleck, Joseph H., & Sawyer, Jack (Eds.). (1974). *Men and masculinity*. Englewood Cliffs, NJ: Prentice-Hall.

Randall, Vicky. (1987). *Women and politics* (2nd ed.). London: MacMillan.

Restak, Richard. (1986, May 4). Women doctors: Their growing numbers will improve medical care. *Seattle Times*, p. A21.

Reynolds, Pamela. (1989, May 14). Career-family balance is dads' issue, too. *Seattle Times*, pp. K1–K2.

Rich, Adrienne. (1975). Toward a woman-centered university. In Florence Howe (Ed.), *Women and the power to change* (pp. 15–46). New York: McGraw-Hill.

Richards, Janet R. (1980). *The skeptical feminist: A philosophical enquiry*. London: Routledge & Kegan Paul.

Rowland, Robyn. (1984). *Women who do and women who don't join the women's movement*. London: Routledge & Kegan Paul.

Schaef, Anne W. (1981). *Women's reality*. Minneapolis: Winston Press.

Scobey, Joan. (1986, May). Cut from a different cloth. *New Woman*, pp. 76, 77, 78, 80, 82.

Segal, Lynne. (1987). *Is the future female?* London: Virago.

Sheehy, Gail. (1976). *Passages*. New York: E. P. Dutton.

Silver, Jane. (1989, July 23). Love your colleagues as yourself? *London Observer*, p. 37.

Spender, Dale, & Spender, Lynne. (1986). *Scribbling sisters*. London: Camden Press.

Spicer, John. (1988, January 6). Women bosses would reduce stress at work. *London Times*, p. 16.

Syrett, Michel. (1988, March 27). Flexibility in hours works for men too. *London Times*, p. E1.

Tavris, Carol, & Wade, Carole. (1984). *The longest war: Sex differences in perspective* (2nd ed.). San Diego: Harcourt Brace Jovanovich.

Toffler, Alvin. (1980). *The third wave*. London: Collins.

Walczak, Yvette. (1988). *He and she: Men in the eighties*. London: Routledge.

Wallach, Aleta. (1975). A view from the law school. In Florence Howe (Ed.), *Women and the power to change* (pp. 81–125). New York: McGraw-Hill.

Ward, David. (1989, 25 July). Building in the school yard. *London Guardian*, p. 21.

Weisheit, Ralph A. (1987). Women in the state police: Concerns of male and female officers. *Journal of Police Science and Administration, 15*, 137–144.

Wheeler-Bennett, Joan. (1977). *Women at the top*. London: Peter Owen.

Willett, Roslyn S. (1971). Working in 'a man's world': The woman executive. In Vivian Gornick & Barbara K. Moran (Eds.), *Woman in sexist society* (pp. 511–532). New York: Basic Books.

# INDEX

**About the Author**

PATRICIA W. LUNNEBORG is a retired Professor of Psychology and Adjunct Professor of Women's Studies at the University of Washington. She has written more than 100 publications and is the coauthor of *To Work: A Guide for Women College Graduates*.